Manliness

Manliness

Harvey C. Mansfield

Yale University Press
New Haven and London

Designed by Nancy Ovedovitz and set in Galliard Oldstyle type by Integrated Publishing Solutions. Printed in the United States of America by Vail-Ballou Press, Binghamton, New York.

Library of Congress Cataloging-in-Publication Data
Mansfield, Harvey Claflin, 1932–
Manliness / Harvey C. Mansfield.
   p.   cm.
Includes bibliographical references and index.
ISBN-13: 978-0-300-10664-0 (alk. paper)
ISBN-10: 0-300-10664-5
1. Masculinity — Philosophy. 2. Masculinity — Political aspects. 3. Sex role.
4. Assertiveness (Psychology) 5. Nature and nurture. 6. Feminism.
I. Title.
HQ1090.M365 2006
305.31 — dc22   2005023687

A catalogue record for this book is available from the British Library.

The paper in this book meets the guidelines for permanence and durability of the Committee on Production Guidelines for Book Longevity of the Council on Library Resources.

10   9   8   7   6   5   4   3   2

For Delba

Contents

Preface

This book is about manliness. What is that? It's best to start from examples we know: our sports heroes, too many to name; Margaret Thatcher, the British prime minister who is the mightiest woman of our time (What! a woman, manly?); Harry S. Truman, who said "the buck stops here"; Humphrey Bogart, who as Rick in *Casablanca* was confident and cynical — cool before "cool" was invented; and the courageous police and firemen in New York City on September 11, 2001. Manliness seeks and welcomes drama and prefers times of war, conflict, and risk. Manliness brings change or restores order at moments when routine is not enough, when the plan fails, when the whole idea of rational control by modern science develops leaks. Manliness is the next-to-last resort, before resignation and prayer.

We today inhabit a society with a very new justice, long overdue: the gender-neutral society. In this new society your sex does not determine your rights, your duties, or your place. The gender-neutral society regards sex as an irrational hindrance to freedom because it subordinates women to men, and to efficiency because it misuses their abilities. Manliness, the quality mostly of one sex, gets in the way of an equal or reasonable distribution of tasks and rewards; it seems to promote a bias in favor of men over women. In this book I begin from manliness as the irrational obstacle to a rational project that seeks to remove this bias. By the end I hope to convince skeptical readers — above all, educated women — of the reverse: that irrational manliness deserves to be endorsed by reason.

I was going to call this book "a modest defense of manliness," but manly men are not modest, and I do not want to sound like a wimp or to begin by looking down on manly men. "Modest defense" is my conclusion, however, in view of the good and bad in manliness that most anyone can see. The good — the manly rescuers on 9/11 — seems necessary to us, just as the bad — the manly attackers on that day — seems very unnecessary. But can you have the good without the bad? Most good things, like French wine, are mostly good and accidentally bad. Manliness, however, seems to be about fifty-fifty good and bad. If it is good, maybe that's because it's the only remedy for the trouble it causes. This is what I mean by a modest defense.

Manliness is something that affects us all, something that most anyone can see. Common sense has a lot to say about it. For the most part, I take the side of common sense. I like its forthright defense of stereotypes regarding the sexes. I am not so friendly to the two sciences that treat manliness, social psychology and evolutionary biology, even though they, too, largely support those stereotypes. The evidence the social psychologists compile on the differences between the sexes is useful for refuting those who deny sex differences or regard them as easily changed, and there is fascination in being shown small but significant differences in the ways that men and women do the same things in daily life. These differences are observable by anyone who cares to look and available in the stereotypes of common sense, but it is reassuring to see science catch up with truth and confirm in interesting ways what we already know.

On the whole, however, I am quite critical of the scientific understanding of manliness, whether in social psychology or evolutionary biology. These sciences see manliness at its lowest as aggression and altogether fail to consider the phenomenon of manly assertiveness. A manly man asserts himself so that he and the justice he demands are not overlooked. He rouses himself and seeks attention for what he deems important, sometimes something big — in the case of the New York uniforms and the Islamic fascists, the nature and value of Western civilization. These sciences, and science generally, are uncomfortable in the presence of big questions of human importance like this one. This is a severe limitation for the study of manliness that I cannot accept.

And science does not even understand aggression correctly or fully because it is completely ignorant of the phenomenon of *thumos*, known to Plato and Aristotle but later abandoned because it was inconvenient to the agenda of modern science. *Thumos* is a quality of spiritedness, shared by humans and animals, that induces humans, and especially manly men, to risk their lives in order to save their lives. That's a paradox familiar to all human beings who ever get angry. But it is a fact almost unknown in the scientific literature on manliness. As manliness is made out of that paradox, it is, to say the least, more complicated than the simplistic drives of aggression, domination, and self-preservation to which science tries to reduce manliness. I have done my best to develop assertiveness and *thumos* as features of manliness, and my book—here's an example of a manly assertion—is the only ready-to-hand treatment of manliness in these two respects and as a whole that you will find.

When I say that I develop these two features I mean, first, that I go beyond the scientific treatments of manliness, interesting though they are. After offering criticisms of social science and Darwin's biology I turn to the many productions of literature and philosophy that will teach us about manliness. Here is such profusion that I must select only a few among those that might be relevant. Not many books have been written solely on manliness, but almost every great writer or thinker has had something to say on the subject. I bring together a certain number of them: some whom I find striking, such as William James and the Stoics; some who are too good to miss, such as Teddy Roosevelt, Tarzan (not a writer but smarter than you think), and Hemingway; and two who are essential, Plato and Aristotle. I know that some readers will doubt that you can really learn anything solid from high talk lacking in numbers and graphs, but my advice is to wait for the results. While waiting, try out the thought that fiction and nonfiction are alike in aiming to present the truth.

Drawing from a number of sources, I present them in episodes that do not follow chronological order but are connected by the argument. The argument develops from what we appreciate best, the stereotypes of manliness, to what we appreciate least but need most, the wisdom of Plato and Aristotle. Do not be surprised, then, if the definition of manliness changes as the argument ascends from aggression to philosophical courage.

Another peculiarity in my book is to treat the levels of manliness. Most studies search for unfailing characteristics of all males and are thus confined to the lowest common denominator, which might be maleness or masculinity. But manliness has more than one level. Manly men are given to passing adverse judgment, and not only on women but also on other males who do not meet their exacting standards. Manliness at one level might be universal to all males but at another level common to only the few most manly males — and these few might be joined by a few manly women. Beyond these levels manliness is a virtue (despite what I said above about its being neutral between good and evil), the virtue of courage or perhaps of gentlemanliness; and beyond that might be found manliness in thinking, the courage to challenge conventional beliefs.

I do not make it my business to lament the decline of the gentleman in our day. I might agree with those who do lament it, but the gentleman presupposes manliness — he is a manly man with polish and perfection — and manliness is in question. If you want to know what a gentleman is, look up Squire Allworthy in Fielding's *Tom Jones*. In our day a man has to struggle to assert himself. The difficulty is not to make the man into a gentleman but to know what is a man. Manliness is below the gentleman, since many manly men are coarse and rude, but I believe it is also above him in the unfamiliar, uncelebrated manliness of the philosopher.

Because most studies do not address the levels of manliness, they do not get beyond a very elementary understanding of nature versus nurture. Looking for the lowest common denominator of masculinity, they either find it and call that "nature" or fail to find it and call manliness "nurture." Or, since it is obvious that some variation in the forms of manliness can be observed — from medieval knight to Connecticut Yankee — they say in statesmanlike fashion that it is both nature and nurture, and stop. In my book I go further and give an account of the dispute over nature and nurture in which manly assertiveness has a starring role and politics is key. I try to do justice to the scientists dressed in white who say manliness is nature and to the advocates of deconstruction and creativity in their rumpled suits or black jeans who say it is nurture. The crucial point missed by both sides in the dispute is that nature and nurture cooperate as well as conflict. You cannot isolate them as if to say that spitting by male athletes on television (not done by female athletes) is 25 percent nature and 75 percent nurture.

My book aims to comprehend the whole of manliness but not to cover everything. One aspect omitted is homosexuality, a topic I leave to others.

Another aspect left out is the science of neural physiology with its study of sex differences. Also, instead of Freud I give you Nietzsche, a bargain for the reader. And certain great authors I have not discussed, above all Shakespeare and Cervantes, deserve to be examined for their wonderful thoughts on manliness. The authors I have examined in the brief episodes of my book are not treated in full but used to illustrate aspects or problems of manliness. I want to show a different, more ambitious method of political science, duly cautious but unafraid of big questions.

Switching from apologies to thanks, I am grateful for the many valuable suggestions I have received from friends and strangers who heard I was writing a book on this subject. An author takes a risk when he writes on a subject on which everyone has an opinion, but then, one could say, it's manly to take risks. Or is it foolish—and manliness is foolish? Will I be grateful for every adverse comment made against this book? Manliness loves, and loves too much, the position of being embattled and alone against the world. That is another fundamental thought in my book.

Far from being alone myself, I would like to acknowledge the help of a number of my students: Sammy Ford IV, Rachel Friedman, Bryan Garsten, Susan Hamilton, Maria Konnikova, James Kruzer, Mary Rosaleen Lawler, Hugh Liebert, Catherine McCaw, Bronwen McShea, Melissa Moschella, Chad Noyes, Richard Regina, Kathryn Sensen, Rashmi Singh. I must also express my gratitude for support from the Lynde and Harry Bradley Foundation and the John M. Olin Foundation as well as from Harvard University, my generous employer. The dedication is to my wife.

All this has been preview, and the beginning of the book on the situation of manliness today is just ahead.

Chapter One The Gender-Neutral Society

Today the very word *manliness* seems quaint and obsolete. We are in the process of making the English language gender-neutral, and manliness, the quality of one gender, or rather, of one sex, seems to describe the essence of the enemy we are attacking, the evil we are eradicating. Recently I had a call from the alumni magazine at the university where I work, asking me to comment on a former professor of mine now being honored. Responding too quickly, I said: "What impressed all of us about him was his manliness." There was silence at the other end of the line, and finally the female voice said: "Could you think of another word?"

We now avoid using "man" to refer to both sexes, as in the glowing phrase "rights of man" to which America was once dedicated. All the man-words have been brought to account and corrected. Mankind has become human-kind; man of the year, person of the year; and so on. But even when "man" means only male, "manly" still seems pretentious in our new society, and threatening to it as well. A manly man is making a point of the bad attitude he ought to be playing down.

The attempt to make our language gender-neutral reveals something of the ambition of our democracy today. A gender-neutral language implies a gender-neutral society, marking a pervasive change in the way we live our lives. Our society has adopted, quite without realizing the magnitude of the change, a practice of equality between the sexes that has never been known before in all human history. The principle of equality, born in modern times, is several centuries old, but as its application to the sexes is very new, we can see that even democratic peoples were long content to ignore very obvious inequality between the sexes. That inconsistency is no longer accepted. Much more has occurred, and is yet under way, than a mere adjustment of law to ensure equal access of women to jobs. Some women want a law of affirmative action to give them an advantage in competitive situations from which they have been so long excluded, and for which they may not be prepared. But that adjustment — not accepted by all women — is considered temporary and transitional even by its advocates. New attitudes are recommended, new behavior is required, if only to sustain such a law and make it work. The long-term goal, however far in the future, is gender neutrality. Now what does that mean?

Let me try to fashion an answer from diverse strands of present-day thinking, keeping things simple for now. Gender neutrality in theory is abstracting from sexual differences so as to make jobs and professions (especially the latter) open to both sexes. Wherever your sex used to determine your opportunities, it must now be seen as irrelevant. How can you regard sex as irrelevant when it used to be considered highly relevant? The answer is that one must oppose the traditional thinking and "raise consciousness" as to what women can or ought to do. To overcome prejudice against women, they must be said and shown to be equal to men. It is not enough merely to set aside sexual differences. That is the principle. But since the new principle, like everything new in morals and manners, will meet resistance, it is necessary in practice to abolish or lessen sexual differences, at least the important ones. The meaning of gender neutrality, therefore, is transformed to some degree by the effort required to attain it. From a formal, negative, principle abstracting from sexual differences it becomes an actual, positive reformation so as to do away with them. Because there are no gender-neutral human beings, the gender-neutral society cannot simply let nature take its course: take off the pressure to be your sex, one might think, and both sexes will relax, everyone will become gender-neutral. This will not work; pressure in favor of gender neutrality needs to be applied. For some feminists, we shall see, the refashioning goes very far; they believe that gender neutrality can be achieved only if women are as sexually free as the most adventurous men.

Women today want to be equal to men, equal in a way that makes them similar to, or virtually the same as, men. They do not want the sort of equality that might result from being superior at home if inferior at work. They have decided that work is better than home. To think that home is better is no more than the "feminine mystique," the notion Betty Friedan attacked when she began the women's movement in the United States. Any woman who believes in that is being fobbed off by men who don't themselves believe that home is better. No, men are right to think as they do, and they deserve to be imitated by women in this fundamental point. Work gives you more money, more recognition, more freedom than home. The last advantage is decisive; work offers you more choice. "Choice" is the byword of modern women, and not only in regard to abortion. But being devoted to "choice" as a principle also limits your choices in practice because it requires you to choose work, which has more choice in it because you can change jobs, over home, where a woman is stuck with her husband and children. To the woman always at home, her husband is absent during the day and sometimes longer, engaged in activity that is more lucrative, more interesting, and more important than hers—while the children remain with her, all too present and ever-demanding, a constant worry and a constant occupation.

Thus the true, the effectual, meaning of women's equality is women's independence—which in turn means, so far as possible, independence from men and from children. Complete independence is obviously not possible, at least for women who want a family; but to gain maximum feasible independence, women will want to imitate men, lead the lives of men, and seek to reduce family responsibilities to the level that men have been inclined to accept for themselves. An alternative strategy is to get men to do more housework, to behave more like women, both partners making equal sacrifices of their independence. In such arrangements, women's independence is sustained by the idea of a contract, in contrast to an imposed role. In the old society, marriage was called a contract but the woman had a servile role she could not escape. Now she can specify what she expects of her partner and how much she will cede to him. Her concessions, made knowingly and voluntarily, will be less bruising to the soul. Each marriage can be lived more freely and happily on its own terms, and these terms need not, ought not, be dictated by society. If a man finds a complaisant woman, let him rejoice while it lasts. If he does not, too bad; he, not the woman, needs to adjust.

A gender-neutral society is a society of independent men and women, especially the latter. Although modern women still have some of the ways of traditional women, they behave much more as only men used to behave. The sexual difference is not so much set aside as actually *diminished*. Not only are women behaving more like men, but also men are more welcoming to such women, more *sensitive* toward them, as we say. The sensitive male is above all sensitive to the desire of women to be like men (though also, in a lesser degree, to their desire to remain women and to combine this with the main desire). Such a fellow is no longer the Male Chauvinist Pig he was accused of being when this great change got underway. Men have had to curb, if not totally suppress, their sense of superiority to women. And having done this at the behest of women, they have in a way abandoned the contest and acknowledged the artificiality and fragility of their superiority. By their failure to resist they admit that it is easier to live equally.

A society of independent men and women, in which the sexes are converging and surrendering their sense of difference, in both the grand projects and the routines of life, surely has its attractions. The central one is greater freedom. The women's movement in its initial phase in the 1970s released women from the oppression of millennia, let them be angry, and with exhilaration seized the task of starting a revolution. Both leaders and followers in this movement were full of fire, fight, and ambition, for they were opposed by traditional conventions that included alleged natural differences in the sexes supporting those conventions. All nature and convention had been arrayed against women, all of society's spurious wisdom joined with its hypocritical morality, and now was the time to throw them off and create something new. This was the heyday of feminism when, excited by a spirit of transgression, women were none too pleased with men and not shy about letting them know it.

One thing women let men know was that sexual harassment had to stop. Sexual harassment has existed ever since predatory males have been around, and until now it has been contained by the code of a gentleman. The new law on sexual harassment, intended to secure women's independence as well as their honor, replaces that code so that women no longer have to rely on it to restrain predatory males. For a traditional example of sexual harassment, not of course taking place at the office, one need only think of Jane Austen's *Pride and Prejudice*, in which Mr. Wickham, a man somewhere between a fool and a villain, takes advantage of Lydia Bennett. This case of ungentlemanly behavior was offered for our dismay and indignation and contrasted to a standard of how a gentleman would behave. The gentleman, as opposed to a cad or a lout, does not take advantage of those weaker than himself, especially women. He declines opportunities to push himself on others by means of a stronger will, to say nothing of greater brawn. Although he is expected to take the initiative — since in the relations of men and women someone at some point always has to make the risky first move — he allows time for choice or second thoughts by the woman and does not proceed if he is not wanted. He may not give up easily, nor will he seek written permission for his every advance, but he mustn't complain if he is turned down.

The gentleman, however, is an embarrassment to the gender-neutral society. A gentleman, we now think, has the same pretension to inequality as the harasser, and because he carries this infection within himself, it may get the better of him on some future occasion. The old ideal of gentlemanliness was tolerant of male pretensions, seeking only to transform them, not remove them. We now believe it is safer to rely on the law rather than an ideal. The new law shows respect for the equality of the sexes and drops the odious presumption that men are stronger, women weaker. Thus gender neutrality came into being, replacing gentlemanliness as the standard of both morality and common courtesy.

The gender-neutral society has lately produced softer, more comfortable freedoms, too. Ambition has subsided from making a revolution to making one's career, as the movement has lost its feminist passion, and with that some of its antimale and antibourgeois resentments. In moving up the ladder, the two sexes do not compete as sexes, and they rather fancy seeing more of one another in freer circumstances as they do now. The sexual revolution allows them to act on what they see. Both sexes, not just the males, can harbor ulterior motives, which now can become perfectly frank. A new egalitarian mutual respect has appeared, in which men find out that women are capable and women see that men can be fair; and as the blessing resulting from mutual respect, it's very nice for the family (or its substitute) to have two incomes. Although both men and women work hard, harder in fact than they used to, a new sense of ease is replacing the sense of duty that men used to struggle with and the sense of being constrained and generally put upon that women labored under. Life is pleasant and less demanding even as work is longer and more productive. The gender-neutral society of independents has more choice and less necessity. Its obligations are those one sets for oneself; they are fewer, more easily postponed, and more satisfying than they used to be.

A gender-neutral society can, we might think, lose its partisan character. In its mature phase it can leave behind most, perhaps all, of the specific, divisive theses of the feminism that brought it to be. It can simply base itself on the obvious truth that men and women have more in common than not. Of course, you can see sexual differences if you look for them (as we shall do), but why look? It would seem wiser and easier to rely on the overlap between sexes than to make a point of the differences. In one generation women have shown that they are quite capable in the occupations to which they were previously denied access; the exceptions are few, the discrepancies minor. Women may not be equally qualified with men to be firemen, say, but they are not disqualified for the job, and they may have advantages of temperament and finesse over men — if not there, then elsewhere.

To justify the gender-neutral society we can rely on the authority of great men who in previous times wrote on its behalf, so to speak, without meaning to. Who knows more about American democracy than Alexis de Tocqueville? He said that the American dogma is this: "Providence has given to *each individual,* whoever he may be, the degree of reason necessary for him to be able to direct himself in things that interest him exclusively."[1] Forget the masculine pronouns and look at their reference, "each individual"; are not women included in this? And as to the social advantages of believing in each individual's reason, take the word of Alexander Hamilton (not a gender-neutral but a man who gave up his life in a duel because he was a gentleman): "When all the different kinds of industry obtain in a community, *each individual* can find his proper element, and call into activity the whole vigor of his nature."[2] Again the language can be applied without correction to our condition today. One might say, then, that it is no longer necessary to raise the general question of equality between men and women, as did the feminists. Let women succeed as they will without counting up the results, without making a fuss. It does no good, no good at all, to revive and replay on every occasion the battle of the sexes. Let there be a division of labor not between the sexes but within them, so that differences between the sexes can be treated in the same way as differences within the sexes. Many men, after all, are not cut out to be firemen. The question of equality between the sexes doesn't arise on its own if there is no one to insist on it.

It's a pretty picture. It's the one we hold of ourselves, and it is to some extent, even to a considerable extent, true. If it does not quite represent how we behave, it shows what we want and where we intend to go. It is the truth we wish for, and the wish is potent enough to silence would-be critics.

Nonetheless, a certain resistance to the gender-neutral society has been noticed by its admirers. One of them speaks hyperbolically, and preemptively, of "backlash," but there is no backlash; there is only inarticulate resistance in the form of reluctance, a residual, bodily, behavioral unwillingness on the part of men to do their share in the upkeep of gender neutrality.[3] For the picture drawn above is of work, not of home. It takes for granted the standpoint of what has been called the "ideal worker," one who has somebody else to deal with the distractions of home.[4] The ideal worker is now a woman as readily as a man. At work the men have been told to move over, and they have, but at home things are different. The independent woman does not have a wife to make her independence viable — to do the housework, cooking, and child rearing.

As women always said and men often admitted, the independence of men rested on the dependence of women. But now that women are independent, or mean to be, these former dependents are no longer available. So it's not enough for men to move over and make room for women. The logistical support team men used to have must be reconstructed. The government can be called in to provide funds for day care, and with these or with income from her job, a woman can begin to cover the tasks she used to do herself. The people she hires, often women, are employees and not so dependent as she used to be.[5] Even if they do everything — not a likely prospect — they have to be managed. Who does that? The woman does because her husband does not want to do women's work.

What! How is it possible that men will let women do men's work but not reciprocate and do women's work when women are perfectly willing to let them do it — when women even invite them to do it? The answer is that *men look down on women's work*. They look down on it not because they think it is dirty or boring or insignificant, which is often true of men's work; they look down on it because it is women's. Working around the house is not objectionable if it is the sort of thing men do, for example, a man's trying manfully to fix something. But in this enlightened age, the age of raised consciousness, men still do not care for what they regard as women's work. It is not correct these days to say such things (perhaps it never was), but men's sentiments are strong if mute. Women should not have been surprised at this as they, too, now officially prefer men's work. Their complaint was that in being excluded from men's work, they were denied access to better things in life. But for some reason women were unprepared for men's reaction. They thought that men could accommodate themselves to the new situation and make the best of it without too much complaint. Women used to put up with injustice; surely men could tolerate justice? One shakes one's head sadly at such naïve confidence.

Proponents of gender neutrality—feminists of all stripes—must be distinguished from its beneficiaries, who include all grown women today (for now, let's not mention men and children). The beneficiaries tend to be more moderate than the proponents, as well as somewhat ungrateful to them. Neither group has been much concerned at first with changing our idea of men's behavior, and the leaders of the women's movement, especially, had little or nothing to say about manliness. They denounced men as oppressors, but they did not try to understand what makes men want to be on top. Other women saw no reason to denounce in universal terms particular men they happened to love, but this was perhaps because they saw no reason why these men could not behave more reasonably than men have behaved up to now.

By some accounts, American men are doing more around the house than they used to do (which was, in democratic America, more than in most any other society). A recent study speaks revealingly of "household chores" rather than something more dignified such as homemaking, of which a woman could be proud. It finds that although nine-tenths of both men and women believe that the chores and child care should be shared equally, in fact women do two-thirds of the work (or give two-thirds of the time), with no change from 1955 to 2002. Men contribute two-thirds of the family income and one-third of time devoted to the family—still.[6] In household tasks a considerable degree of sexual division of labor remains in force.

Women still do the cooking; men mow the lawns. The new freedom permits and encourages a great variety of arrangements within households, and necessity (which in the form of divorce and single parenthood still somehow attends the new freedom) pushes both sexes into what once were considered unmanly or unladylike tasks. The lines between men's and women's tasks vary from one society to another and from one time to another. Today they have certainly been blurred, especially for women. But they have not been effaced. Men still hold to, and seem to insist on, the difference between men and women, and they want to apply it to matters outside sex, to home if not work. This is their manliness still operating in a society that has no legitimate place for it.

Betty Friedan, the founder of American feminism, wrote of "the problem that has no name," by which she meant the boredom of the suburban housewife.[7] But, to repeat, we have lost the name we used to have for what mainly resists gender neutrality, which is *manliness*. I do not say that manliness is the only obstacle to the new dispensation; the consequences for society generally and even the preferences of women may also get in the way. Nor do I say that manliness is defined only by insistent sexism. Far from it: this book has much more to say about manliness than that. But men's disdain not only for women's work but even for *women* — which let us hurry to say is unjustified and irrational — has shown itself to be neither ephemeral nor transitional. This is the point from which to open our inquiry.

From one angle, the attempt to create a gender-neutral society, never before recorded in human history, has been an amazing success. It has aroused virtually no open opposition. There were segregationists to defend the Old South and its unjust ways, but the universal order of patriarchy found no spokesman to set forth an ideology on its behalf, let alone defenders to mount a countermovement. There was no George Wallace, no Bull Connor, no massive resistance to oppose the women's movement. No men of our time had the nerve to make fun of the feminists as men did of the suffragettes a century ago. True, conservative women under the leadership of Phyllis Schlafly did succeed in defeating the feminists' campaign for an Equal Rights Amendment in 1982. But Schlafly's campaign was based on women's traditional protections and exemptions, such as not having to fight in wars and not having a man with you in a public toilet, rather than on women's traditional virtues that thrive only in the home. Opposition to the ERA was compromised by the fact that the most educated women, conservative as well as liberal, were leaving homemaking for careers. Jane Mansbridge's classic study, *Why We Lost the ERA* (1986), concludes that a constitutional amendment was perhaps unnecessary, that its aims could be accomplished through legislation and judicial interpretation — and this seems to have been correct.[8] Even conservative women, I have been told on good authority, want two items from the collection of innovations in the new society: the two Cs, career and contraception. If that's all they want, it's still a lot.

The conquest in thought was accompanied by a massive shift of women into the workplace beginning in the 1960s, and it was quickly followed by wholesale changes in law and custom requiring us to get used to gender neutrality. Altogether, it seemed, there was a sudden and universal collapse of even the mildest forms of patriarchy. The American patriarch, if you want to call him that, was perhaps at that stage nothing more formidable than Dagwood Bumstead, bumbling husband of Blondie, manly only when tackling his hero sandwich. But such as he was, the dominant patriarch was overturned and he readily succumbed.

Yet from the standpoint of the complete gender-neutral society, how little has changed. The late feminist political scientist Susan Okin stated the principle of such a society as "a future in which men and women participated in more or less equal numbers in every sphere of life, from infant care to different kinds of paid work to high-level politics."[9] For "high-level politics" and the like, the truth is that men are still in charge. Men have the highest offices, the leading reputations; they make the discoveries, conceive the theories, win the prizes, start the companies, score the touchdowns. Men run things; women follow, accompany, imitate, elaborate, develop. This is not to say that women do not excel, but they seem still to excel as women, in accordance with the traditional stereotype of women and not the new gender-neutral stereotype. Although the line between male and female occupations is much more blurred than it used to be, particularly in the white-collar professions — lawyers and doctors are now 30 percent women, college teachers, 43 percent — significant traces of the old ways remain. Legal assistants are 83 percent women; nurses, 93 percent; dental assistants, 98 percent. Pilots are 96 percent men; truck drivers, 95 percent; construction trades, 96 percent;

car mechanics, 98 percent. As children grow up, their teachers are 98 percent women in kindergarten, 83 percent in elementary school, 58 percent in high school, and as we saw, 43 percent in college.[10] In business, women excel in small enterprises, in finding a niche for a specialized ambition. They seem to be less interested in becoming numero uno for its own sake. This is not true in every case, to be sure — think of Margaret Thatcher — but it is true on the whole.

In going to work, women have not deserted the home and most of them show a secret liking for housework. They continue to do more than their share of it, that is, more than an equal share. What they have abandoned is not the home but domesticity — the virtues of the home, the justification for staying home. Cheryl Mendelson's large book *Home Comforts* praises the home virtues that produce home comforts. Its title is a rejoinder to promoters of gender neutrality who would describe home comforts as disagreeable "household chores."[11] The book is a subdued but still very manifest claim on behalf of women to rule the household not from the top by making big decisions but from beneath by assuming the right to declare when it is clean. Even more pronounced than women's penchant for nesting is their desire to take loving care of the babies to be reared in the nest. They take nature's pleasure in giving milk, and they generally enjoy greater intimacy with their babies than do men. This applies, in one recent survey, to women assistant professors, a group likely to be loyal in principle to gender neutrality, and it includes among specific tasks changing diapers, which a majority of the women said they actually enjoyed.[12]

To these reservations against gender neutrality, we may add women's hesitancy to condemn manliness. The gender-neutral society permits, or rather requires, women to be independent, to carry on their own lives without following in the wake of some man. But suppose you have to fight to maintain your independence? Suppose it is not enough to agitate the community, shame the males, and raise everyone's consciousness? With the disaster of September 11, 2001, Americans were sharply reminded that it is sometimes necessary to fight, and that in the business of government, fighting comes before caring. Women were reminded that men can come in handy. The heroes of that day were (apparently) exclusively male — as were the villains. Does this mean that the gender-neutral society is valid only in peacetime?

The situation might make some women wish for the disappearance of men, so as not to be subject either to the threat of their aggression or to its remedy. And the wish has long ago been thought out in Charlotte Gilman's *Herland* (1915), a manless utopia. But the extirpation of males might have to be carried out with the aid of males like our hijackers, seeking the new world of justice by suicide.[13] Women on their own are not ruthless enough. One suspects, moreover, that many of them have a sneaking admiration for manliness when it comes to the fore in time of need. Some women may welcome it with open arms. Women's manliness may take the form of appreciating manliness in men and — a further point — of censuring its absence when required.

Two notable instances of such reproach may be recalled. As the Moor Boabdil was being expelled from the city of Alhambra in Spain, he turned around to gaze at it and heaved one last sigh, whereupon his mother said, "You do well to weep as a woman over what you could not defend as a man." And Lady Macbeth, fearing that her husband was "too full o' the milk of human kindness," found it was true, and she told him that when they had decided to kill the king, "then you were a man."[14] Are women in the gender-neutral society more tolerant of unmanliness in a man? I would not count on it. Think of Margaret Thatcher's public advice to George H. W. Bush that it was "no time to go wobbly" on war in the Persian Gulf.

Women still rather like housework, changing diapers, and manly men. The capacities and inclinations of the sexes do not differ exactly or universally, but they do seem to differ. These differences are, one could say, all the more impressive now that they are no longer supported, indeed now that they are denied or opposed, by society's ruling conventions. The old Adam is still effective and still visible despite all that Hollywood and the media (when they want to be serious) do to instruct us in gender neutrality.

Or is this judgment made too soon? We are still in transition from the old patriarchal society to the new gender-neutral one, it might be objected, and it will take time to see the change completed. But it's just a matter of time. To this the answer is, we shall see. Right now there remains an obstacle to gender neutrality — manliness — which does not seem easily removable, even in time. Gender neutrality seems at first to disregard sexual differences, but it also wants women to be more independent, more like men. It assumes that what was until recently specific to men is actually common to both sexes.

It requires that we guide ourselves by what is common to the sexes, and this is what we are presently trying to do. Everywhere in the media we see portrayed the aggressive female and the sensitive male—Xena the Warrior Princess and Alan Alda or Warren Beatty (sometimes together). Both roles are difficult to play, but somehow the latter is more so. Women may have trouble in playing the aggressor, they may not be consistent, they may not be as pleasing to men in the new format; but despite the difficulties they can usually manage. Women are more malleable; they are able to do what men do while still maintaining an identity for themselves specifically as women. Yet men reject and resist the expectation that they should abandon their manliness. They do not so much mind sharing their traditional opportunities with whoever can exploit them, and they have shown newfound respect for women who can. But they draw the line at doing what women have left behind.

In sum, a serious discrepancy exists between what men and women, and especially men, believe, or say they believe, and what they are in fact willing to do. Their unofficial desires are not what they should be officially to maintain the gender-neutral society. Democracy as a whole, Tocqueville tells us, overthrows the legitimacy of unequal privilege much more easily than it establishes a legitimacy of its own, for one equal person does not see why she should obey another.[15] Today it seems generally admitted that gender neutrality is the only legitimate way to live—yet we are not living that way. This means that every woman has, or is entitled to, a grievance against her man and against men in general. The fact that her man is probably no worse than any other she can find may induce her to be resigned to her fate, or it may not. Either way she cannot be happy in the society that was supposed to bring the liberation of women. Men, too, are not altogether happy. They have shown themselves willing to accept women's liberation verbally as long as it does not subtract from men's satisfaction at home. But of course it does.

Why couldn't a woman content herself with rough justice in the family that finds more money from men an equal exchange for more time from women? With the higher incomes men receive they get more honor than women, more "recognition." Manliness prevents men from giving equal honor to women: this is the issue behind inequality in housework. If housework were equal in honor to the sort of work you "go to," instead of being considered necessary chores, a woman could be satisfied with doing more of the first and less of the second.[16]

Once upon a time women received recognition of a sort from a gentleman, and it is not clear that women want to do away with manliness in this more moderate form. It is for them, I suspect, still something of a treat to be in the company of a man who behaves like a gentleman. Women are quite expert in the interpretation of small courtesies, and they are in the habit of awarding points to men who offer them, especially in the early stages of acquaintance. Are you *showing interest,* and if so, how? Moreover, precisely in times of greater sexual freedom, it is good to be with someone you (as a woman) can trust. A gentleman is a man who is gentle out of policy, not weakness; he can be depended upon not to snarl at or attack a woman when he has the advantage or feels threatened. It can be delightful, of course, to be surprised, as long as one is *pleasantly surprised.* With a gentleman you can hope, perhaps even expect, that most of the surprises will be of that sort.

We have come to appreciation of the gentleman, the manly gentleman. What is he doing in the gender-neutral society? His chivalry is not only obsolete but also dangerous. The protection he offers women comes at the price of recognizing his claim, usually unspoken, that certain things must be left to men. Most of the time the gentleman conceals his superiority with chivalric irony; he pretends to defer to his inferiors. He opens doors for women when nothing is at stake, but when a crisis comes his very utility commands women to "get out of my way!" The gender-neutral society cannot afford a price that affronts its principle. Hence it cannot remain passive while members of both sexes individually choose which occupation they want to pursue. That society, like any other society, has rulers, and it matters who rules in it, above all that men and women rule equally. If it turns out that the gender-neutral society is still ruled mostly by men, that fact may be fatal to it. It may not matter that firemen are mostly males and dental assistants mostly females, but presidents, legislators, and justices give a character to the whole; if they are mostly males, the society is not really gender-neutral.

Thus, prompted by costly nostalgia for the gentleman, one must raise the question of power. The gender-neutral society must secure itself despite the reluctance of men to conform to it. One must be sure that it is held and defended by people who believe in it. Its rulers must be equally male and female at the least, and perhaps a surplus of females would be safer. In any case, there must be no gentlemen with their dangerously attractive courtesies.

Now supporters of the gender-neutral society (call them feminists) are torn between showing that they are as competent as men and doing away with gentlemen who might oppose them. In the first mode, they want to show they are manly; in the second, they want to deny there is any such thing. The first mode predominated in the early wave of feminists in the 1960s and 1970s led by Simone de Beauvoir and Betty Friedan, which was more critical of women than men. In the 1980s, however, an attempt began from within academia to "deconstruct" manliness and to replace it with *masculinity*. Many books appeared with "masculinity" in the title, and an academic subfield called "masculinity studies" popped up in the near vicinity of women's studies. In the anecdote recounted at the beginning of this chapter, I should have replied "masculinity" when asked for a word other than "manliness," but I wanted to honor the man I was describing, and somehow "masculinity" is not a compliment.

The process known as deconstruction addresses the question of power. It assumes that the notion of manliness has nothing to recommend it but the power of those who dreamed it up or "constructed" it. Their power does not come from their manliness, but rather their so-called manliness comes from their power. Let's dub it masculinity, say the deconstructers, to signify that it has no particular virtue or attraction. But this might seem to be a bad move. Power is gender-neutral and masculinity is not. Why should power-seeking be especially male? If so, that would be very damaging to a gender-neutral society because it would imply that women are not so gifted as men when it comes to shoving rivals out of the way. And yet if it is not so, how do we explain the apparent fact that all previous societies have been ruled by males? When one deconstructs manliness, is the effect to expose manliness as mere aggression, and therefore bad, or is it to deny that manliness has any intrinsic quality, and therefore doesn't exist except as an illusion?

We should be grateful to feminist deconstructionists for insisting on the question of who rules. That question can easily be lost in the delusion that choice is nonpolitical, that you can choose one thing, I another — and nothing follows. But a society of choice could not be one where it does not matter to me whether, say, you choose to be manly or not. If it were, choice would be unimportant even though it is put forward as the very principle of human life. In such a society, you would think hard about what to choose and then find that your effort was wasted; there are no consequences to choice, or choice is of no consequence. When people are free to choose how they live regardless of their sex, it matters how they choose because the choice affects others; the choice of the majority rules everyone. Manliness tends to be insistent and intolerant, and it is truly a threat to the gender-neutral society. Those who want to "deconstruct" or do away with it may be wrong but they are not anxious over nothing. If manliness exists, it is probably a greater threat than these critics believe. For even if manliness is a social construction, it does not follow that it can be done away with, and reconstructed, overnight. Darwinians, as we shall see, believe in a kind of social construction of manliness that has taken place gradually over millions of years. Why would it take less time to reverse the construction? Deconstructing manliness to "masculinity" may rob it of virtue but only confirms its power.

I conclude that we must confront manliness. We cannot escape the gender-neutral society, and we cannot ignore the challenge to it. To establish choice we have to clear away the obstacle to choice. So, what is this manliness, today no longer so chauvinistic as it once was but still disdainful and yet perhaps still appreciated? We need a definition — something provisional — from which to begin.

Manliness is still around, and we still find it attractive. To begin the search for a definition that will continue through this book, let's consider what we like about manliness. Two things, I would say, for a start: the *confidence* of manly men and their ability to *command*. The confidence of a manly man gives him independence of others. He is not always asking for help or directions or instructions (for it is out of manliness that men do not like to ask for directions when lost). The manly man is in control when control is difficult or contested — in a situation of risk. He knows his job, and he stands fast in that knowledge. If he doesn't really know his job, his confidence is false and he is just boasting. If he knows it but lets himself be pushed around, he's also not really confident; he merely has the basis for confidence. The first case of boasting is a manly excess, the second is a defect of manliness. For some reason manliness includes, or is hospitable to, too much manliness, but it emphatically rejects a person who has too little of it. Perhaps it is because a manly man wants his manliness to be visible. So he is often portrayed in novels, in the movies, or wherever, in exaggeration, even though too much manliness is also a defect and can have disastrous consequences.

The independence of a manly man would keep him from getting involved with other people. He would be aloof, satisfied with himself and none too interested in other people's problems. At the least, he would wait to intervene until he is called upon to do so. But that degree of independence is in tension with the other manly element, the ability to command. The manly man is good at getting things done, and one reason is that he is good at *ordering* people to get them done. In politics and in other public situations, he willingly takes responsibility when others hang back. He not only stands fast but also steps up to do what is required. In private life, in the family, this ability makes him protective of his wife and children because they are weaker. Being protective (as opposed to nurturing) is a manly form of responsibility in private life analogous to getting into politics in public life. In both there is an easy assumption of authority. Manly men take authority for granted — the need for authority in general and their own particular authority. To the extent that all of us recognize the need for authority, whether emergency or everyday, we are attracted to those who seem to radiate authority and thus inspire confidence.

John Wayne is still every American's idea of manliness. That tells you something about the standing of manliness because John Wayne is not of our generation; in fact, he's dead. He is so far from gender-neutral that one's imagination balks at picturing him as him/her. How could his manliness be abstracted from his easy male swagger? His characters are more manly than the frenetic heroes of today's action movies who do not know how to stay quiet. The typical John Wayne movie shows the conflict between manly independence and manly command, as the question is whether he will be trapped into marriage or some other responsible situation (*Stagecoach*) or remain aloof and wild in his independence (*The Searchers*).[17] Manly men are often not hard for women to catch, but they are not easy to corral. So too in politics, the manly one is often disgusted at the irresponsibility and incompetence of those who got themselves into a mess, and he is strongly tempted, like Gary Cooper in *High Noon,* to leave them there where they belong.

We are attracted to the manly man because he imparts some of his confidence to everyone else. With his self-assumed authority he vindicates justice and makes things turn out right or at least enables us to get even. He not only knows what justice requires, but he acts on his knowledge, making and executing the decision that the rest of us trembled even to define. He knows what he is doing, himself, but in a large sense he represents human competence to all of us. He is manly man asserting the worth of man the human being (perhaps this is why, in English and in other languages, male and human being are both called "man"). In asserting his own worth, he makes us feel worthy too. While admiring him, we come to admire ourselves, since we have someone or something to look up to. Admiration is quite different from sympathy or compassion for someone's suffering. Admiration makes you look up to someone in control, compassion makes you look down to someone in distress. As with manliness, we have lost the idea but not the practice of admiration.

Let us not be too sure about manly confidence, for not everyone finds it attractive. Manliness, like suffering, deals with fear. The Greek word for manliness, *andreia,* is also the word the Greeks used for courage, the virtue concerned with controlling fear. When we come to fear, we enter the dark side of manliness. Manly men rise above their fear, but in doing so they carry their fear with them, though it is under control. Some say that manly men do not truly control their fear; they continue to struggle with it. The struggling takes the form of boasting they can overcome fear. But can they? In this view, manliness is based on the anxiety of losing one's manliness. Manly men are not confident but actually fearful. When they try to command, they become bullies. In our century, these critics say, we have seen the epitome of manliness in fascism, the theory and practice of loud, boastful, bullying, swaggering — and murderous — men.

Recalling the men who fought fascism and recoiling from this extreme of distrust, we realize that manliness is not all bad. Let's take a more complex view and consider two well-known authors who show their doubt of manliness in two well-known writings.

First, recall the incident in the first chapter of *Tom Sawyer* between Tom and the new boy in town, the one with the "citified air" that Tom could not put up with. When they meet in the street, Tom finds it necessary to challenge the new boy. The result is a dispute over nothing, arising merely for the sake of superiority: a meaningless argument, vain boasting on both sides, a line drawn in the dust, the dare to step over it accepted, a scuffle followed by recriminations and threats. It is not hard to guess that this is Mark Twain's picture of manliness done in childish caricature. He seems to say that manliness *is* childish, only perhaps not so funny and its irrationality not so obvious or so innocent when assumed by adult males. In the adult version, the scuffle is a war. Twain's critique — though this is just a glimpse of a wonderful book — resembles a woman's disdain for men's foolish daring.

Another view of manliness, more negative than it appears, can be found in Shakespeare's *Julius Caesar,* at the end, in Mark Antony's tribute to Brutus. The speech ends: "His life was gentle, and the elements so mix'd in him that Nature might stand up and say to all the world, 'This was a man.'" His life was gentle, says Antony — not anxious. What man would not want to have this said of him! But of course, Brutus has just lost the battle and has died by his own hand; any tribute from nature would be a kind of consolation in defeat. Indeed, we perhaps especially reserve tributes to manliness for noble losers; nothing more substantial is left to them. But we human beings have to make the tributes. Nature, unfortunately, does not stand up and speak for itself, as Antony seems to wish; Antony, a man, has to speak up for a man and say how perfect he was.

Actually, it is Shakespeare, speaking through Antony, who speaks for nature. Poets must assert the dignity and excellence of man against nature because nature on its own preserves no memory of the best human beings. It is only through Shakespeare (and other poets, aided by historians) that we know of Brutus, only through Homer that we know of Achilles. Manly men like Antony have a tendency to believe that manliness speaks for itself, as if manliness were a natural perfection that all can recognize implicitly, that nature makes perfectly obvious. In Shakespeare's view — again, nothing but a glimpse of one speech — manliness looks better than it does in the scene from *Tom Sawyer.* Because it serves the function of defending us against tyrants like Julius Caesar, it is not merely foolish. But manly men tend to exaggerate the naturalness of their behavior, believing that their deeds speak for themselves and need no explanation. They know how to "tell off" an opponent but not how to understand his opposition. They forget the need for poets, who are not men of action. Manliness is biased in favor of action over reflection. That is a severe criticism when you think about it. One could even say that thinking is by itself a challenge to the superiority of manliness, which is too confident of itself. Yet one could also say that imagination is in need of fact, that poets need the men of action to serve as examples of superiority, and that Shakespeare depends on Antony and Brutus to show us human greatness and individuality.

So we are beginning to get a picture of manliness, neither altogether favorable nor repellent. Manliness can have something heroic about it. (Tom Sawyer, the boy who caricatures manliness, is nonetheless Twain's hero.) It lives for action, yet is also boastful about what manly men will do and have done. It jeers at those who do not seem manly and asks us continually to prove ourselves. It defines turf and fights for it, sometimes for no good reason, sometimes to defend precious rights. And it exaggerates its independence, as if action were an end in itself and manly men were the best or only kind of human being.

This is only the beginning of a definition, but it is solid enough from which to see that manliness is both good and bad. Manliness has always been attractive, but equally it has always lived under a cloud of doubt. The doubt is raised perhaps by men who do not have the time or taste for manliness. This suggests that it is possible that manliness is not in the interest of men, or of all men, let alone women.

What prevents a woman from being manly? Today we must explain what has for so long, for millennia, been taken for granted. Are not women as confident as men? They are in their way. A lady has been defined as one who never loses her dignity regardless of the situation. But this virtue does not encourage her, may even prevent her, from seeking out situations of risk in which her dignity is challenged. A woman would not risk her dignity for no reason, like Tom Sawyer and the new boy. But this means that she might not risk her dignity for good reason, like Brutus in killing Caesar to save the Roman republic. Let us not presume that killing Caesar was done for good reason as it led to the murder of the philosopher Cicero and did not, after all, save the Roman republic. A prudent woman with confidence in her judgment might have foreseen this bad outcome, but to forestall it she would have had to take a risk or act through men who are in the habit of taking risks. Manliness is knowing how to be confident in situations where sufficient knowledge is not available.

Most people are either too enthusiastic about manliness or too dismissive of it. They think that manliness is the only virtue, and all virtue; or they think it is the last, stupid stereotype, soon to be dead as a dodo. To study it well, the trick is not to get carried away to either extreme. Yet manliness is a passionate quality, and it often leads to getting carried away, whether for good or ill. A sober, scholarly treatment risks failing to convey the nobility of manliness — it's so easy to make fun of. That's particularly true today when the picture of manliness conveyed to us is as direct and unsubtle as the actor Russell Crowe in *Gladiator,* the singer Ted Nugent in *Cat Scratch Fever,* and the wrestler Jesse Ventura in *Governor of Minnesota.*

So, we are confronted with a manliness that in refusing an equal share of housework disdains women as such, irrationally and indiscriminately — stereotypically. A manliness, too, that seeks glory in risk and cannot abide the rational life of peace and security. And a manliness that yearns for deference from the women it looks down on. In the book of an educated woman I came across this piece of wisdom quoted from another woman, not deeply educated: "The problem is that men need to feel important."[18] Exactly! Now what is the cause of this feeling and is it justified?

Chapter Two

Manliness as Stereotype

I t is a big change we make, a heavy responsibility we accept, when we go to gender neutrality and abandon manliness. In doing so we call manliness a stereotype. The word *stereotype* is a term of science, but it is also a word at large in our speech, used disparagingly to designate a construction of folklore or alleged common sense. When we call manliness a stereotype, we invoke or imply the authority of science. What does science say about manliness?

To support the change to the new society we call upon science to supply us with a study, for in our day a "study" usually means a scientific study. But there are no scientific studies of "manliness." Manliness, a quality of the soul, is not something that science looks for by that name, for science likes to refashion and rename the objects of its inquiries, and its assumptions exclude qualities difficult to measure. Science is neither poetic nor philosophic; it does not care for drama, nor does it waste time in deep thought. It wants exactness, which to it means numerical exactness, and it looks for exactness everywhere. What kind of support, then, does gender neutrality get from science? Has science verified that manliness is a stereotype? In considering these questions we will get a view of how science treats a controversial topic like manliness, subjecting it to measurement. Science does not always speak with one tongue, though apparently it always wishes to do so. On manliness, social science is hardly of one voice and is quite shaky in its conclusions, and its concerns differ markedly from those of evolutionary biology, a "natural" science. But there is general accord between the two sciences of social psychology and evolutionary biology that we will address. Although neither science is able to say clearly whether manliness is a social construction or a permanent feature of human nature, they concur that it is here to stay.[1]

Before turning to the scientific treatment of stereotype, let's first see what the manliness stereotype is. What do we nonscientists say? The definition of manliness I have given — confidence in the face of risk — is composed of a number of qualities thought to belong to men. Some apply to all men, others only to certain men, manly men. All are thought to be more or less characteristic of men, not equally true of every man. These ingredients of manliness make manliness specifically male. Without them confidence could as well be womanly (and I have said there is a womanly confidence). These qualities are, however, typically contrasted to womanly qualities, so that the stereotypes come in pairs. Stereotypes are about differences, and differences are more pronounced in contrast. Stereotypes give women an excuse for not being manly; after all, they're women. At the same time, of course, they take away any excuse for a man who is unmanly. Manliness is an exclusion of women but a reproach to men, to unmanly men.

The basic stereotype is surely that men are aggressive, women are caring. This is what you would first think of and perhaps also the basis of the others. That men are promiscuous in sex, women faithful or at least unadventurous, follows from the basic stereotype. So too do the beliefs that men are hard, women soft; men assertive, women sensitive; men seek risk, women security; men are frank, women are indirect; men take the lead, women seek company; men don't cry, women do; men are aloof, women sympathetic; men are cold, women warm; men boast and show off, women are modest; men are forceful, women persuasive or seductive; men are loud, women quiet; men are laconic, women are loquacious; men are stoic, women complain.

It's also said that men are rational, women emotional. One can easily imagine a sexist male saying that in exasperation to, or about, a woman. A more refined version of this pairing might say that men are abstract and idealistic, women are empirical and realistic. How is that related to the basic stereotype of aggression and caring? One might suggest that men use their reason to yearn beyond, and to seek to abstract from, the present situation, while women use theirs to study and make the best of the present. Men are more decisive because they can reject what they see before them, and women are more perceptive because they hesitate to do that. Thus both men and women have both reason and emotion, but differently. Yet to make this refinement moves beyond stereotyping into analysis, which stereotypes as such are supposed to avoid.

I have given a sexist accounting of the stereotypes merely by listing the male quality first in each case. To do so reflects the meaning of aggression, which is trying to be first in any situation of possible advantage. But in coming second, the womanly quality shows the need for the manly quality to be seconded, or rather, to have a counterpart. The traditional stereotypes thus aggressively assert that women are the second sex, just as Simone de Beauvoir noted in the title of her book, yet because the stereotypes come in pairs, "being second" seems to mean not merely "less" but rather providing the counterpart. Though caring is less aggressive than aggression, it is more truly a positive quality—and one not always less valued than aggression. In my list of stereotypes men do not necessarily have the advantage even though they are thought to be more aggressive in seeking advantage. Men come first, but second is sometimes better. We mustn't make a stereotype of the stereotypes by making them seem more prejudicial to women than they are.

Still, being aggressive will usually get you ahead of those who are not aggressive, especially if they defer to you. That is the traditional stereotype of a man in relation to women. It gives him his sexist disdain for women and for their effeminacy. It makes him unwilling to give women their due and generally to cooperate in the gender-neutral society. It may inspire the superiority that is responsible for the manly man's confidence discussed in chapter 1. What is the response of the gender-neutral society?

The response is in the word *stereotype,* and what is that? As used popularly today, a stereotype is a prejudice. *A stereotype is an unreflective, self-serving generalization made by someone who is too lazy or too stupid to think carefully.* That definition is too plain and much too judgmental to be found in social science, where the notion of stereotype has been developed. But let's begin from popular speech even though it has been infected by science. The gender-neutral society we have been discussing rests on the belief that manliness, the quality of one sex, does not really exist; it's only a stereotype taught to us by our patriarchal tradition, and serving the interest of that tradition, in which women are held to be unequal to men. We have lived with it up to now, but there is no necessity, there is nothing in nature, requiring us to continue living under a delusion that so drastically limits our freedom of choice.

The *word* stereotype came originally from printing: a stereotype is a kind of impression. As we use it now, the word implies that society impresses us with our notions, hence that different societies impress different notions. A stereotype is a convention, and conventions vary. You don't have to be a scientist to suppose that manliness might be a convention varying in both time and place. It's easy to see that a knight differs from a cowboy, a soldier from a priest, an aristocrat from a hardhat, a nerd from a jock, and a scholar from a pirate. The question, though, is how deep convention goes. Are these men totally diverse or are they various versions of one quality—of manliness? Does society's impress create the form, as if molding putty, or does it work upon, or from, a model made by nature, as if dressing a doll?

The gender-neutral society regards, and is obliged to regard, manliness as a stereotype in the deepest sense. The deepest sense is also a pejorative sense, for it implies that society makes a distinction between men and women that it need not have made, one that is wrongly and unjustly imposed. For a society to be equally open in all aspects to both genders, there must not, strictly speaking, be any quality pertaining to one of them that gives it an advantage or a disadvantage in life's occupations. Of course, science, wishing always to be open-minded, does not care in any case to speak either for or against a social arrangement or political proposition. Moreover, science earns its reputation for benefiting humanity by opposing common sense. After all, if unscientific common sense were enough to guide us, why would we need science with all its expensive apparatus, complicated concepts, and trained personnel? These are reasons why science would be neutral or hostile to the stereotypes of common sense. On one hand, science shows its neutrality by not insisting that common sense is prejudice; on the other, science shows its hostility by diminishing common sense to the status of imposed, inflexible stereotypes.

In the case of manliness, however, the sciences on the whole confirm common sense; they generally repeat the common-sense view that the sexes differ: men more aggressive, women more caring. This is no surprise, one could say — but no surprise is precisely the surprise. One must qualify this conclusion, of course, to accommodate diversity of results and controversy among scientists. One also senses that most scientists, whatever their findings, favor the gender-neutral society. But what they say does not really sustain it.

The *concept* of stereotype was first employed by the journalist Walter Lippmann in his 1922 book, *Public Opinion,* to give a name to the effect of culture on our perceptions and to contrast that to an appeal to reason.[2] It was then picked up by social science, notably by the Harvard psychologist Gordon Allport in his 1954 book, *The Nature of Prejudice.*[3] Allport spoke of stereotypes regarding sex; but his main interest was in racial prejudice.[4] The feminists then applied the concept to sex, which they renamed "gender" (borrowing a term of grammar) to give emphasis to the point.[5] "Gender" refers to one's sex without resort to stereotypes. It is a word that maintains contact with the bodily shapes one sees with one's eyes while refusing to draw conclusions from them. "Gender" goes with the possibility of being neutral between the sexes, while "sex" would be reserved for having fun. (No one speaks of "having gender.")[6] The traditional sex roles were stereotypes, the feminists said, both masculine and feminine and especially the latter. Betty Friedan's "feminine mystique" was the no. 1 stereotype, but next to it was its counterpart, manliness, insofar as it excluded women from occupations formerly reserved for men.

In the 1970s, the influence of feminist belief began to show in new psychological research on stereotypes, much of it by women. An important book by psychologists Eleanor Maccoby and Carol Jacklin, *The Psychology of Sex Differences* (1974), found some sex differences but was skeptical that they matter much or even that they exist. They blamed the belief in sex differences on the power of stereotypes.[7] Others attacked previous work, for example, patronizing male posturing on the "maternal instinct," as biased, erroneous, and prescientific.[8] But as the new research developed, the results were not as expected: sex differences did not disappear under the pressure of scientific experiment. The researchers did not abandon their feminism or go back to their nurseries and kitchens, but they were fair-minded enough to report conclusions that must have disappointed them. Alice H. Eagly, a Purdue psychologist, gave an account in 1995 of her change of mind, speaking calmly and objectively when in fact she was the heroine of a drama, "a political story."[9] Not only were sex differences found to persist, but some of them were also declared to be "large," according to a measure that compares all psychological differences (which tend to be small).[10]

As a result of these disturbing findings, many of them produced by women researchers, the word *sex* has not been replaced by *gender*, and usage is now quite variable. When you hear the word *gender*, you don't know whether it means sex in the sense of what is fixed or in the sense of what is changeable. You only know that it represents the aspiration of the gender-neutral society to declare that everything concerned with what used to be called sex can be remade. Deborah Tannen says, "Gender is a category that won't go away."[11] But the name for the category has changed or become confused, and perhaps that won't go away either.

Eleanor Maccoby published *The Two Sexes* in 1998, changing the view she had held in 1974. She found to be spontaneous, not imposed by our culture, the behavior we all remember of boys aged eight to eleven: they "hate" girls and refuse to have anything to do with them. Schools can sit boys and girls alternately in the classroom, but when recess comes, they separate (led by the boys) into two clumps refusing to mix. Here is the germ of manly disdain for women that endangers the gender-neutral society—but Professor Maccoby mostly leaves interpretation to others.[12]

What other sex differences, apart from boys hating girls, have been confirmed? One fine example is the "water-level test," in which a child is asked whether the level of the water in a glass half-full will be horizontal when the glass is tipped sideways. Boys are much more likely to recognize that the water will stay horizontal (if it didn't, how could you drink?); girls even up to college age, influenced by the movement of the glass, do not grasp this as quickly.[13] Women, it seems, are more "contextual," just as the stereotype says. They see the water as in the glass, not abstracted from it—in which they are wrong but not foolish. Women, so expert in noticing, remember the location of objects in a room better than men.[14]

Most of the time one sex is not more correct than the other but rather sees or acts from a justifiably different viewpoint. Women smile more than men: of those who smile more than average, 65 percent are women.[15] But isn't it defensible both to smile a lot and not to do so? Would you want to do away with either the welcoming types or the reserved and have everyone in the middle like Goldilocks smiling just the right amount? Anyway, what is the right amount? It might be to smile always, because everyone needs to be assured he is welcome, or never, because nobody deserves that assurance. It seems better to have the variety in our lives arising from diverse temperaments. And diversity is not just a range of behavior along a continuum from snarling to sycophancy but also contains couples or counterparts, such as welcome and reserve, that are represented in the two sexes.

Two kinds of sex differences relevant to our later analysis of feminism have also been confirmed. First is the sex difference over having sex. Today men are still more promiscuous than women, despite what the gender-neutral society says. "I don't pay them to come over . . . I pay them to leave," said the actor regarding the prostitutes he patronizes. Women want to stay and have to be paid to leave; men want to leave and have to be induced to stay. The studies say that men think about sex more often than women do, and what they think about is not marital bliss but "an active sex life." When men do think about marital bliss, they focus on lots of sex rather than the mere kissing and hugging that women prefer. Despite official disapproval of the double standard, the studies say it is still considered better to be a stud, like the actor, than a slut, like the women he sleeps with. Above all, in fantasies in which men can dream of their exploits with impunity and unfailing success, men show the life they really hanker for; and it's not what women dream of.[16] That men are more promiscuous than women in both attitude and behavior is perhaps the oldest common-sense fact there is, and the most useful for men and women to know. It is good to have it confirmed by science.

Steven Rhoads concludes that despite the gender-neutral society there has been no decline in sex stereotyping by people in general, who see men as more competitive and ambitious than women. The sexes still use the traditional stereotypes to describe themselves, men seeing themselves as more aggressive, women seeing themselves as more tender. Women are more likely to want to nurture, as shown in studies confirming that girls like dolls and boys like cars and guns, and that boys play rough and girls do not.[17] Eleanor Maccoby says that you never hear a mother saying to her son, "Don't play with the girls; they're too rough." By one name or another it seems true, and confirmed by science, that women have a "maternal instinct." The Census Bureau, trying to keep up with the gender-neutral society, no longer inquires "who is the head of the household," but instead wants to know who is "the family householder." Nonetheless, in 1994, Rhoads notes, 91 percent of American couples said it's the husband.[18]

Second, let's take note of the sex difference over assertiveness. There are language differences in assertiveness that the linguist Robin Lakoff brought to light in her influential book *Language and Woman's Place* (1975) and that the sociolinguist Deborah Tannen described in her best-selling *You Just Don't Understand* (1990).

Lakoff pointed out certain distinctive features of women's speech. Women use a more specialized vocabulary for female tasks, such as cooking; they use milder expletives than do men; they use more empty adjectives like "cute" than men do; they attach tag questions at the end of assertions (don't you agree?); they use a wider range of pitch and intonation, as if avoiding flat statements; they employ "superpolite" forms, such as "I wonder if you would mind"; they sort of hedge their assertions; their grammar is more correct than men's and avoids vulgar or coarse words; and they do not tell jokes.[19] Lakoff believed that these differences showed hesitancy and ingratiation in women toward men, which she deplored as weakness. But Tannen in her work attempted to rescue "women's speech" from Lakoff's indignant scorn and to restore its value and legitimacy. Whereas Lakoff thought that women's speech submerged their identity, Tannen shows how it expresses their womanly ways.[20] Her title, *You Just Don't Understand,* says that there is something being conveyed and worth understanding in the ways men and women talk.

Listening to ordinary conversations, Tannen finds two "equally valid styles," even two "worlds" that distinguish women from men.[21] She does not begin by looking for stereotypes so as to test their accuracy, thus looking down upon her subject; instead she asks what men and women mean when they converse. Men and women live for contrasting ways of life: men want independence, women intimacy. When men speak, they report what they know or believe, as if lecturing in public to an audience. When women speak, they seek rapport with their listeners so as to connect with them. As men are always speaking as if it were in public, so women treat every audience as if the discussion were private. Both men and women speak in context, there is always a "frame" in which conversation occurs, but women are more "contextual" than men. When men say something, it's take it or leave it. Men's speech is more *assertive* than women's.

By omitting Tannen's excellent examples I have made her book seem more abstract than it is, less contextual, perhaps more manly. Tannen sometimes uses her own reactions to illustrate the way women think, especially when it is a question of how the two sexes misinterpret each other.[22] For her theme is *misunderstanding* in human conversation. The two styles are equally valid because each appears sufficient to itself; both men and women, if uninstructed by experience or by Tannen's book, are satisfied with their style of conversing. Thus they do not really listen to the other sex; even women, who are supposed to be listeners, mistake disagreement in conversation for hostility. The two sexes misunderstand, misinterpret, each other. The same action, say a polite request, that looks like subservience to a man looks like sensitivity to a woman.[23] If a woman is silent, a man thinks she has nothing to say; if a man is silent, women think he does not need to speak. Silence means lack of power in the first instance; confident power in the second.[24] Somehow, as Tannen notes, women get the short end of the stick. This is not because women are frightened out of demanding their just deserts but because they want something different—intimacy rather than domination. Men with their seeming indifference to the context are actually very concerned with hierarchy; they want to rebel against it, show their independence of it, climb to the top of it, or establish an equality within it. Women are more democratic, or more effortlessly democratic, because they do not begin from the desire to contest.

Involved as it is with context, Tannen's psychology constantly threatens to become political and shrewdly stops short of politics just when it might become partisan. On the whole, it can hardly be said to endorse the gender-neutral society. Although she does not directly address the question of whether the talking styles of the two sexes are fixed in nature, it is fairly clear that for her they are.[25] These ways are not imposed on men and women or on women by men; they are spontaneous and congenial to both sexes. More than that, they go beyond routine, habit, or unconscious custom; they represent two ways of thinking. The thinking is implicit and has to be elicited by Deborah Tannen, but it is there. In regard to women, we can say that Tannen "valorizes" the feminine mystique that Betty Friedan named and attacked.[26] Women are not moping in their suburban homes with nothing to do; they are doing what they like to do. What they like is the caring that the stereotype says they like, just as men enjoy being aggressive.

Yet Tannen, a very successful professional woman, does not stay at home satisfied with the intimacy of her family and friends. Nor is she bound by the feminine character she describes so well. *You Just Don't Understand* implicitly promises understanding of the other sex, not just your own. At several points in the book Tannen suggests that it is possible to do this and that two good results would follow.[27] One is that the sexes will stop blaming each other so easily, and the other, more interesting, is that having learned both styles, we will be more flexible in our choice of strategies and thus freer.[28] This, I have to say, is a Machiavellian idea. After being persuaded at length of the integrity of the two styles, it is disconcerting to be told that one is free to be one or the other. And is this flexibility truly symmetrical? I can see how a dominating person could make use of the ability to seem caring, but how could a caring person be dominating without ceasing to be caring?

Pursuing the opposites of aggression and context, let us examine the sex differences in verbal fluency (advantage to women) and spatial ability (advantage to men). Women are more fluent with words than men; they are better at producing rapid and accurate speech.[29] Stuttering is almost entirely a male problem, as is dyslexia. Women can think of synonyms and do anagrams more quickly, and they compute faster. Their verbal facility helps them to keep contact with their context and to achieve and maintain a measure of intimacy. Men, on their side, excel at verbal analogies (of the kind recently abandoned for precisely this reason on the college SAT examinations), at mathematical problem solving, and especially at mentally rotating objects in space. Hence men are better at navigating—which is good, considering their proverbial resistance to asking directions (noted in chapter 1). But how is spatial ability in men related to their aggression? Aggression is selfish or self-centered. But to be self-centered, you need to be free or make yourself free from the environment in which you find yourself. Whereas infant girls look at what surrounds them, infant boys orient themselves to objects. Boys have better mechanical ability than girls. For these things you need to be able to abstract yourself, you need to be able to think abstractly, to see things as they might be in different contexts or without a context. That is the connection I see between aggression and abstraction. Aggression and abstraction are two forms of being single-minded.

This has been a quick survey of what the science of psychology tells us now about sex differences. In sum, it says that men are aggressive, women contextual. Other terms used for men are agentic, instrumental; and for women, expressive, communal, intimate. The various studies focus on narrow items like the water-level test because these can be quantified, but when you add them up — in what is called "meta-analysis" — the result is the same contrast. This contrast between the sexes follows the stereotypes, both in sum and in detail. In fact, as well as I can see, of the stereotypes listed at the beginning of the chapter not one has been disproved (including men's boasting and women's weeping).[30] Common sense has been vindicated by science, and I will add that, vice versa, science has been validated by having discovered in its way what everyone knows without science.[31] For if science had discovered that women were more aggressive than men, one would rather believe one's eyes than that science. Some scientists speak of "relational aggression" in women, referring to women (and girls) who attack other women indirectly; they "shun, stigmatize, gossip, and spread false rumors." But relational aggression is not bold, and what is aggression without boldness?[32]

Stereotype is a social-scientific concept designed to improve upon common belief, and yet we find that in regard to manliness the psychologists end up endorsing common belief. Are we to think that in this important matter science is no better than common belief? Is it possible that science falls short of it? The fact that science cannot speak of manliness by its name tells us something about science as well as manliness: science wants to be exact and manliness wants to boast. Because science desires never to overstate a point, it has trouble understanding the human desire to overstate. Common sense, as we have seen, can appreciate the desire to "feel important."

Let's return to the disdain for women on the part of the manly man, the superior feeling that makes him unwilling or unable to cooperate in the gender-neutral society. He will carry out the garbage and do other tasks he recognizes as his, but only those and not what he sees to be women's work. The psychologists who admit sex differences are far from drawing the conclusion that manly disdain of this kind is legitimate, but some of them, we have noted, remark on the surprising accuracy of sex stereotypes. From the outset Lippmann and Allport had stipulated that stereotypes may have a "kernel of truth"; fewer Jews are drunks than Irish, said sober Allport in the free-speaking 1950s. These writers had understood stereotypes as categories, and anyone who thinks needs categories. How then do we distinguish the categories of the prejudiced from those of thinking persons who are not prejudiced? Allport, in liberal fashion, tried to describe "monopolistic" categories held inflexibly from "differentiated" ones open to new knowledge.[33] But if we accept the accuracy of sex stereotypes, it seems that people prejudiced in favor of manliness were right to hold that traditional belief inflexibly; and in doing so they held substantial truth, not a mere kernel. More recent psychologists have invented the notion of "cognitive shortcut" by which it makes sense to use hasty generalizations when one doesn't have time to think carefully, with "differentiation," as Allport wants. Psychologists habitually label "cognitive" every excuse for knowledge, in which they are partly right. It's important to remember that prejudice is a claim to know, in that sense "cognitive," but one mustn't forget that it's also an evasion of any attempt to learn. "Cognitive shortcut" is a psychologists' evasion of the duty of science to sit in judgment over popular prejudice.

The psychologists suggest, too, that sex stereotypes are not acquired or practiced without thinking. One authorial foursome says that women's language may not always be uncertain but sometimes deliberately sensitive. In order not to annoy an attractive male, a woman might play dumb so as not to offend him, thus thoughtfully and perhaps ironically conforming to the stereotype.[34] Such behavior is not correct in the gender-neutral society, but it may occasionally occur nonetheless. Maccoby points out that children first select spontaneously the sort of toy they like, and then, after becoming aware that it is the sort that boys or girls like, they apply the stereotype consciously.[35] The stereotype is the consequence, not the cause, of the behavior — or perhaps it is an interaction; and it shows awareness, not rigidity.

The same general sex stereotype appears in the much-read work of psychologist Carol Gilligan, *In a Different Voice*. Her plea, directed particularly to feminists, is that their demands for the justice of equality should not overlook and thus devalue the characteristic "voice" of women, the ethic of care and attention to relationships. Gilligan does not tell us about the manly voice that is perhaps not so caring, and she does not infer that the caring voice of women disadvantages women in any way when in competition with a manly voice. Her work leads her to the stereotype of women, but it does not provoke her to reconsider hostility to stereotypes as such, still less to question the gender-neutral society. Her research has been criticized for lack of rigor as if rigor were possible. The most successful studies, such as those of Eleanor Maccoby and Deborah Tannen, have departed from strict science and accepted common sense in an uneasy alliance of professional rigor and the plain citizen's naïvete. They are based partly, or mostly, on observation of behavior as it appears to us rather than on experiment under laboratory conditions intended to abstract from the ordinary appearances of things. They smack of phenomenology, a philosophical movement dedicated to "saving the phenomena," that is, the way things appear to us humans as opposed to the theories and categories of quantifiable psychology. A sign of the difference is that Maccoby and Tannen use ordinary words for the most part and not the concepts — the jargon — of science.

The jargon of science is part of the ambition of science to examine what is obvious to us and to restate in more precise terms the words we normally use. Nobody objects if a botanist wants to call a daffodil *narcissus pseudo-narcissus,* and botanists do not care if we continue with the common name. But when it comes to human society, science is not, and cannot be, so tolerant. Here the common names stand for prejudices that protect society as it is and has been. At a certain point, social science decided to rename prejudices "stereotypes." The scientific word then passed from books of science to everyday talk and was applied by the women's movement to sex in order to change society. But change was already implied in the scientific usage. Social science invented the very idea of stereotypes in order to impugn common prejudice. It wanted not only to deny prejudice the status of common sense but to wave it out of political debate, which henceforth would be conducted exclusively among scientific hypotheses. Social science does not as a rule listen to prejudice. With such terms as *stereotype* it prejudges the truth of nonscientific opinion; it has a prejudice against prejudice. It is therefore in general hostile to the status quo and friendly to change toward the new gender-neutral society. The gender-neutral society, in turn, is very welcoming to social science and to such concepts as "stereotype" or such constructions as "he or she" that express neutrality—or should we not say scientific objectivity? Isn't objectivity akin to neutrality? Objectivity requires one to put aside one's personal attributes, including one's sex, in understanding what is to be expected of the male or female sex. And neutrality toward the sexes presupposes that it is possible to look at them objectively, which means to judge by their behavior and not by outworn social expectations set by fuddy-duddies ages ago.[36]

The ambition of science is thus to change society as a whole. It is no surprise that in everyday speech "stereotypes" are often called "traditional stereotypes," especially in regard to sex. The tradition of different roles for the two sexes is impressively long—long enough to comprise all societies except advanced liberal democracies today. That tradition survived every democratic revolution except the most recent one of the women's movement. But the knowledge that this would be the first sexually just society did not compel social scientists to hesitate, nor did it sober up the revolutionaries; on the contrary, it added to their exuberance at making a truly radical if perfectly obvious liberation. Both groups shared the optimism of Lippmann, Allport, and the others that society did not have to live by stereotypes. Previous thinkers were aware that society might not be resting on simple truth. Plato in his image of the cave said that all societies live by artificial shadows rather than knowledge.[37] It is nothing new to suppose that people are prejudiced, but the concept of "stereotype" amounts to a scientific denial that they have to be. Our use of "stereotypes" still carries with it the incautious optimism that science, with its objectivity, does its best to conceal. The concept recalls the original eighteenth-century Enlightenment that began the attempt to bring science to society so as to replace prejudice and superstition with knowledge.

Science so understood can make society competent to govern itself. It can give fresh justification to democracy, now no longer despised as the rule of an ignorant multitude but capable of becoming the rule of the enlightened. For the hidden ambition of social science is not only to make society more democratic but also to enlighten democracy. Being so apolitical, social science does not understand how democratic it is, and its ambition is hidden to itself more than to outside observers. The stereotype itself is a very democratic idea, presupposing both the dominance of democratic opinion and the possibility of correcting it. Stereotyping occurs when people prepare categories of "people perceived to differ significantly from one's own"; stereotypes are made by the in-group to categorize the out-group.[38] With these categories they justify "discrimination," meaning unjustifiable discrimination and assuming democratically that *any* discrimination is likely to be unjustified. Stereotyping is a democratic failure to be sufficiently democratic. In an aristocracy where the aristocrats are disdainful of the people as such, one would not speak of stereotypes. But the theory of stereotypes assumes that all people are alike and do not deserve to be held inferior.

The real problem in a democracy, however, may be just the opposite of stereotypes: considering those who are unlike to be alike. Tocqueville said that democracies tend to generalize, meaning that they generalize too far; they tend to make everyone similar (*semblables*) to one another.[39] Perhaps the gender-neutral society is an instance of overgeneralizing, in which democratic impulse and scientific objectivity go hand-in-hand, each deferent to the other but regarding itself as superior. Yet in fact we see that the psychologists of sex differences, most of them women, have mostly concluded that the sex stereotypes are generally accurate. They do not go so far as to question the idea of a gender-neutral society, but they know that their results do not favor it and are not congenial to its promoters. Democracy, too, has its pretensions, and the main one these days is that sex differences do not exist.

Yet even the best of the psychologists' studies do not go beyond the rudiments of manliness. They suffer, in lesser degree, from the defects of scientific studies that use jargon, embrace statistical regressions, and close the door to common sense. There are five faults in the scientific studies I have read that greatly undermine their utility and authority. These are not imperfections of an immature field that could be remedied with more research of the same kind, nor do they result from the limitations of individuals (all of whom know science, in their sense, much better than I). They are systematic failures of method that hinder or prevent the understanding of manliness.

Scientific studies of sexual differences, we recall, are not about "manliness" so called. Why not? "Manliness," it seems, is not a scientific word. It is said of an individual as a whole in consideration of all his manly actions, or better, manly deeds, and with a view to his disposition to such deeds. But the studies, seeking quantifiable precision, split up the sexes into discrete aspects or behaviors, such as spatial and verbal abilities or violent and nonviolent tendencies, and then *never reassemble the pieces into a whole*. They begin with man and woman but never return to man and woman as wholes. Men have better spatial abilities than women and are also (surprise!) more violent. Are these two things connected? Sometimes, using meta-analysis, the studies try to connect two aspects, but not these two; and they always stop well before they return to the whole individual being they started from. They focus on qualities they can isolate so as to measure them, but their precision is only in carving. Regarding individuals as wholes, the studies are so imprecise as to say almost nothing.[40] These studies stand in need of the precision they would gain from biography and history, showing manly individuals in action. What does John Wayne or Theodore Roosevelt show us about manliness in its completeness? A manly man is nothing if not an individual, one who sets himself apart, who is concerned with the honor rather than survival of his individual being. Or, better to say, he finds his survival only in his honor.

Lack of interest in wholes shows in the scientific rejection of the term *natural*. It is a term we shall soon need, and one long said to be harder to dispose of than you might think. The nature of a thing displays it as a whole to which its parts contribute. A whole with parts, like an apple, must be something fixed. Some time ago, the famous anthropologist Margaret Mead wrote a book in which she distinguished the layman's typical remark, *"naturally* no human society" from the anthropologist's statement of scientific caution, "no *known* human society." Yet she went ahead and titled her book *Male and Female* as if there were no difference between the two statements. The reason is that she wanted "man" to mean men of many kinds or rather of diverse combinations of qualities so that man could be "open-ended." Yet open-ended is still a fixed description of man's . . . nature. Mead published her book in 1949, before feminism got started with its assertion of the possibility of creating one's identity, and Mead herself was sure that there were "basic regularities" in the sexes that would limit our creativity.[41] But the point is the same. The overcaution (or pretended caution) of science, based on its dogmatic assurance that nothing is for sure, lends credence to the revolutionary's desire that anything be possible.

Instead of looking at men and women as wholes, the social psychologists put their diverse qualities on a unisex continuum and add them up. Alice Eagly speaks of the change in the 1970s from narrative studies to quantitative ones and remarks, "By implying that a continuum is the best metaphor for thinking about sex differences and similarities, . . . psychologists . . . escape the more simplistic debate about sameness versus difference."[42] These psychologists dislike *versus;* they prefer a continuum by which they assume prior to inquiry that every difference is a matter of degree. A boy is a wee bit more of this than a girl and a wee bit less of that. Thinking like this will prevent us from overstating the sex differences as do the stereotypes. But in fact it prevents us from coming, or even attempting to come, to a conclusion about the sameness and difference of the sexes. Nothing is more simplistic than the assumption of a soupy continuum from one sex to the other, whose purpose is to avoid debate. Later I shall speak of the manliness of modern science, but here we see unmanly evasion.

Unconcern with the best is another failing. Just as the studies focus on isolated qualities, so, relying on the deceptive precision of statistics, they consider mainly averages. But in the vernacular, "manly" is a term of praise usually reserved for the few best. Manliness is not so much what all males share, or what most males share with a few females, as what a few males have superlatively. The rest merely show traces of these few, and the few manly types look down on the rest whom they think unmanly. Now is a manly man the best man — as he plainly believes (and as Antony believed of Brutus)? Does he have in greatest measure the qualities that, as a whole, make one want to call a man a man? Should the rest of us share his opinion of himself? Many a woman has had to face the choice between romance with a manly fellow and security with a more careful, prudent type. Which is best? Which is more of a man? Can the two be combined?

The scientific studies looking at the average overlook the best, and therefore also the ambivalence of the best. They want concepts that cover all instances of what appears to be "man," but they forget that the defining qualities of man are those of the best man as well as, or more than, the average. In no case is this truer than in that of the manly man, who is inspired by perfect examples of his own type. The manly man may be seen better in fiction, where a poet can exceed reality, than in science, or the kind of science, which confines itself to the universal case. Is the manly man Achilles or is he Socrates?[43]

The studies *lack nuance and subtlety*. In order to establish sex differences they have to measure different behaviors, and what is measurable has to be unmistakable. It does not matter if the difference is tiny, but it has to be unmistakable so that it will not be open to interpretation. Any discovery open to interpretation tempts disagreement, and that we must not have. Science seeks agreement even as scientists disagree. Women, for example, are found to have greater verbal abilities than men, meaning greater fluency, or volubility, or persuasiveness, or eloquence, or something else. But what of the grace with which women persuade, contrasted with the authority of a male voice? "Verbal ability," though divided into particular aspects, is a broad, clunky quality designed to measure rather than describe. It says nothing of the diverse ways men and women speak—or sing.[44]

These studies are also *too far from human life*. *Verbal ability* and *spatial ability* are terms abstracted from the use of words and the manipulation of images in actual life. These are concepts constructed for the sake of scientific observers, not for the use of human beings. They suffer from the fatal need to "operationalize," that is, from the need to restate the facts a scientist encounters in terms that he, as opposed to the human beings he observes, can operate with.[45] So "verbal ability" is fluency operationalized, made abstract so as to be measurable in experiments. Betty Friedan, by contrast, speaks of real human beings when in her famous book she raises "the problem that has no name." She may be wrong in her analysis, but she looked at things the way human beings look at things and correctly sensed that women wanted or needed something new. In our studies, however, the problems are scientific; they are generated from difficulties of scientific observation and discrepancies of results. They are not the problems that human beings face and define. This means that the scientific studies abstract from the culture in which we live, the "regime," as Aristotle called it. Their authors are aware, of course, that we live in a democracy now very suspicious of alleged differences between men and women. They step carefully because they know that they are writing for the gender-neutral society. But they do not address that society or its democratic demand; with the exception of Alice Eagly and a few others, they do not directly consider the importance, or unimportance, of sex differences. It might be apes we are talking about, and in fact they do frequently discuss "primates," and it seems with equal sympathy, too. There is some, but not enough — to repeat a word — *phenomenology* in the study of manliness now.[46]

Some of the social psychologists, we have seen, refer to stereotypes as cognitive shortcuts. We haven't the time to learn better; so we use "an implicit personality theory" and decide men are aggressive.[47] Social scientists often say that science differs from common sense only by making explicit theories that nonscientists hold implicitly. The true distinction, they claim, is not between common sense and theory but between theory that is unaware of itself and explicit theory that follows scientific method. To say this, however, understates the difference between science and common sense (as if there were a continuum between them) and causes science, not common sense, to be unaware of itself — unaware of its pretensions as well as its limitations.

I could have said at once that the studies *do not evaluate what they try to describe.* Here is the most obvious difference they have with the vernacular stereotypes, which are the basis of moral judgments about how men and women should behave. The scientists are professionally required to subscribe to the fact-value distinction, known loosely as "positivism," a position in philosophy that sensible people never believed and that trendy people no longer believe.[48] Take, once again, the deficit in aggression to be found in women when compared to men. Is this sex difference commendable modesty in women or blamable timidity? No doubt it is both, sometimes one, sometimes the other. But modesty is not just a positive spin, nor timidity a negative spin on the same fact of nonaggressiveness; they are quite different facts, the first showing control in a woman, the second not. The difference may be difficult to discern but it is very important. Anyone who is satisfied with a broad, behavioral, allegedly value-free description, such as "less aggressive," will not describe accurately but will mix together phenomena that are distinct. The same is true of men described as "more aggressive," when we want to know whether they are properly so or not. Our everyday speech is more objective than scientific objectivity; it uses terms that do not hover hesitantly over an area of meaning but that bring things to a point. "A point" refers both to accuracy and to judgment. To evaluate well you must pay attention to the facts; but to describe well you must do so with the intent to evaluate.[49]

Thus the social scientists take for granted the superiority of their theory without considering what it consists in. They try to condescend to common sense while taking advantage of its insight (for example, that men are indeed more aggressive). I will try to do the reverse. I will treat the scientific studies in manliness as imperfect versions of the stereotypes. I think that manliness is part stereotype or prejudice and part common sense. One difficulty is to sort out one from the other; another is to go beyond both.

Now it should be clearer why I am not offering another new "study" like those the press so frequently reports. One reason is that there is wisdom in the thought of the past. Another is that in the scientific methodology of the present there is a kind of guaranteed imprecision and unwisdom. It may seem ungrateful for me to say so because the sex difference studies I am denouncing do in general support a moderate manliness by telling the world that men and women are different, and more, that they differ pretty much in the ways that we have always supposed. To remove this ungracious impression, I will accept their support as far as it goes. I have nothing against science or against the good intent of scientists today, but I do think that their method, applied to human beings, gets in the way of science. By "science" I mean not a huge, well-financed, cooperative, corporate, enterprise, but mere understanding, the goal rather than the apparatus of science.

Assuming, then, the general accuracy of sex stereotypes, let's ask why sex differences persist. What explains them? The gender-neutral society does its best to destroy them but only succeeds in minimizing them or in suppressing overt reliance on them, as when husbands abandon male privilege and say they will do half the housework but don't actually do it. In the case of sexual promiscuity, the gender-neutral society by giving women an equal privilege makes it harder for them to say no, thus facilitating the aggressive fantasies of males and aggravating the sex difference in that regard.[50] The best efforts of social construction by the gender-neutral society have in some ways reduced but have not done away with sex differences. Hence, one concludes, social construction did not cause the differences. They must be traced to a deeper cause, to what is unchangeable, to nature. That is why some of the psychologists and sociologists turn to evolutionary biology to support their findings of sex differences still persisting in a society that wants to be rid of them.[51] Manliness, we shall see, is not sufficient to itself but needs and sometimes wants the support of nature. So, too, social science in order to explain manliness (which it cannot name) goes eagerly if sometimes inexpertly to natural science in search of fundamental theory.

But before we do that, we can look at observable facts of plain biology showing that nature seems to put the equipment of aggression in the hands of males rather than females. Men have more strength, size, and agility than females, who in turn have greater dexterity, delicacy, and endurance (they live longer). It is no small help to an aggressive disposition to have the means available to express it in powerful fists, a sturdy chest, a head to butt with, and feet that can kick. Imagine the frustration of having a male's desire to fight implanted in the yielding body of a female — an anomaly occasionally seen. Of course male aggression is mostly directed against other males, and a manly spirit in a very small male might cut a ridiculous figure, like a hare trying to lay down the law to lions.[52] But in the relation between the sexes the physical superiority of males to females will give impressive support to their more aggressive wills. Despite the laws, the customs, and the morals that we live under, it is still a considerable fact that almost any man can beat up almost any woman. A man can be caught unawares (which happens more often than one would think), but "battered men" is not a general problem men complain of. The physical discrepancy sets the terms of a relationship, not preventing women from getting their way but requiring them to be indirect, persuasive, and "contextual." Women have to smile and be reasonable or make a scene. Either choice is harder than just doing what you want.

That male's willful will, too, is not just a concept, an airy, bodiless wish with nothing behind it. It has been found to have a chemical basis in the hormonal differences between men and women: men have much more testosterone. The political scientist Andrew Sullivan, who suffers from a condition requiring him to inject himself with testosterone, has written a graphic account of the leap in vigorous spiritedness that results. While it lasts he becomes a living, strutting stereotype.[53]

Let's turn now to the theory underlying sex differences. In our time the strongest scientific opposition to the gender-neutral society comes from evolutionary biology, a field that descends from the theory published in 1859 by Charles Darwin. It might seem strange that this should be so because "evolution" was first set forth in opposition to the opinion of both Aristotle and the Bible that the species were fixed and had always been as they are rather than coming to be by evolution. A theory of evolution would seem, then, to resemble a theory of social construction, which also features change. If manliness has not always been as it is but has been made, it would seem not to matter much whether it is made by nature's evolution (actually, women's choices in sexual selection) or by society's artificial construction. But in fact it does matter. Nature's evolution takes place over millions of years, whereas the changes demanded by the gender-neutral society are expected to occur soon or immediately.[54] Darwin's theory may have been radical when first conceived, but now it serves the conservative purpose of defending manliness against those necessary changes. In my view it goes too far — oddly enough, it goes further than its great enemy, Aristotle — and is much too adamant in justifying a much too primitive manliness.

It is best to discuss Darwinism by consulting Darwin. Darwin himself may have evolved by chance, but his theory descends to us by design. Darwin makes the issues clearer than do his present-day followers because he wanted to build the edifice that they live in, and he saw the alternatives and made the choices that they accept as given. Darwin's thinking is critical for modern beliefs about manliness, and we shall be returning to him frequently.

Darwin sees nature, or organic nature, as a "struggle for existence" in which the result is "the survival of the fittest."[55] These two famous phrases (the second adopted by Darwin from Herbert Spencer) reveal the nasty character of nature together with its happy ending. Manliness in its aggressive stereotype proves to be not something artificial or accidental but the very essence of nature; and manly aggression is excused by the end that it does not wish but nonetheless brings about — the perfection of each species, especially the human species.[56] Nature has a good intention, but it does not use good means to that end. Nature takes care for the preservation of each species yet cares nothing for the individuals of that species. Its care for the species shows in the geometric rate of increase that the species would achieve if unchecked. That increase, however, is checked by other species, by others of the same species, by the shortage of available sustenance and space. So to each individual, and Darwin looks at nature from the viewpoint of the individual, life seems threatening rather than sweet. Nature's generosity to the species is the cause of its lack of generosity to individuals. The species survives by reproductive oversupply in the midst of which every individual must scramble for his own life with the aid of natural instinct, in the case of man haunted by awareness and fear of death.

Here one might expect a complication arising from the discrepancy between nature's goal for the species and man's conscious goal to pursue his perfection as he sees it. But no, there is nothing special about man. Man has intelligence and "social habits," but these do not free him from evolution. Darwin says that he is the dominant animal, but he is an animal nonetheless, differing in degree and not in kind from other animals.[57] His life, like any other form of life, is dominated by the struggle for existence. Darwin adds the concept of "sexual selection" to that of "natural selection." Natural selection is nature's preference, better to say insistence, that the species survive, and it is shown in the small improvements that constitute evolution. Sexual selection consists of the aims or "strategies" of individuals for reproductive success understood not as survival of the species but of the individual's genes in following generations.[58]

In sexual selection men and women devote themselves to self-preservation in an extended sense. They want to preserve not only their bodies but also — not their souls, of course! — their genes. They may have to risk their bodies for the sake of having offspring. This means that for Darwin as contrasted to Thomas Hobbes the state of nature has a competition for women as well as a war of all against all. The struggle for existence changes its focus from life in your own body to the life of the bodies to which you give birth. The struggle thus takes different forms for men and women, since women because of their bodies have care of gestation and lactation and men, because of theirs, do not. Men compete with other men for women in a struggle that does not, like the struggle for existence, end in death. But it does make man "more courageous, pugnacious and energetic than woman," and gives him "a more inventive genius."[59] Hence we have in Darwin, very much contrary to the gender-neutral society, natural sex roles. These are ways of life in which each sex specializes and must pursue lest any individual fail to preserve, which means propagate, his own genes. Self-preservation for Darwin seems less futile than for Hobbes because it does not end in the mortality of man; one can be preserved in one's children. But the genes — one's immortality — are dispersed in following generations.

In the end aggression is all there is. Man is not, as Aristotle said, a pairing animal who takes pleasure and finds utility in the company of one member of the opposite sex.[60] There are different versions of aggressiveness, but the underlying motive is the same. Women may not use their fists, but they use their attractions. Men have manliness so as to compete with other men; women use the manliness of men to protect themselves and their children. And if women consciously manipulate men for their purposes, men dominate women for theirs. A woman may look as if she is surrendering, but in truth she is indulging her relational aggression. The sex differences studied by the psychologists are apparent but not fundamental; both sexes are aggressive. As we know without psychology, you can smile at someone while getting one up on him. Still, the fundamental truth that all human beings are aggressive does little for the gender-neutral society. The apparent difference between manly domination and womanly manipulation must be maintained despite their fundamental similarity or else the strategies will not work. Women must continue to smile and defer while looking for a quality mate. For in their strategies for reproductive success, men need quantity and women need quality. Men must sow their seed as widely as possible, but a woman must choose carefully as to whose seed she bears and rears. The double standard rears its ugly head.[61] It is not that man and woman form a couple and have a common good to which they contribute differently, which is the double standard Aristotle describes. It is rather that nature compels them to make use of each other: in Darwin's view marriage is not a kind of friendship, and fidelity to it is not in the interest of the male. What man and woman have in common is the aggression in two opposed forms that divides them.

So far I have been looking at Darwin's theory from a moral or human standpoint, one from which aggression is fully endorsed and justified as good for the species. From this standpoint, however, the manly man would hardly recognize himself. As we have seen him so far, he is preeminently an individual concerned with himself and the circle of those within his protection (which might be as large as his country). In his self-concern he wants the credit and glory for his deeds from those he benefits; he does not care about the preservation of the species or even that of his own descendants much beyond his grandchildren. A theory like Darwin's that pretends to be based on individual decisions as to what will enable one to survive is strangely distant from the purview of actual individuals. Actual males do not care for nature's purpose, as explained by Darwin, of perfection in the species. Their aggression is neither so selfless nor so selfish. It is for the sake of advantage now and in the near future for identifiable humans instead of in the indefinite future for his invisible, uncollected genes. Darwin's theory adopts the idea of manly aggression but distorts it by truncating and abstracting it almost as if it were — a stereotype. The theory does not see that manly men want to protect themselves and theirs, that manly aggression does not want to survive by adaptation, that it is essentially defensive. Darwin's theory tries to connect the individual with the ultimate collectivity, the species, while ignoring the bonds of friendship, family, and politics that are in between.

To explain this criticism, let us look more closely at Darwin's theory and consider its difficulties as science. There is no space to elaborate but for our purpose there is no need. Darwin's theory says that the species evolve; they are not fixed. The species evolve gradually by the "natural selection" of minute, chance changes from prior species, those changes that are "adapted to" the "survival" of the species being the ones selected. The gradualness of change by small adaptations is required not so much by the facts as for the theory itself, by the scientific understanding of causation; for each effect must be brought about by the conditions preceding it.[62] If change were not gradual, one could not explain the later species on the basis of what came before it; one would have to assume a leap from one species to another by "special creation," a concept smacking of divine intervention that Darwin set himself to oppose.[63] "Evolution" is not a consequence of Darwin's theory but presupposed by it.[64] And yet how does evolution explain the existence of the species, which must be to some extent, or mainly, fixed? If there were very many chance mutations, why would they settle or cluster into the recognizable whole of a species? A species is a going concern, a whole being with functioning parts that can reproduce itself. It is not a cluster of mutations that happen to fit. A stock car can be adapted to become a hot rod by a teen-age mechanic, but how can an elephant be caused by chance fiddling with a pre-elephant? There is a distance between the mastodon and the elephant that cannot be bridged by mincing steps of evolution; at some point a distinct new being must be organized. The new being does not simply represent the survival of the old being, which according to the theory becomes extinct because it cannot compete with the new one.[65]

In speaking of survival it is always necessary to specify *survival as what?*[66] Survival of the mastodon is hardly assured by its turning into an elephant. This is survival only in a perverted sense. Something is saved, one supposes, but more is lost; the previous organism was found not to be viable and it disappears. But of course it may not disappear. Not only do species have fixity, but they also have hierarchy. The fact that elephants, let alone cockroaches, cannot compete with men in the struggle for survival does not mean that they disappear. Evolution does not erode all the species into the one all-adaptive being—whether human being or cockroach—that has the highest capacity to survive. In sum, Darwin does not account for the species when he claims to explain "the origin of species." He takes them for granted.

Thus Darwin takes for granted human beings as they are today; *theirs* is the origin to be explained by his theory. He does not show, as he claims, that the higher species evolve from the lower; he works backward from the species as they have evolved. The origin of the species refers to the species as they are now, especially the human species. Because *The Origin of Species* (1859) did not say much about human beings, Darwin wrote *The Descent of Man* (1871), to make it clear that man descends "from some lower form." But the higher form, man, is the thing to be explained—*this* higher form. According to the theory, man is an accident and could have been other than he is. Yet without man, a being capable of science, there would be no science; so Darwin needs to show how a scientific being could have evolved out of some lower form. He does not really begin with the lower form; he knows beforehand that it is going to result in, and be capable of, science or intelligence. He begins from the awareness that the lower form is lower than what is going to evolve, a higher form. He is not, as he thinks, free of presuppositions but, in fact, takes for granted the intelligible hierarchy of nature somewhat as Aristotle laid it out. This is why he can speak of the grandeur and perfection of nature, and especially of man.[67] I do not mean to say that

Darwin, the enemy of fixed species and of teleology, is a secret Aristotelian; what I say is that he had more difficulty than he knew in escaping Aristotle's elaborated common sense.

Darwin's theory should tell him that man is not a definite stopping point, that he is bound to evolve into something unknown.[68] Yet the difference between the higher form and the lower ones seems quite definite. When Darwin finds such human attributes as curiosity and dread in monkeys, he does so by measuring the distance down from the higher form rather than up from the lower one. He does not really derive the higher from the lower. Darwin himself spoke of the difficulty of explaining the evolution of the human eye, which seems so far ahead of any other animal's eye.[69] In general, it is hard to conceive how mind could evolve from nonmind, how the ability to think, to make images and to see what is invisible ("I see your point!"), could evolve, bit by bit, from the absence of these advantages. Nor, *pace* Rousseau, is there evidence of such evolution.

These matters of theory may not overthrow Darwin, but they complicate the Darwinian picture of man and make a puzzle of the "struggle for existence." Manliness in his view is aggression that is valued and chosen by women for their protection and thus "selected" by nature for survival to the next generation and beyond. Although men survive by attacking an enemy, species survive by being "adaptive." But could not clever men take a hint from nature and survive by pretending to cooperate with others and concealing their aggression under cover of fraud? One could answer in the voice of morality and say that a fraudulent person does not preserve but only compromises himself. Some tincture of this voice is in the behavior of a manly man. Survival is self-preservation, which is self-defense, which presupposes that the self is worth defending — as it is. One defends a fixed, not an evolving, self. In defending it one risks it, for a half-hearted defense will soon be recognized by one's enemy and overcome. Manliness is steadfast; it is taking a stand, not surrendering, not allowing oneself to be determined by one's context, not being adaptive or flexible. In Darwin's view manliness is not as we see it. It is subjected to the flexibility contrary to its nature that allows species to survive; and then he does not explain why manliness itself could not become flexible. "Existence" and "survival" become dubious when the "struggle" is among the "fittest" and the fittest are the most flexible.

Manliness understood as aggression instrumental to nature's goal loses contact with males. If manliness is aggression instrumental to nature's goal, we do not know how it is related to human goals. In this regard social Darwinism, though much despised, tells us something that Darwin does not. Is not "the female of the species" more deadly than the male when lesser capacity to fight is made up for by desperation and lack of scruple? In the poem of this name (1911), Rudyard Kipling writes that woman must be made "in every fiber of her frame" to protect her child "lest the generations fail." That is Darwin in spirit if not in letter.[70] Her advantage over men is her total disregard of "some God of Abstract Justice" to which men are unable to be indifferent. Every man is his mother's son and thus better defended by her than by himself. But he would not be better ruled by her. A woman's disregard of justice gives her license to command but not to govern, since governing has to do with justice. Despite the deadliness of females and the cowardice of men, for Kipling women cannot win and the sex roles remain.

Speaking of Abstract Justice reminds us of the absence of politics in Darwin's theory. All we have is the individual and the species.[71] Each cares only for itself and not for the other, though the individual, being mortal, is obliged to care for his progeny if he is to survive. There is no country, no common good to consider, and manliness is kept in thrall to survival, not permitted to be deflected into patriotism, let alone greatness. Recently Darwinians have attempted to fill the obvious vacancy in an ingenious enterprise they call "sociobiology."[72] To sum it up, one would have to say that they have not found a place for Abstract Justice except in the form of dire necessity or ferocity that Kipling described as female and maternal.

Manliness is not mere aggression; it is aggression that develops an assertion, a cause it espouses. The cause arises from the risk the manly man confronts, for if you risk your life to save your life, your "life" must be some immaterial cause, some version of Abstract Justice. You still want to survive, but with honor. Your survival is not dictated for you by nature's command, like that of the female of the species (as Kipling presents her), but it is chosen by you. It is your survival because you state its terms. Unfortunately the men and women of science—manly in their abstractness whether they are stereotypers or evolutionary biologists—cannot appreciate manly abstractness in the form of assertiveness. They seem to have a set aversion to politics.

Chapter Three

Manly Assertion

Let us now leave the gray, flat, featureless domain of science to look for something new. Our science rather clumsily confirms the stereotype about manliness, the stereotype that stands stubbornly in the way of the gender-neutral society. But we already knew before science told us that men are more aggressive than women: is there also something to be learned in this fact? In this chapter I will elevate manliness from aggression to assertion and thereby discover its connection to politics.

Aggression is a vague word because it applies to any action that increases your power. *Power* is a vaguer word because it doesn't tell you for what purpose power will be used. Any action, even a smile, can look like aggression if you don't see the point of it; and if you deliberately refrain from looking at its purpose, like the scientists we have studied, you leave it to be inferred that its only, all-purpose purpose is to increase power. But let's suppose, against that view, that power has a point. Let's suppose that it is used to assert something, which means to assert the worth of something, to make a claim on behalf of someone or something. Pay attention, says the manly man, which means pay attention to *me*. Manliness is not mere generalized pushiness but rather a claim on your attention. That is why the male animal displays and the manly man struts and boasts.[1] He has a point to make and the point is important! His aggression takes the specific form of an assertion of importance applying both to himself and to the matter he raises. If you want to be manly, you have to be assertive (so a fashion among women for "assertiveness training" arose in the 1970s). Modern science overlooks assertiveness because it feels uncomfortable with the notion of human importance. It wants to explain human events by means of universal laws that give no respect to our sense of self-importance and offer no solace for our delusions of grandeur. Manliness, too, is about the universe, but it claims a place in it for human importance.

To see assertive manliness, we will look at literature rather than science. Continuing on from Kipling's poem, we will go to Ernest Hemingway, the writer in our time (or just before) most celebrated for manliness, and to Homer, whose hero Achilles is the paragon and paradigm of manliness. Literature has the same aim as science, to find and tell the truth. But literature, unlike science, also seeks to entertain—and it could not entertain if it did not know some truth not well known by science about the human resistance to hearing the truth. Literature uses fictions that are images of truth while science tries to speak truth directly and succeeds only in speaking abstractly. Literature requires interpretation, and interpreters will disagree, a situation that science cannot abide and literature welcomes. Literature is open to different degrees of understanding from a child's to a philosopher's, while science speaks in a monotone and wants its audience of other scientists to be on the same level so that its results will be replicable. Science relies on nonscientist publicists to address the multitude of nonscientists. Science has fruits that benefit the body; literature nourishes the soul. Literature takes on the big questions that scientists set aside and ignore, and so literature has more to say about manliness. The evidence literature offers for its insights comes from the intelligent observation of those who produce it. Great writers are both witnesses to truth and judges of what they see. We readers can replicate their insights according to our capacities, and we have to do so without the guarantee supposedly provided by scientific method that the truth conveyed is the same as the truth received. In studying human affairs, the trouble with the scientific guarantee of replicable evidence is that it's also a guarantee of clumsiness and mediocrity.

Manliness is not too modest to assert itself, to tell us the value of the manly man. Here is a small collection of manly assertions: "It is what a man must do." "But I will show him what a man can do and what a man endures." "And pain does not matter to a man." The most famous one: "But man is not made for defeat. . . . A man can be destroyed but not defeated."

These quotations come from Ernest Hemingway's masterpiece, *The Old*

Man and the Sea, a novel published in 1952.[2] They would probably not be written today, but Hemingway is almost today and his book, though out of fashion, is still read. It offers our most convenient access to manliness as something we do not quite recognize but is not yet over the horizon. Hemingway was a macho fellow and a seeker of adventure when coupled with fun; he was ridiculed in his own lifetime — by Noel Coward, for example, in a special rendition of Cole Porter's "Let's Do It" — when manly foibles were received more with amusement than indignation.[3] But this book is a serious work and we should consider it.

It is clear from its title that the book is about man and nature. Man is the old man and nature is the sea. The old man fishes for marlin, a big fish that is a challenge to catch and that can also be sold for food. The old man is named Santiago and is called so not by the narrator but only by the boy he mentors, who is called Manolin by the old man. No mature man is a character in the book although two or three persons are mentioned and there are several references to the "Great DiMaggio," the Yankee baseball player whom the old man admires. The old man stands for man because of his intelligence and his experience, working together. A mature man would be closer to his physical peak, but the old man has just enough strength and more know-how, "tricks" of the trade. One particular thing he knows is to be patient. If you want to catch a big fish, you must wait for your luck to come. To be sure, when after a succession of failures the old man finally goes out by himself — the boy having been discouraged by his family from going along with one so unlucky — he quickly hooks his fish. The manliness of catching a big fish can be taught but has to be done alone.

The old man goes out on the sea, which represents nature because the land is divided into countries with various regimes that do not permit direct contact with nature. To be manly on land you would have to deal with a particular social context, as Hemingway did in his earlier book on bull-fighting, *Death in the Afternoon,* which is about Spain.[4] In this book, Hemingway's manliness is unpolitical. The old man fights with a fish and as a fisherman he stands for man more easily than if he were Cuban or American. He contends with a marlin and several sharks, and he dreams of lions on the beaches of Africa. It is not that he is not Cuban, but he is described in a way that makes his manliness accessible to all regardless of political differences or diverse "values." The old man's love of baseball is shared by both Cubans and Americans.[5]

Is man the dominant animal, as Darwin says? No, the old man thinks (for sometimes he thinks and sometimes he talks to himself) of the marlin whom he kills as his brother. The battle could have gone the other way, but the old man won through trickery. The marlin is a more noble thing than man, whose integrity is compromised by his intelligence. Human intelligence works with nature as well as against it, for the stars that show the old man where he is are his friends, as is the bird that helps him catch his bait. After he has caught, fought, killed, and taken possession of the marlin, the old man has to bring him back to shore. He runs the gauntlet of sharks, who are not his brothers; he fights them off, but there are too many and they succeed in stripping the marlin of flesh, leaving the old man with its skeleton. He comes back with the evidence of his exploit but without profit from it. It is a trophy he deserves because he won the battle with the fish and because he did not conquer all nature to do so. What he won, he won fair and square.

Through the sharks nature gets even with him. "And what beat you, he thought. Nothing, he said aloud. I went out too far." He went out too far because the marlin pulled him out to sea, but the old man takes responsibility as if this had been his error. Then he can say aloud — *assert* — that nothing beat him, only himself. "I went out too far," says this very reflective manly man of himself. Manliness is the willingness to challenge nature combined with the confidence, inspired by the knowledge, that one can succeed. It is also defined by the knowledge that one can fail, depending on the chance of catching a great fish and handling it successfully. Chance prevents nature from dominating us, and us from dominating nature. You win some, you lose some. If we could conquer nature and eliminate risk, we would not need manliness.

Manliness is an assertion of man's worth because his worth does not go without saying. So too, because worth needs to be asserted it needs to be proved; in asserting, one must make good the assertion. Did the old man go out too far, as he admitted? He did; he could not bring back his prize. Yet of course most of Hemingway's readers — those who do not think him sentimental — will not agree that the old man went out too far, and the marlin's skeleton proves that his deed was not a dream or a fisherman's lie about the one that got away. The old man thinks a lot; he seems to be a kind of self-taught philosopher. He has thought out the difference between being defeated and being destroyed, and he has decided that despite what you might think, being defeated is worse. The boy "keeps him alive," being a sort of student, and the old man found it pleasant to talk to him after his battle with the great fish. His manliness includes the analysis and the teaching of manliness. It does not have much religion. "I am not religious," the old man says before reciting his prayers "mechanically." He thinks (and does not say aloud) that he has no understanding of sin, but "there are people who are paid" to think about sin. He does not oppose those people or the Church, and in describing his story Hemingway actually supplies obvious parallels to Christ's agonies on the hill of Calvary.[6] He shows, however, that the old man suffers for his manliness and not to redeem himself from sin. It seems the old man does not like the idea of being dependent on divine help but does not object to others' belief. His manliness is full of contrivance in the clever ways he knows to subdue the fish, but it does not rely on advanced technology. It happened today; it could have happened in any age. Manliness does not depend on newly acquired power over nature; it is if anything endangered by such power. Manliness contends with nature but respects nature because it is prompted by nature. We, Hemingway's readers, can see the manliness of Hemingway's hero because we, too, are prompted by nature to appreciate it. The old man is aware that he serves as an example to others who will be inspired by the news of his deed. It inspires us too, Hemingway's readers, but it also makes us envious. We see the definition of man summed up — displayed in deeds and asserted in accompanying speech — in the best one of us.[7] Hemingway is enough of a Christian to want to displace Christ.[8]

Hemingway's old man gives us access to the heights of manliness that cannot even be glimpsed by modern science. The old man is not necessarily of our time but he is not repugnant to our time. His humanity, unlike Christ's, is somewhat withdrawn from what most people feel and know. At the end of the story, a woman tourist and her male companion look ignorantly at the long backbone of the great fish and mistake it for a shark. Not having read Hemingway's book, they do not appreciate the old man's feat. The old man's manliness is not political; it cannot claim the recognition of a community as opposed to that of a young student.[9]

Next we go to Achilles, the manly hero par excellence without whom a book on manliness can hardly be composed, the archetype of the he-man and the asserter of his worth and the worth of his kind.[10] Achilles, let's admit, is a bit difficult for us. In contrast to the old man, Achilles is a warrior in the prime of life; he has a name and especially a lineage; he consorts with gods; he distinguishes himself undemocratically from the hoi polloi, the *anthropoi* or the human beings; and he finds himself not alone but in combat and competition with other heroes and in a relationship with nonheroic human beings, thus for both reasons in a political situation.

Achilles is a he-man (*aner*) above and distinct from human beings. We are used to holding the broader designation to be higher: humanity, mankind, humankind are nobler and more generous than any group of humans, which as such will necessarily have parochial interests at odds with the whole. To be devoted to humanity is a life well spent. But in Homer's *Iliad* the he-men of the Greeks (Achaeans) and the Trojans are presented as nobler than mere human beings, who lack individuality because they are incapable of great deeds. *Humanity*, it appears, is a collective word that has no singular, for to be an individual you have to be a great one. He-men are few, and they are identified with heroes. All the he-men are males, but most males are mere human beings along with all women and children. You could taunt he-men by calling them women, much as we might say to an adult, "stop acting like a child." When Hector, hero of the Trojans, challenged the Greeks to a duel and none responded, Menelaus rebuked the Greeks as women, calling them Greeks in the feminine plural.[11]

Instead of submerging themselves in the category of humanity, he-men or heroes connect themselves to the gods. They are sons of gods or they can trace a lineage to a god. Achilles was the son of Peleus, who was the son of Aeacus, the son of Zeus. There you are: Zeus is his great-grandfather. Not surprisingly, Zeus takes an interest in Achilles and the other heroes. He and other gods intervene on behalf of heroes; for example, at the beginning of the *Iliad*, Athena directly prevents Achilles from killing Agamemnon, appearing to him while invisible to others and pulling him back by his hair. Zeus is a father to the he-men, the heroes, but a ruler of human beings, who do not get his individual attention. Human beings suffer neglect and would be excluded from the care of the gods if they did not constitute a kind of audience before which the he-men display their heroism. Thus patriarchy in the style of the *Iliad* is not the fatherhood of God over the brotherhood of men but a compound of fatherly care of heroes and fatherly indifference to human beings outside the family. The gods care for the best men, and the best men seek to resemble the gods; they are even called demigods.[12]

Among the Greek heroes, however, there is a quarrel between Achilles and Agamemnon over Bryseis, Achilles' slave woman, stolen by Agamemnon. Agamemnon is king by virtue of his lineage, and when first presented in the *Iliad,* he is not called by his name but his father's, "Atreides lord of men."[13] Achilles, knowing himself to be the better man, disdains Agamemnon's claim to his respect and obedience, and the two exchange furious insults. We see enacted the "wrath of Achilles" with which the *Iliad* begins, a wrath said to be "divine" and prompted, or supported, by the wrath of Apollo, who is also involved in the incident. The quarrel is not so much over the woman as between the two parties, Agamemnon claiming the authority of his lineage and Achilles the power of his virtue. The eternal dispute between ancestral and natural right opens up among the he-men because lineage, even to the gods, does not guarantee virtue, or as we would say, birth is one thing and merit another. Agamemnon relies on his scepter, symbol of his authority and made by the god Hephaestus, but Achilles swears by a scepter of his own and relies on his spear.[14] Manliness appears first not as a claim of authority but as the assertion of virtue against authority, an assertion always required because authority is always in the way of virtue and virtue never gets a free welcome from authority. In the course of asserting itself against authority, virtue becomes a possible claim on the basis of which one can assert one's worthiness to rule, thus a claim to authority. Even then it is only one of several claims and must expect to face resistance from other claims.[15]

Or does virtue not need to be asserted when it can be recognized, as today, in a competitive examination taken by all? Our "meritocracy" may seem to have solved Homer's problem of combining virtue and authority without fuss from the virtuous and condescension by those in authority. But to do this, meritocracy must understand virtue in conventional ways so that it can be recognized and scored by those in authority. We are aware that true virtue is rarely the winner of a competitive examination; and if it is, it cannot take

success for granted and still needs to assert itself. Meritocracy does not eliminate the necessity of advertising one's merits, and we should not look down
upon Achilles' boastful vaunts.

To vindicate his wrath, to make good on his claim, Achilles faces great risk
as it has been foretold to him by his mother, Thetis, that if he returns to war
to avenge the death of his friend Patroclus, he will die soon after.[16] He has a
choice between returning home to live in peace or staying at Troy and going
to battle to be killed with great glory. Eventually he chooses glory, dies, and
goes to Hades.[17] When Odysseus later sees his shade there and asks him how
things are going, Achilles replies, "Better slave on earth than king of hell!"
He was dissatisfied with the choice he had made. Manliness rejects the safety
of self-preservation in favor of the glory of risking one's life to vindicate
one's rights and deserts. Homer shows us Achilles ruing his decision, and he
wrote in the *Odyssey* of Odysseus' finding his way home through many risks,
having made the choice that Achilles declined. Homer does not endorse either the wrath or the repentance of Achilles, it seems. He sings of his wrath
and its consequences to remind human beings of the need for heroes, and
heroes of the need for humanity. Achilles' assertiveness causes him to sulk in
his tent—which is the aloofness of the manly man, as we have remarked—
and to vindicate his right by avenging the death of his friend, a return to
battle and a kind of entry into politics. For Odysseus, the return home permits him to resume his family life and his rule in Ithaca, after asserting his
right to both against the suitors of his faithful wife.

What most obviously distinguishes Homer from Hemingway is the presence of the gods as actors in the story. The gods are a reminder of the need
for authority in human affairs, of a higher power to which human beings can
point when claiming their rights. Gods are necessary to manly assertion because without them assertion is mere assertion, arbitrary and unsupported.
But gods also get in the way of manliness, as Hemingway indicates, by forcing
men, even he-men, to call on and thus depend on them. Possibly Hemingway's readers are supposed to supply the prayers of thanks that the old man
seems to forget after he returns from fishing; in this way prayers ratify what
heroic men have already done on their own and do not imply dependence
on the divine. Even so, Hemingway seems less humane than Homer, more
adamant in his aristocratic disdain. His manliness, while not trampling on the

weak, offers them no succor, no recognition. Those who cannot catch a big fish are to admire those who can, perhaps in the way we all—all of us fans— admire the grace of Joe DiMaggio. A baseball player doesn't threaten us but doesn't help us either. By hobbling the heroes, the Homeric gods keep them restrained within our category of the *anthropoi,* not the same, not equal, but comparable and subject to human weakness. Achilles thought himself human only because he was not immortal and not because he was weaker than a god. That's a delusion Homer makes us see—makes Achilles see.

In our time there are many who say that heroes lack humanity and few who will admit that humanity needs heroes. But at all times heroes have to assert themselves. The question is, what is in it for us?

We have seen two instances of manly assertion, one recent, the other ancient, one outside politics, the other political. They have in common the assertion of oneself and the desire to prove a point to others, even if the point is not directly political like the demonstration by Hemingway's old man of how to catch a big fish. To make the point, the manly man stubbornly insists on himself, and when he does that, he *stands for* stubborn insistence on himself. Not only is he manly, but he also represents the need for manly men. He does this against any rational arrangement—including that of our gender-neutral society—by which one might wish to dispose of the irritating self-centered stubbornness of manly men. Yet manly assertion is a mode of speech and speech has a certain rationality: it makes sense, though often in deplorable fashion. What we must understand now is the combination of stubbornness and rationality in manly assertion. Out of that combination comes the political.

Let's start from the example of *patriarchy,* a political term used today. *Patriarchy* referring to male domination, is the name by which the women's movement has dubbed all previous human societies, somewhat as the French revolutionaries gathered all preceding eras in one category, "the old regime," to designate the age-old castle of oppression. And the women's movement is right: every previous society, including our democracy up to now, *has* been some kind of patriarchy, permeated by stubborn, self-insistent manliness. Even our reason is infected and effectually controlled by the manly types; contrary to reason, for example, men have dominated the professions that require learning, not excluding the academic profession that is supposed to be devoted to learning. In protest, some of the braver sisters turned against reason itself, calling it "phallic," accusing it of a bossy attitude toward women's feelings, and condemning it for trying to direct or foreclose their choices.

It may go too far to accuse reason itself of being patriarchal. As Socrates said, a reasoned argument has a "logic" of its own that the reasoner cannot control but has to follow. But the accusation is right to suggest that stubbornness is added to rationality in manly assertion. An assertion, one could say, is a statement or proposition that the asserter *tries* to control. So there's no doubt that "Father knows best" is the very spirit of patriarchy, in which Father's authority is mixed with Father's knowledge. The phrase is usually spoken by Mother, often ironically, though Father is not above saying it himself if the occasion seems to demand the assertion of authority. Think of Jackie Gleason on the *Honeymooners* saying "I'm the King" to his ever-skeptical wife Audrey Meadows. "Father knows best" is a family motto that is easily translated into politics when those in power claim to know what's good for those in their control. The claim to knowledge is not added on like an accidental extra, however. Manly assertion appears first as stubbornness, but it is more than that; it claims to be knowledge. Patriarchy would not have grown up and flourished everywhere if there were not more to it than the tyranny of fathers. We will easily underestimate the difficulty of getting rid of patriarchy if we are not more careful about the reasons why it has survived.

What are those reasons? *Reasons* — because the one reason of survival is not enough; it no longer holds in the leisurely ease of our civilization, and in any case, it never was enough. Human beings want quality time in their sojourn on the planet; they want more than self-sacrifice for the sake of keeping the species going. They are interested in *why* the species should be preserved — the point overlooked by Darwin. Why did primitive peoples, desperately poor by our standards, living on the margin of existence, and subject to daily risks we can hardly imagine, waste their time and substance on religion? They wanted to know that they matter, that's why; and they were willing to spend heavily for the answer to that question from time and resources they might have saved for their material well-being. Other animal species seek to survive; humans want to survive with honor. It is through manliness that humans insist that they are worthy of the attention of the gods or have an honored place in the scheme of things.

Manliness might not seem to be involved in the meaning human beings want for themselves. The stereotype tells us that manly men are not necessarily the smartest or cleverest of human beings; they are men of action like John Wayne, not thinkers. Indiana Jones is an anthropology professor but seems to spend most of his time in the field. Hemingway's old man is a thinker, an exception to the rule, but then the professorial critics of the work, who don't care for men of action, don't notice that this one thinks (and thinks more than they do). We will not ignore the fact, as do the scientists who study sex differences, that the best thinkers, the philosophers, have been almost exclusively male.[18] But let us put it aside for the time being. The philosophers, though male, do not seem to be manly men of action. And the men of action, in their irrational, very unphilosophic way, seem to represent stubborn resistance to any reasonable scheme such as a gender-neutral society that sets aside sex. The more extreme feminists may be wrong to imply that philosophers can never rise above the self-interest of males, but they would be right to say that *manly* reason is assertive ("phallic").

What, then, do manly men contribute to the meaning of life since they do not think deeply or objectively about it? Strangely, their very stubbornness is a contribution. Instead of thinking deeply, and acting often in a petty way, the manly man makes an issue of himself; he asserts himself in some way. That is what his "aggression" means; he is stubborn for the sake of something and yet also and always on his own behalf. He connects himself—his personal stubbornness—to something bigger than himself—the issue in which, he claims, he and his honor are involved. When the scientists of stereotypes say that men are more aggressive than women, they leave out the end for which men are aggressive and the reasoning by which they support it. It's what men do with their aggression that matters, for however childish and self-interested they may be, they advance a cause for their complaints. Manly stubbornness is often, even usually, negative and selfish, but it is never merely that. To make an issue of something is a positive act. Even with a sulker like Achilles you can work out the principles by which he lives. Manliness is both irrational and rational: irrational because the manly man insists on his own importance no matter what; rational because he has reasons for doing so.

Now, to make an issue is a political act. It is to bring to general attention some unnoticed injustice done to you. The injustice harms you, but in making an issue of it you claim that it affects others too. Achilles expands his complaint against Agamemnon from stealing his girlfriend to not honoring the best of the Greeks.[19] The latter is a more serious matter as it implies a general proposition that rulers should honor the best, a proposition of course including Achilles, in his humble opinion, but not confined to him. This claim transforms a private wrong, which you might suffer patiently, into a public wrong for which you insist on a remedy. The injustice will sometimes be done by society or the government, the powers that be; so to make an issue of it suggests that you are willing to challenge authority to get justice done. How far would you take this challenge? If you are a responsible person, and not a mere complainer, you might decide that it's up to you to step in to straighten things out. Not only do you make your claim public, but to be consistent, and to carry your point further, you take up the reins of control yourself, perhaps even leading a revolution against the status quo in extension of your manly logic. This is manly aggression when it is carried out to its conclusion, good or bad. What manly men contribute to the meaning of human life is its actualization in society. Biased as they are, they may not see justice well; they may be guilty of disastrous mistakes, as was manly Ajax in the *Iliad*. But when confronted with a problem, manly men get busy.

We in our liberal society speak often of the distinction between private and public, believing as we do that our liberties are safe only when a line is drawn to keep the public from interfering too much with the private. We don't want people to pick up the habit of crossing this line, of raising issues too often on subjects for which we have an established law, custom, or policy. The right of private property builds fences that protect us from overmuch interference either from fellow citizens or from the government, reacting to their pressure. But we also have a right of free speech, a right to address our fellow citizens, to raise issues, and thus to create a public question out of a previously private matter. It takes a certain quality of soul to do this, and the quality is manliness, the manly responsibility we have defined. The feminists had a slogan, "the personal is the political." They meant that what had previously been considered private, male-female relationships, had to be redefined by political means. They meant, too, that the original relationship had been defined by an act of political oppression done by males. The redefining from private to public is a manly act, in this case done by angry women who had a grievance and wanted a new society that would make room for their remedy. There are many injustices — such as this one, done to women — that remain latent until someone has the gumption to speak up and "act up," as the gay activists say.

One cannot assume that the distinction in our society between private and public is where it is because it has to be there. Surely there are matters that are private in all societies — somehow sex comes first to mind — but still, they are treated differently in different societies. Coming of age in Samoa is not the same as in an American high school.[20] The difference is enacted and enforced by the public either in legislation or by custom. But the American high school is not the same as it used to be. When it is changed, the source of change is either public, the public changing its mind, or private, when the previous public is persuaded to change its mind or is just plain overthrown. In the latter cases, what was private opinion becomes the public rule, for example, our new gender-neutral society. The gender-neutral society replaced patriarchy, which also got its start from a previous change. There are different kinds of patriarchy, and the one that allowed women to vote in 1919 took over from the one before that time that did not.[21]

We must not look at public and private statically as a distinction that never changes; we must remember that the public emerges from private, latent interests or opinions that find expression. The public, the political, needs to be asserted; what is public now was once asserted, what will be public in the future will be asserted against what is public now. Politics is assertive, and assertiveness is a kind of aggression — the kind that is unwilling to let things be as they are. It is aggression that has received a certain form in an organization or regime and that acts for a certain end or ends.

Yet because the public emerges from the private, it does not follow that the public is created by the private, as most modern political thinkers say. No, the public is always there; always a ruling status quo exists that establishes for any society what is public and what is private. Aristotle said that man is by nature a political animal. He connects this to the fact that man is by nature a rational animal, with opinions on good and bad, just and unjust, harmful and advantageous.[22] When you have an opinion you have a reason, and the reason applies not only to yourself but also to others like yourself. If you, a male, assert "my wife shouldn't fight in the army," you need a reason why wives or women generally should not do this. That reason keeps your assertion from being a mere whim, and it transforms your assertion from a personal statement to a principle that ought to rule others besides yourself. Our rationality prevents us from living on the basis of idiosyncratic preferences. Of course our reasoning may be unsound or biased; it usually is. But the attempt to reason renders us political animals. We cannot live without giving reasons to justify how we live. So we cannot live without a notion of the public, of a political association that attempts to enact and enforce what we assert, using reasons. Without reasons, our assertiveness would be mere unfounded aggression, a pure power move; without assertiveness, our reasoning would be dormant and ineffectual.

Aristotle is more assertive about the rationality of man, more discreet about the assertiveness. He tells us directly that having reason or speech (*logos*) makes us naturally political animals. But he doesn't set forth the argument for assertiveness that I have made. He doesn't want to encourage assertiveness. In his time, he thought, men were already tougher than they needed to be. As we shall see, the philosophers generally take a dim view of manly assertiveness. When Aristotle says "man" is by nature political, he says "human being" (*anthropos*), including women, not he-man (*aner*). Using the same distinction as Homer in the *Iliad,* Aristotle disagrees with Achilles that only he-men have the virtue to be political. Women share in human rationality, and they also share in assertiveness. Aristotle admits this latter fact in a subdued manner, and we have seen it again in the manly assertiveness of the women's movement in our day.[23] It would seem that we have the basis for the gender-neutral society in the very call for that society by the women's movement. If women can take their personal grievance and make it political, isn't that enough to show that women are as assertive, and therefore as political, as men?

Not so fast. Though it's clear that women can be manly, it's just as clear that they are not as manly or as often manly as men. Women, we have seen, have less of the brute spirit of aggression when compared with men. That is what the studies show and what our hormones confirm. The statistics on crime make it plain as a pikestaff that men surpass women by far in the reckless aggression that draws the attention of the law.[24] This shows that men have aggression to spare; they keep it in stock so as to have it ready when it is needed and even, or especially, when it is unneeded and unwanted; like Tom Sawyer, they offer it on slight occasions as a free gift, useful or not. Not all men are like this, but very many more of them are like this than women. The ready excess of aggressive assertion in men reveals the strength of their habitual inclination. Men can spit, cuss, tell dirty jokes, read porn, and drink beer. Modern women are doing their best to catch up with men in these attainments, and they do seem to have made modest progress in cussing, I say condescendingly. But they remain way behind men in natural, easy-going, effortless vulgarity.

Lacking as women are, comparatively, in aggression and assertiveness, it is no surprise that men have ruled over all societies at almost all times. It may seem wrong and unfair to cite the ungovernableness of men as their title to govern, and the moderation of women as the proof of their unfitness. I am not quite doing that. Modern biologists, overlooking what is specifically human, have taught us to say that manly types defend their *turf*.[25] Thus they connect aggression to defense of whatever is one's own. They point to the behavior of other mammals, which first create their own turf, marking out its boundaries with any convenient means, and then defend it. The biologists are not wrong to point to our human animality and to draw inferences from the differences that can be observed between males and females in almost all species of animals. It's an impressive fact that aggressive masculinity is not unique to humans but runs rampant throughout the animal kingdom among both wild and tame beasts. If one thinks in the mode of evolution, the fact that defending one's turf is animal makes it older, deeper, and more ingrained than anything merely human. If, like Hemingway, you think outside that mode, you see nature repeating the male-female distinction with interesting variations.

What is specifically human in the defense of one's turf? Tom Sawyer, we recall, in marking his turf very decently drew a line in the dust with his bare toe. "Turf" is what people say today to refer to their honor. Impressed as we are with the evolution of humans from animals, and democratically inclined not to put on airs, we are drawn to the biological idea of defending turf, the generic rather than the specifically human trait. Yet it's honor that manly men want to defend. Like a dog barking from his yard, we humans are parochial and patriotic, loyal to particular communities if not to masters. But honor differs from turf by asserting the defense of a general or universal principle or cause that is attached to the community. Honor is attached to a particular territory, but by the same token the territory is attached to honor. We honor different things in different societies, but we all know what honor is. Honor has to be asserted and claimed because nature does not make it clear to all concerned what truly deserves to be honored. You have to stand on your hind feet and raise your voice. Of course, if you are placed where your honor is not contested, you don't have to make a fuss; you simply accept the result of a previous effort by somebody else on your behalf and to your benefit.[26]

Honor is a claim to protect one's person, family, and property—and the beliefs embodied in them. A sense of honor is the source of the protectiveness so characteristic of manliness. Honor joins together private circumstance and public belief so that those who desire it feel entitled to act as they do; through the assertion of honor they surpass mindless aggression not devoted to a cause. Yet because honor always has a particular attachment, it is always somewhat arbitrary. Tom Sawyer didn't have to draw the line where he did. He didn't have to draw one at all except that he is something of an honor-lover. Honor comes to a focus on a point of honor, a point on which you decide that your honor is engaged. Often there is a code of honor that tells you what you mustn't tolerate, where your honor is engaged, and that you must take a stand. The point and the code of honor are conventional; they could be otherwise than they are. But honor itself is part of human nature as it develops and perfects animal nature.[27] In assertiveness for the sake of honor, human nature requires a supplement of convention made by human choice and legislation. Our nature is partly determined by us. The biologists are wrong to try to understand honor in terms of turf. They should reverse the point and try to understand turf in terms of honor, as honor lacking in rationality.

Manly protectiveness is the responsible side of manliness discussed earlier.

A man protects those whom he has taken in his care against dangers they cannot face or handle without him. He makes an issue of some matter, engages his honor, and takes charge of the situation either as a routine or in an emergency. Not every activity of protection carries a risk, as when a man provides peaceably for his family. But the willingness to take on risk is the primary protection enveloping all other ways of providing for someone. From this fact we recognize the connection between turf or honor and politics. Honor is an asserted claim to protect someone, and the claim to protect is a claim to rule. How can I protect you properly if I can't tell you what to do? This is how manliness leads to patriarchy, a form of rule in which the rulers behave as if they were protective fathers. Here I use "patriarchy" in the expanded (feminist) sense of every government based on manliness, not merely those governments staffed by males.

Part of the patriarchal code of honor of society before it became gender-neutral was male gallantry toward women. Gallantry is a formality of protection, sometimes extravagant, which is a sign of readiness to protect should protection really be needed. It continues in faded and diminished form today because women like it. Women know it's inconsistent with their independence to have a man open a door for them, but out of the goodness of their hearts they allow it — while at the same time allowing themselves to be inconsistent. What is the true nature of gallantry? Sometimes "gallantry" is used euphemistically or ironically to refer to sexual conquests like those of Don Giovanni. Is gallantry really an admission of the superiority of women as it appears to be, or is it fundamentally insincere because it always contains an element of disdain? The man who opens a door for a woman makes a show of being stronger than she, you could say (Kant said it); but on the other hand, the woman does go first.[28] We shall return to the possibility that being a sex object is not the worst fate in the world.

I seem to have drifted into, if not a defense, then a sympathetic explanation of the way men have traditionally treated women. But cannot women protect men? It's clear that in the home women take care of men in a ratio well beyond fifty-fifty. Can't women also rise to the occasion in dangerous emergencies? All of Elmore Leonard's novels explore manliness in its ordinary American excesses, both bad and good, when men are committing vicious crimes and when, endearingly, they are preventing or avenging them.

In *Killshot* he tells of a woman who saves herself and her manly but tardy and somewhat unwary husband from being murdered. How does she do it? By asking herself what he would do and then doing it. Let's look also at *High Noon*. At the end of this film celebrating manliness, Grace Kelly, a Quaker lady, shoots a criminal in the back just as he was about to shoot her husband in the back. The manly man needed help and got it from a refined woman who did not believe in the use of violence but still shot pretty accurately.[29] It seems, moreover, that women also defend their own honor. In our day they have their own personal codes as to what they will and will not "do," that is, allow to be done. "No! Not on the first date!"[30] Yet though women have honor, they need society to vindicate it through shame and punishment; and society sometimes needs to be activated by manly men. In *High Noon,* the whole town is frightened and it's up to Gary Cooper to act. And though Grace Kelly saves him at the end, one cannot imagine their roles reversed; only in a pinch does she, like Leonard's heroine, do what a man would do.

Is it possible to teach women manliness and thus to become more assertive? Or is that like teaching a cat to bark? It is hard to persuade someone to abandon or acquire a trait that he or she holds or lacks not through persuasion but generically, as an animal. But one can persuade a human someone to modify, rather than eliminate, an animal trait. That is the specifically human way to treat an animal endowment. To modify a trait you have to accept that some underlying ground for it exists and will continue to exist; you must respect that *essence.* You may have no proof or even any thoughts about essences, but for practical purposes you go along with a manly essence. In that case you are trying to form willful, wild manliness into a more manageable variety — or to find a hidden reservoir of manliness and bring it to the surface. In the 1970s some psychologists and therapists tried to get women to take "assertiveness training" to prepare themselves for the new gender-neutral society.[31] Women were being asked to accept the manly essence and to take measures to share in its advantages. Far from doing away with manliness, they would adopt it and use it for themselves.

The idea had its critics, and one can see why it did not succeed. Assertiveness training presupposes that women have a defect in that department. While men have excessive assertiveness and need to be tamed, women have too little and need a boost. Their training aims to teach them to make their own case, a habit one takes for granted in men. If that's so, it's no wonder that men have dominated business and politics. With or without training in moderation, men were just doing what comes naturally. But if women don't take steps to reduce their assertiveness deficit, will they succeed as well as men in the formerly manly occupations? Perhaps their true policy is to assert themselves as women and not try to become artificial men, but that policy requires a certain distance from manly assertiveness.

A mass-market effort began in the early seventies to offer books and workshops on assertiveness training for women.[32] It found support from the linguist Robin Lakoff's influential book *Language and Woman's Place,* describing a "woman's language" of weak and ingratiating speech. Lakoff and other feminists deplored this unassertive style and wanted to see it corrected. They did not give much thought to what America would be like if both sexes tried to "get ahead," as Americans say. Or is it that women used to get ahead vicariously through their men but now want to get ahead on their own? That would suggest there never was appreciation in either sex for the good things you get by giving rather than taking. Yet perhaps women do retain something of their traditional critical attitude toward the ways of assertive men and toward the value of the worldly goods you get by being assertive. Which is better for women, love or money? Perhaps there is a middle thing, neither love nor money but combining both: *recognition* (an important word, we shall see, for some feminists). But recognition for what? For being successful in love or with money? The question cannot be avoided.

The gender-neutral society with equal assertiveness for women results, it seems, in an unreflective embrace of commercialism and other forms of mundane ambition. Was there really nothing to the objections that used to be made, by both left and right, to the exploitation and the pettiness of a bourgeois society? There is, to be sure, a New Age feminism that is in principle quite contrary to feminist careerism. It opposes bourgeois society as wasteful and exploitative and seeks to reconnect with nature respectfully as women used to do in olden times of tale and myth when women were fairies, witches and goddesses.[33] New Age women sometimes sell souvenirs of this bygone age, but their career plans go no further than this. They keep their distance from the artificial manliness delivered by assertiveness training.

The feminist psychologist Mary Crawford, an intelligent observer, says that women are less assertive because they have less power. It's not that they have less power because they are less assertive. Assertive women, she adds, meet disapproval; so it makes sense for them to ingratiate themselves, instead of asserting themselves, with the men who have power. If only women had fine offices with secretaries and limousines with chauffeurs, as men do, they would develop a robust sense of entitlement and easily slip into the habit of self-assertion. Here Dr. Crawford disagrees with Dr. Samuel Johnson, who thought it ridiculous for a woman to assert herself. That's what he meant when he made his famous remark quoted in Boswell's *Life of Johnson,* "Sir, a woman's preaching is like a dog's walking on his hind legs. It is not done well; but you are surprised to find it done at all." Aristotle played to the same sentiment when he reported that the magnanimous man is expected to have a deep voice.[34] Do women become shrill when they assert themselves and thus fail to impress others with their authority? In my experience it is difficult for a man who is attracted to a woman not to find her cute, rather than intimidating, when she gets angry. But "formidable women," as we call them, do exist. Expelled members of Margaret Thatcher's cabinet might think they had met one of them.

Perhaps Crawford is mistaken to focus on the overall power of men. She is thinking that men are — were — those in power. But powerful men assert themselves against other men as well as women, for example, Achilles against Agamemnon, and to be assertive is not simply to sit down calmly in the seat of authority. To get to that seat you have to compete, and in a competition there are losers — usually more of them than winners. To assert yourself you must take the risk of losing.

Today's women want power, but they are not so eager to accept the risk that goes with seeking power. An indication of this failing is the willingness of women to claim solidarity with other women in the "women's movement." Women today take pride in "our" power, "our" advances, as they become ever more like men while remaining ever the same as women. A men's movement would be more divided against itself, each individual man looking out for himself and caring less for the general cause of his sex. Some men do complain of the plight of the male sex, but they are thinking of themselves. Both women and men like to reflect on their paths to the top. Successful women often speak with commendable gratitude of the "support" they received from other women, possibly a "support group." Men are more likely to exaggerate their independence, or if grateful, to mention lessons from sources they were perspicacious enough to consult and take to heart.

Even to speak assertively is risky. To initiate or to dominate a conversation you must take the chance that your remarks will not be well received. People may not laugh at your joke, and perhaps the risk that they will not is the reason why women don't usually tell jokes. But I cannot accept that they never make jokes. Women excel in put-downs. Crawford gives an example to which she does not give enough weight. During the trial over the Profumo scandal in Britain in 1963, counsel asked Mandy Rice-Davies, a witness to prostitution, whether she knew that Lord Astor had denied any impropriety in his relationship with her. Her answer: "Well, he would, wouldn't he?"[35] It's a put-down joke, reactive to male bluster, even equipped with an ironic tag question.

The staple of feminine humor is the put-down of complacent males: dreams of glory! — but dating from the feminine mystique. That kind of assertion ensures that women hold their own when men speak or act first. But it's less risky. One has only to think of Jane Austen to be assured that women have a sense of humor, distributed in lesser quantities to lesser brains. Women do make jokes, only not so noticeably as men. Women have the humor of the wise; they observe and remark in subdued or ironic fashion. Men have the humor of the powerful; they expect everyone to laugh aloud. Today's woman thinks she can have wisdom and power together: wisdom without modesty, power without risk.

Facing risk is a feature of manliness that goes with holding power. More than most women, indeed, more than most men, the manly man accepts — nay, welcomes — a risky situation. He is not looking for the life of Riley. And he does not, as has been alleged, fear competition from women, though no doubt he is wary of women who have found a way around competition. Only power in its nonhuman, physical meaning — the power of gravity, for example — is power that cannot fail, that carries no risk. Human power has the freedom that comes with indeterminacy, but freedom comes at a cost, the risk that you may not get what you want. All of us accept risks in small things, but those who welcome risk in large enterprises do the rest of us a great benefit. They give effect to our desire not to be determined by outside forces however beneficent; they represent human freedom.

In the smaller, piecework enterprise of reproducing the human race, men take on the duty of insemination (where the risk is mostly with women) and before this, in a ceremony not fully considered by Darwin, the business of asking for a date. When you ask someone for a date, you risk refusal; you put your ego on the line. Traditionally, men ask and women dispose; each sex has "power" of a kind. It was thought that women would not have the gumption to take the first step, make the first move, and men would not have the realism to sit by the telephone and accept their fate. Lately, women are showing more gumption while men still lack realism. Confusion reigns in the gender-neutral society; as Jimmy Durante would have said, everybody wants to get into the act. I have the impression that the forwardness women display — immodesty is too severe a label — still differs from manly confidence. It is called "showing interest" as if it were a response to a man who was just about to ask you for a date. Or is this splitting hairs? In any case, the liberated woman takes advantage of the general retreat from the formality of dates, specifying one sex as the initiator. But someone still has to ask or move first: assertiveness is a feature of human reproduction, and, so too is modesty, to keep it in check.

Assertiveness training aims to toughen speech rather than actions. This fact accords with Aristotle's reason for why man is by nature a political animal, which is that man has speech, not merely voice like other animals. With speech men assert opinions and make claims as to why their opinions are better than other people's. Politics is expressed in speech, assertive speech in which we claim that our policy, our party, our regime is superior to someone else's, the other party, the rival regime. But although politics is mostly speech, the assertive character of political speech directs it against others. Assertiveness means *against* someone, some other human or set of humans. You are not merely expressing yourself, saying what's on your mind, contributing to a discussion, offering a comment. You are making a claim against others in order to justify the way you do things, which in the full sense means to justify the way you rule. Assertive speech justifies the way you live; it indicates why you defend your way of life; it leads to action. So, assertiveness training that merely taught women how to put a point across would not be sufficient. A sign of this is the recent popularity of training in karate (or some variant) for women, an activity intended to show willingness to fight to defend one's independence, one's right to say "no" — together with the competence to back it up. Hollywood has been supporting the action side of assertiveness training with films where star actresses like Angelica Huston, Kathleen Turner, and Geena Davis appear as hit men well versed in the ability to kill.[36] Of course hit men do not really fight or defend themselves, and they take care to give themselves every advantage. They are not like John Wayne but rather are just the sort of professional thug he typically takes care of. They are manly only insofar as they do not suffer from squeamishness and do not favor gun control.

Our line of thinking makes war or conflict central to politics and manliness the inspiration of both. It has behind it the evidence not only of males ruling over all societies at almost all times but also, as we have seen, of male preponderance in crime and in the prison population. For good and for ill, males, apparently impelled by their manliness, have dominated all politics we know of. Is there something inevitable about this domination or is it merely experience up to now, creating a stereotype from which we are free to depart? Does patriarchy have a future?

One reason to doubt its future is that manliness seems undemocratic, while the direction of history in America and elsewhere seems to be toward ever more democracy. To put oneself forward, even in behalf of someone else or a higher cause, seems to require a display of ego. The manly man will take it personally if you do not pay attention to what he says. But a display of ego implies that one is not satisfied with what satisfies most people; it is at base an aristocratic impulse. Women, having less "ego" (in the popular sense of willingness to display it), are more democratic than men. They display themselves cosmetically so as to attract men, and vain women are certainly egoistic. But attractive or vain women merely expect you to pay attention to them (and will be disappointed if you do not); they do not insist on it peremptorily, like the manly man. It is take it or leave it. They do not say "c'm'ere" with the authority of Gary Cooper speaking to Katy Jurado in *High Noon*. There are, to be sure, many shy men and women. The shy men wish they could display their egos, and the shy women believe they should not as they think modesty becomes them. The traditional stereotypes take their cue from the ego man and from the modest woman, and not due to arbitrary "privileging" but because the man's ego is more directly dominant than the woman's.

For confirmation we can look back to the wisdom in Aristophanes' play *The Assembly of Women* (392 B.C.). Athenian democracy differs from ours in that women did not vote or share in rule, but Aristophanes was able to imagine what would happen if they did. In the play he shows that women are more democratic than men.[37] Praxagora, she-general of the women of Athens, leads them in a plot to take over the conventional government by men and replace it with a new one manned by women. Surely a manly deed? But the women take command by pretending to be men—wearing false beards, applying imitation tans (women then were pale because they worked indoors), arriving at the Assembly before the men, dressed as men, and voting in the new order as if it were a legitimate decision of the old one. The totally novel design of rule by women is arranged and appears to be a last resort of the corrupt government of men, always eager for innovation and willing to try anything however fantastic. The women do not publicly claim to rule as women; this is not a women's movement but a successful plot of women pretending to be men.

Before the takeover, Praxagora gives a speech to the women she has assembled in a rehearsal of what she will say later in the Assembly. Despite having a "feminine heart" that might hinder public speaking, she says that women have great experience in delivering erotic speeches to their lovers in bed. They know how to say "I love you" and also how to give excuses—two necessary skills for a politician. Then, still in rehearsal to the women only, she says that women ought to rule because they are not equal but superior to men—and superior in what? Women are more conservative and law-abiding and also more devoted to the common good than the corrupt men running Athenian democracy, who live off public handouts and by suing prominent persons. In a list of women's political qualifications, the only item relating to rule is the ability to henpeck their husbands, a form of indirect rule. Once installed, Praxagora's new order proves to be as novel as the new rulers: attempting to do away with all causes for being bad, it introduces communism in property and in the family. Nobody will be envious of others and no disputes will arise. Free dinners will replace democratic deliberation in the Assembly. Politics will be abolished and will be replaced with free love. Our 1960s slogan of make love not war is realized — and there's no politics, either.

Aristophanes presents women as lacking manliness, which means lacking not so much the desire to rule as the desire to claim publicly for oneself the right to rule. Even Praxagora, the remarkable leader, makes no claim on her own behalf for the office to which she is elected. Halfway through the play she disappears and we see her rule as it applies in practice but not in person. The new order she installs transforms Athenian democracy in accord with women's lack of desire to raise issues. Her communist design removes disputes from city life, abstracting the democracy from politics; democracy is made more democratic by being feminized, depoliticized, so as to make everyone happy. As long as there are political decisions to be made, those who do not benefit will be unhappy.

It turns out, however, that some are unhappy under Praxagora's regime as well. Implementing the sexual communism of that regime, the new law prescribes that men and women will be sexually available to one another. But in order to compensate for the sexual advantage of the young and beautiful, an affirmative action provision in favor of the old and ugly allows them to claim a right of sexual access ahead of those who are naturally more attractive. A scene develops in which three hags, each uglier than the one before, squabble with a young woman for first dibs on the service of an appalled young man. By following out the logic of the antipolitical feminine heart together with the egalitarian logic of democracy, the Assemblywomen have squelched the love of beauty that adorns human life. Aristophanes rehearses the women's movement of our day and perhaps gives us a glimpse into the future of affirmative action. The difference between him and us is that he has no idea of gender neutrality. Somehow, despite his poet's love of the individual and aversion to essences, men and women have distinct political natures, men being more direct and assertive than women.

Two facts in American politics today reveal that the stereotype is still tolerated in our gender-neutral society. *The* stereotype is that women are less aggressive, less assertive than men, and it appears in our refusal so far to employ women in combat as well as in the gender gap in voting. As to the first, our thinking about manliness leads us from assertiveness to the political to conflict. Raising an issue may well be tantamount to picking a fight. One could say, then, that manliness is best shown in war, the defense of one's country at its most difficult and dangerous. In Greek, we have noted, the word for manliness, *andreia,* is also the word for courage. Aristotle says that courage is best shown in battle.[38] What we call political courage, the willingness in a democracy to face unpopularity, is lower on the scale than facing death for the sake of one's country. Yet courage in battle may have a political consequence. Those willing to face death for their country have often asserted that their courage gives them the right to rule or to share in rule. The issue raised today over women in the military concerns the sovereign claim of manliness as the title to rule. For if women can fight as well as men, why can they not govern as well, and as deservedly?

It is some time since women have had the right to vote without the right to fight. Now it would seem that this situation must be corrected to solidify women's equal claim to rule. If we survey the gender-neutral society as a whole, the exclusion of women from combat stands out like a sore thumb. What can justify this anomaly? Yet who can reasonably deny that women are not as accomplished as men in battle either in spirit or in physique? The partisans make much of the issue. Conservatives say that this proves women are not the same as men; liberals just go ahead regardless, making the competence of women in everything a point of honor so as to deny (in manly fashion) what cannot reasonably be denied.[39] One can perhaps take a position above the fray and say that the gender-neutral society does not require perfect interchangeability among men and women; it can go along with Aristotle's qualification (on the meaning of "nature") and maintain that men and women are the same "for the most part" if not perfectly. But perhaps, again, this is too superior a view. If the partisans are extreme, they are often more illuminating than the more sensible middle, and right now we are trying to illuminate. Besides, ability to fight is not a mere detail of the big picture. As noted above, it is an important claim to rule (think of the slogan, "old enough to fight, old enough to vote"), and it is the culmination of the aggressive manly stereotype we are considering.

The average male soldier is not a warrior in the manner of Achilles. In peacetime such warriors are called "gung-ho" by other soldiers, with uneasy admiration but without envy. In wartime the warriors come to the fore and by their example lead the others, who fear being shown up as cowards. Women, up to now, have not been warriors nor have they shown any inclination to be led by warriors. They shun risk more than men and they perceive risk more readily than men; they fear spiders.[40] Men, especially warriors, seek out risk as if they could not live without it, and no doubt foolishly they may welcome war. War is hell but men like it. To become the equals of men in combat, then, women would have to become warriors or warriors would have to become obsolete. We see women becoming warriors in the movies and on television: the hit women mentioned above, the film *GI Jane,* and the television show *Xena, the Warrior Princess.* A man watches these performances with a degree of skepticism. He has some experience with the anger of women and with the intrepidity they show in expressing their anger to persons much larger than themselves. But there might come a point when these stronger persons would have to be fought rather than merely told off. The idea of women as warriors would then be exposed as a bluff, and foreseeing this humiliation, the very great majority of women would take a pass on the opportunity to be GI Jane. In the NATO countries where women are allowed in combat units they form only 1 percent of the complement.[41] Whatever their belief about equality, women might reasonably decide they are needed more elsewhere than in combat.

Then, we might ask whether we need manly warriors at all. In the movie *Fargo* (1996), a woman police officer triumphs over men who are either unmanly or whose manliness takes the form of vicious cruelty merely with her plodding but intelligent, asexual professionalism. The movie seems to say that rule-bound professionalism is replacing erratic manliness in occupations that were once manly, and that by this means women, who are steadier than men, can replace them, or at least do as well. Women don't fly off the handle so easily. The argument for professionalism in the police is stronger than for the military because the police enforce the law and need to be seen as respecting it.

What does a professional army do with the warrior? Until recently the professional army tried to make use of the warrior instead of replacing him, and officers exhorted their men to behave as men, by which they meant but rarely said, "be courageous." Nowadays they urge the ranks to be professional in a gender-neutral sense devoted to cool, controlled, dispassionate killing of the enemy, somewhat like the hit men only paid less. When excessive manly passion has been successfully curtailed, soldiers like these may have more quality time for their families. One writer holds out for public adoption an "ungendered vision of aggressivity with compassion."[42] The alternative to women as warriors, it seems, is women as we know them. Nonetheless, women as we know them today do not want to be excluded from the category of warrior even if they do not want to become one. In a recent decision regarding women in the military, Supreme Court Justice Ruth Bader Ginsburg said that any classification by sex, in order to be constitutional, has to be "exceedingly persuasive."[43]

I doubt my words can meet that test. So let us leave this tricky matter for our politics and our necessities to decide. Perhaps we shall be lucky enough not to require an efficient and fearsome military, and instead we can go for equal justice, if that's what it is, like Canada and Denmark. As things are, we do not confine the right to vote to those who fight. In not doing so we imply that women as women (and not as warriors) have something to contribute to our politics. The result of their contribution, we now see, is a gender gap in the voting of men and women.

In the last three American presidential elections, men and women voted for different candidates. In 1996, men were very slightly for Dole and women heavily for Clinton; in 2000, men went 53 percent for Bush and women, 54 percent for Gore; and in 2004 men were 55 percent for Bush and women, 51 percent for Kerry. For elections, the 2000 and 2004 results are substantial differences, as 53 and 55 percent of the vote represent an easy victory. But from the standpoint of sex differences, 53 percent is about equal, somewhat over half. In regard to women in combat the sex difference in capacity is larger, but when it comes to women in politics, the sex difference is muted, and it is a difference in outlook more than capacity. Why should manly assertiveness be less pronounced in politics than in war? Recall that Aristotle said that human beings, not just males, are political by nature.

The difference in outlook of men and women in recent American politics follows the central stereotype that we have been pursuing from aggression to assertiveness. Men, more willing than women to take risks, tend to favor policies of self-reliance and to oppose government programs that provide care and succor to the needy; and men are readier to go to war or to use force in foreign policy. Women, more risk-averse, favor those programs and seek to avoid conflict by supporting policies that promise peace. It appears that in the last two decades of American politics, the gender gap has been created by men turning conservative; women have remained faithful to the New Deal and the Great Society.[44] So, it is said, the Democrats are the Mommy party and the Republicans the Daddy party, as if political parties were like parents and behaved like counterparts rather than opponents. The gender gap in support for the parties is much less for the married than for singles, suggesting that the sexes are more themselves when they live apart. When a woman gets married, she turns right; if she gets divorced, she turns left in search of support from the government, replacing her unsatisfactory husband.[45]

One reason why the gender gap in voting is not wide is that women are divided among themselves. Some observers go so far as to speak of a war between the conservative housewife, who refuses to cooperate with the gender-neutral society, and the liberal, career woman, who wants to extend gender neutrality as far as it goes.[46] In this war each party does her best to hurt the other. The housewife does more than half the housework, which makes it harder for the career woman to teach her husband equality; and the career woman disdains men's fidelity and refuses their courtesies, which are vital to the housewife. So the mom ends up voting for the Daddy party, and the critic of motherhood goes for the Mommy party. Each woman wants security, but one finds it in her husband, the other in the government. Women used to be considered the conservative element in society, the upholders of the common good against manly ambition and of morals against manly aggression. In the *Assembly of Women,* Aristophanes shows how women move easily from conservative morals to radical schemes of big government; a reaction against democratic corruption gives rise to a plot to overthrow the whole manly system of self-interest and to set up a government that takes care of you without your having to exert yourself. It's a comic overthrow that was thought impossible by Aristophanes, as we see from his getting us to laugh at it. But it suggests a connection between the politics of liberal women and conservative women. Though opposed, they are both womanly in their distaste for the politics in which they have become involved.

That marriage mutes but does not remove sex differences suggests that men and women learn from each other. That means they must be capable of learning from each other; there must be something in each sex enabling it to learn from the other. Isn't it possible that a married couple might be in love? And when you're in love, you want in your beloved some things you lack but appreciate; and these might be not only features of the body but also qualities of the soul. A man learns not to charge, and a woman not to flinch, at every danger. Or at least, if you cannot change yourself, you can be glad to have a spouse to do what you won't do. Is it like this in politics too? In any case, though men and women have opposed tendencies, there are plenty of liberal men and conservative women. Among the Democrats, for example, are union members standing up against the bosses and the rich in manly fashion, and also blacks doing the same against the whites who dishonor them by not treating them equally. You can look at the New Deal programs as protection of the weak and also as assertion by the strong.[47] Republicans for their part like risk and competition in the free market, but they also like steady wives and husbands for whose loyalty you do not have to compete. It seems that manly assertiveness is not enough, or not capable of standing alone; a manly person cannot always despise the unmanly, he needs the realism of those who know human weakness. Families and politics are associations that bring men and women together and make them mutually appreciative. As electoral differences go, the sex difference is not great. Certainly in American politics today it is less than the race difference or than the difference between churchgoers and nonchurchgoers. But these differences reflect situation and belief while the gender gap is about natural temperament.

Apart from how women vote, they are less active politically, less interested in politics, less well informed about politics than men.[48] Just as women are less likely to know the names of players in the National Football League (or even the names of the teams!), so too in politics they know less because they care less than men do. Again, the difference is moderate. An interesting study by three political scientists — of the kind I have been disparaging — has made the point. It traces the gender gap not to sex differences but to "participatory factors," such as education and income, that give men greater advantages in civic skills, enabling them to participate politically. But the facts that men are better educated (operationally, make that "formally educated for a longer time") and make more money than women do not close the gap, and the authors have to resort after all to the diverse psychologies of men and women. Resort to psychology implies that men and women make different uses of their education and income. For example, when a woman gets married or has a child she works less, but when a man experiences the same two events, he works more.

The authors believe that if more women were on the ballot, the gender gap in political activity would disappear. As social scientists they need to find an explanation that does not depend on human will or (which is the same thing) chance, and when they have done this, the gender-neutral society will come inevitably into being.[49] It will not require an education in the principles of gender neutrality because the authors do not specify what sort of education. All that is needed is more education of women — whether in public schools, military schools, or nunneries makes no difference to this highly refined but strangely obtuse analysis.[50] Here we see that the liberation of mankind, and especially womankind, by social science will come through the same hapless determinism as did its enslavement to manliness by Darwinism. For only a new determinism of social construction can surely defeat the old determinism of biology. So think my social science friends who constitute a support group for the gender-neutral society.

If we move from political participation to political ambition, we find the deficit of assertiveness in women more marked. To judge by the peak, the character of Margaret Thatcher proves that forceful and successful ambition is possible in women (a fact we knew already from such historical examples as Queen Elizabeth I). But it is also clear that women politicians and rulers are far less than half the total number, and this happens in democracies where women make up half the electorate. Women do not run for office as readily as men do, nor do most women, it seems, call on them to run. It seems that they do not have the same desire to "run" things as men, to use the word in another political sense that like the first includes standing out in front.[51] Women are partisan, like men; hence they are political, like men. But not to the same degree. They will readily sail into partisan conflict, but they are not so ready to take the lead and make themselves targets of partisan hostility (though they do write provocative books). It is interesting that, in contrast to black male civil rights leaders, no feminist leader in our time has run for office. This forbearance has to some extent reduced partisan division within the cause of women, and all women, conservative as well as liberal, can take satisfaction in the next "first woman" to invade a male privilege. Women have made the gender-neutral society more by shaming men than by ruling them, but that very accomplishment leaves them short of equality in ruling. Or does it? Traditionally, women were thought to excel in indirect rule that is not asserted in the blustering fashion of males. Today, women gain in rule as much by practicing modesty as by refusing to be modest — as much by accepting tradition as by denouncing it.

In this chapter we have ascended from manly aggression, discoverable and measurable by science, to manly assertion that is seen and shown better by poets. A wiser, more open-minded science would welcome and incorporate the truths seen by poets, who are spokesmen for human importance and thereby leaders in human assertiveness. That science would not neglect our animality, but it would dwell on what is special about human beings and take particular interest in the assertiveness by which human beings express their strong sense of deserving a share of the best. It would not be so suspicious of exaggeration and anecdote; it would be more aware that to be human is to be individual. It would need to understand manliness, for when manly men assert themselves, they compel us to remember their names. They make themselves, and the rest of us who depend on them, distinct from the nondescript, commodified human beings who are the subjects of our social science.

Chapter Four Manly Nihilism

In manly assertion there is more than a little drama. The old man and Achilles call attention to themselves and their feats. Hemingway and Homer make sure that the stories of their heroes are exciting, their speeches impressive. An assertive speech is a claim on us to vindicate a wrong and to make things right; it's a claim to justice. It may not be directly political, but even Hemingway's old man, not a political type, wants a world in which his knowledge and deed are honored. The manly man, as we say, "makes a statement." It's a statement of significance; this person, this action, should not be overlooked. To work out a manly statement, it is necessary to show its place in the meaning of all things; one has to think, or the author describing the manly hero has to think. The old man is portrayed as thinking for himself and having a relation to the sea, to nature. Achilles lives among the gods, and though he doesn't think much for himself he has a thinking counterpart in Odysseus.

The most dramatic statement of manliness would be the one where the man is the source of all meaning, where nothing else has meaning unless the man supplies it. That is the condition of nihilism—a state in which nothing in itself has meaning; meaning has to be furnished by a human being, the sole source of meaning. The subject of this chapter is the great explosion of manliness that took place in the late nineteenth and early twentieth centuries. The explosion was a particular assertion by the very manly male, and in America he even has a name: Theodore Roosevelt. Who ever was more manly than TR? Who ever spoke more emphatically than he in praise of "manly virtues"? If TR was the foremost champion, he was hardly alone. His theme was picked up by other Progressives, such as Herbert Croly and William

James, as well as by imperialists, such as Rudyard Kipling and H. Rider Haggard. These promoters of manliness were not conservatives defending family values, like those in our day, but progressives rescuing the human race from degeneration and securing the conditions of further advance.

Why did such loud praise for manliness come at this time? We return to Charles Darwin and his influence. Darwin was not a nihilist, but he prepared his generation and later generations for nihilism. His theory of evolution not only denied the eternity of the species but also undermined all eternities, all permanence of meaning. And looming behind Darwin was the greater figure of Nietzsche. Nietzsche declared, and spread the news like a counter-apostle, "God is dead." By this he meant all ideals, everything transcendent or spiritual, as well as God in any religion. The only response to this news, if you believe it, is an assertion that man must go on without God and must make his own ideals to pursue, his own idols to worship, his own substitute God. Thus manliness gets a license from science and philosophy to boast and to act without restraint.

Why so? To sum it up: all meaning depends on human beings, but they have to make an effort of assertion and that, as we have seen in chapter 3, is manliness. Manliness is unrestrained because there is nothing outside manliness, or human assertion, to restrain it. No God with His commands, no nature with its essences stands independently as a warning against going too far and a guide for going the right way. Human invention is left to its own devices and made to generate its own spirit so that manly assertiveness feeds on itself alone and does not serve to protect and defend a cause greater than itself. Of course, decent people—among them TR to be sure—did not use the license they received from Nietzsche to its limit, but they had difficulty explaining why not. And when the manly cannot explain something, they often exert themselves all the more to assert it. Huff and puff are the metaphysics, as well as the physics, of manliness. So we see nihilistic manliness and decent manliness at the same time—early fascism and the Boy Scouts—the one asserted against the other seemingly with equal right and truth. Let's take a tour in history to see manly assertion in action at its most dramatic.

First, we need to understand the context of early twentieth-century manliness. Its immediate context was Darwinism, for in the theory of evolution manly aggression is nature's primary agent of progress. Anyone who mainly agrees with that theory would feel justified in imitating animal aggressors because doing so is doing what comes naturally. It would seem that according to the theory, nature's laws leave you no choice but aggression if you are a man and no choice but to welcome aggression if you are a woman. TR's famous maxim for foreign policy was "Speak softly and carry a big stick." But when it came to the manly virtues, he actually spoke quite loudly. I am not sure there is one recorded instance in his life of his speaking softly, even to his wife; when he spoke, it was always for publication. Why wasn't it enough to carry and swing his stick? It seems that manliness is not something you can just have or be or do; you have to talk or boast about it. Or so TR implies with his loud talk. He openly departs from the strong, silent manly type who disdains talk and especially men who talk. Perhaps the silent type needs to have his silence noticed — spoken of — by someone else, someone who gives the interpretation and asserts the significance. The drama of manliness needs to be dramatized by a poet. Darwin was not a poet but TR in his blustering way was.[1]

To understand the immediate context of Darwinism we need to consider the remoter, more profound context found in Plato. For quite a few things in our time, the context can be found in Plato and his companions. The Greeks studied manliness, for and against, more than we do, moderns that we are. Modernity in its devotion to self-interest does not care much for manliness with its thirst for risk. To understand manliness we must have constant recourse to Greek poetry and philosophy, to Plato as well as Homer. Plato's *Republic* is his treatment of justice, the central human virtue, and it is recognized as his central work. But not many have seen that it is also a critique of manliness, particularly of the manly assertiveness that seems required to advance a claim of justice.[2]

The critique occurs early in the education of the guardians, the future philosopher-kings or their defenders, after Socrates has described their spirited nature. At present, Socrates explains, the Greeks are educated by their poets Hesiod and especially Homer, whom Socrates accuses of a crime of which he was later found guilty, corrupting the youth. Poets undermine the courage of manly youth by teaching them a faulty theology of gods who conflict and commit crimes and of an afterworld in Hades that has no sense to it.[3] A picture of angry, vengeful gods held up to the young males keeps them from being ashamed when they get angry and encourages testy and rambunctious behavior. But what is wrong with a mindless version of Hades? Socrates quotes Achilles' ringing response to Odysseus in Hades, that it is better to be slave on earth than king of hell.[4] Such talk, Socrates says, would make the manly guardians of the best city too fearful of death, hence lacking in courage. They must be taught a simpler, rational theology of gods that are good and simple or inactive. Those gods would leave men alone and not be examples of either good or bad to them.

The crux of the matter, as presented here, is that poets do not believe in, or do not offer for belief, an order in the world, a cosmos. Their theology features a fearful place they call Hades that has no mind, no intelligibility to it. A hero like Achilles cannot count on being treated well, and if he cannot, who can? Generalized, this example means that the cosmos does not have a place for manly excellence.[5] Hades is nothing but disorder and chaos thinly disguised. What does that mean? Since the gods are capricious and human excellence is not rewarded, each of us is thrown back on himself. There being no reliance on anything outside oneself, each must defend himself and his own. This defense of one's own amounts to endorsing and intensifying the spiritedness (*thumos*) that every human being has in some measure but that the manly have in excess. Thus poets justify the fierce loyalties of manly men by teaching all of us that, in effect, no one is watching out for you but yourself. Poets institute the tragic view of life according to which humans, and above all the manly humans, make a drama of their lives and put themselves at center stage. Poets teach us to whine at the ills we suffer and to boast of our successes. No one will notice the silent manly types who by keeping their mouths shut rely on others to give them the credit they deserve.

The lesson of poetic theology is that dramatic manliness is the only way to live. Plato's theology (given through Socrates) opposes the poetic theology — in fact hardly a theology — with a rational theology of gods you can understand even if, not having human form, they are hard to relate to. These rational, dispassionate gods prepare us to understand the forms or ideas discovered by philosophers and presented later in the *Republic*. Knowing or studying the ideas, philosophers replace Achilles as the model for human excellence. Socrates is Plato's hero even though he doesn't beat his breast or tear his hair. Instead of asserting, like manly men, Socrates questions. But also, at least provisionally, he answers his questions with a simplified theology of gods that neither threaten humans nor take sides in their disputes. These gods would be entirely good, so not responsible for evil, and entirely simple, hence unable to assume different forms and meddle in human affairs.[6] The effects of such a theology are to reduce the dramatic intensity manliness craves, to disappoint manly ferocity, and to reassure us that things are not going to hell.

Returning from Plato to Darwin and given the connection between the order of things, or a cosmos, and the education, the taming, of manliness, we ask what is the character of Darwin's theory of evolution? It is not enough to consider Darwin's theory as science, as we have done; we must also see its social or political implications. Although the theory is based on survival and aggression in all species, its effects on human life have to do with manliness. Does it supply cosmic reassurance like Plato's theology, or does it incite excesses of manliness as in Socrates' apparent reproach to the poets? Darwin's theory is complex. It looks at first like a reassurance, but then it turns out to reveal a grave danger.

Darwin's theory is progressive, and Darwin himself is a progressive, on the side of the progress he describes. *The Origin of Species* depicts the development of the higher species from the lower, from simple to complex, from nonman to man. This is progress, and Darwin, who is not a relativist, calls it that. Not only is evolution progressive, but also it progresses without the intervention of human choice (except for choice in the form of sexual selection, a woman's choice of mate that is assumed to be always correct). So it is progress assured. Although progress is initiated by chance mutations, the selection of the best mutation is by nature and not by chance; chance so to speak conquers itself. Contrary to human experience of best-laid schemes going awry, evolution guarantees that the best is always chosen. Achilles will always be preferred to Agamemnon: how could he ask for more reassurance than this? We can therefore surely expect him to calm down and behave himself. The stage is set — not for tragedy, but for ease and surfboarding in a universal California.

On second thought, however, it is far from certain that evolution is progress. Evolution has no end; it extends into the unknowable future where mutations continue and selection must respond. Natural selection has no guide, no criterion by which to select. What will improve, what will degenerate the species? Evolution progresses up to the present with deceptive ease because the end of evolution is presumed to be man as he is now. We forget that man as he is now might have been better, perhaps, with a different evolutionary turn anywhere along the way. Perfection beyond indefinite perfection into the future, however, is beyond our foresight, though we sometimes take a stab at imagining it in science fiction. Evolution works through manly aggression but in a struggle whose outcome is determined. Manliness as a true, chosen virtue is not required. Perfection in the evolutionary struggle comes easily for humanity as a whole, depending only on average behavior from the mass of individuals without demanding moral perfection or heroism from any of them. Darwin's manliness is totally unheroic; it is so functional that it does not have to be controlled or educated. It could better be understood as the *loss* of manliness, particularly in the present when civilization overcomes the struggle for existence, which comes to seem past and primitive. At this point science may take over from natural selection and produce an artificial man like Frankenstein's monster, the imagined creation of a scientist. Manliness either falls back into debility or charges ahead like a madman. The trouble is that Darwin's man is aggressive without being assertive; he cannot speak and if he could he would not know what to say. Someone is needed to speak for Darwin's man of large brain but no thought, and at the end of the nineteenth and beginning of the twentieth centuries, we find a variety of strong voices loudly calling for manliness.

Listen first to William James, an American philosopher who confronts the situation left by Darwin of apparently meaningless evolution from species that no longer exist to species that cannot be imagined. Who will stop evolution and give meaning to man? Only man can do that—only manly men. In 1910 James published an essay better known for its title than its content. "The Moral Equivalent of War" is the title, and the almost unknown equivalent of war is manliness. In the language of Darwin, James says that war was constant in ancient times and "thus were the more martial tribes selected." Not caring for the savagery of war, James declares himself a member of the peace party of our day. He "devoutly believes in the reign of peace" and in "the more or less socialistic future towards which mankind seems drifting." But any future toward which mankind seems drifting seems by that fact alone less than human, and James admits his attraction to the martial virtues, the *manliness,* touted by the war party of his day: intrepidity, contempt of softness, surrender of private interest, obedience to command. These are among "the absolute and permanent human goods."[7] James does not speak of the need for self-defense, which takes war as the means to peace, and thus puts peace ahead of war; he is closer to the "manly art of self-defense," implying that through *contempt of softness* you rather like fighting and might have to be constrained to the use of it only for defense.

Yet James says it is "simply preposterous" to suppose that war is the only stimulus for "awakening the higher ranges of men's spiritual energy." He proposes a kind of Peace Corps, an army enlisted against nature, where our "gilded youths" would be sent, to do hard, risky work and thus "to get the childishness knocked out of them."[8] Some of the work would be women's jobs—dishwashing, clothes washing and window washing—which suggests that women might be included in this corps. The role of women, however, is not to join in but to value these sobered youths more highly on their return from being knocked about. One can smile at the unlucky confidence in James that the year 1910 would be the start of an era of peace and socialism. Still, the wars that followed owed much to the contempt for softness characteristic of imperialism, fascism, and communism that he discerned in his opponents in the war party. He put his finger on the excessive, unnecessary contempt of the manly for the unmanly, so far beyond Darwinian aggression, instinctive or calculated. Whether he was right that there is a moral equivalent for war is less sure. The conquest of nature is an impressive project, as in getting a man to the moon, but a number of philosophers—Aristotle, Hobbes, Hegel (too many to make it "simply preposterous")—tell us that there is no danger quite as dangerous as war, when other human beings come deliberately to kill you. You do not have to love war to doubt that its demands can be artificially reproduced in time of peace.

William James has his own muted contempt for softness, which can be seen in the book he wrote called *Pragmatism* (1907). Pragmatism in its disdain for ideas is sometimes said to be very American, but James gives credit to one American, Charles Peirce, who began it in 1878.[9] Before James, America did not disdain but devoted itself to ideas. America was based on the idea that all men are created equal, which presupposes, contrary to Darwin, a fixed human nature in which we are created equal. Democracy may have made us materialistic, but that, too, as it presupposes a definitely material human nature, should be distinguished from being pragmatic. Pragmatism, it seems, is a new idea that disdains ideas in a country given to ideas.

Instead of a fixed nature, James says, like Nietzsche, that men have temperaments, and he divides temperaments into tender-minded and tough-minded.[10] The tender-minded are rationalistic, intellectualistic, idealistic, optimistic, religious, and so on, whereas the tough-minded are empiricist, sensationalistic, materialistic, pessimistic, irreligious, and so on. These do not refer to qualities of women and men, as one might suppose from a distinction between tender and tough, but the tough-minded are manly. When James says a tender mind is rationalistic, he has in mind our use of reason to provide security and to offer a shield against unwelcome facts. Pragmatism in its humanity understands the tender mind's "need for an eternal moral order" and so remains distinct from a tough-minded scientific positivism that would tell the tender-minded to get over it. Yet it cannot help regarding that feeling as weakness in failing to face facts, given the successful proof of Darwin's theory that rational design in nature arises from "chance-happenings." Pragmatism is a "method," an approach rather than a settled view, and one that has a universal sympathy and dislikes taking sides but also wants to be tough. It sympathizes with the tender-minded, but its very sympathy does not take their tender reasonings seriously and so does not share their temperament. Pragmatism wants to reduce all reasoning to its "practical cash-value," to the bottom line.[11] The cash value is the fit of an idea to reality, when reality includes the real need we may feel for it regardless of its truth. But despite our tender wishes, truth is not at rest and our desire for rest, which means for nature or God, can be only recognized, not satisfied. Pragmatism is a method only and does not stand for any "special results" in which we might take refuge or find comfort. So we have to be tough.

Or do we? The cash value of an idea is what it does for us, how it "fits." What fits for us is what "adapts our life to the reality's whole setting" and keeps us from becoming frustrated.[12] This is the same adaptation or adjustment that Darwin's manliness fell victim to. Being tough or manly means that you *don't* adjust. In James, there is mutual adaptation between reality and our human concerns for security and dignity so that reality is not so hostile to us nor we to it. Science in his view can take its cue from common sense, which generally deals with the face value of things as they appear to us.[13] But the face value of things, their value to you, is greater than their cash value, what others might give you for them; cash always gets a discount. When you take things at face value in human perspective, you run the risk of merely conforming to what people conventionally say in praise of themselves. What's so tough-minded about that?

The suspicion remains that underneath it all William James is not so manly but just a nice guy, not a tough guy American. True, he *wants* to be tough. His pragmatism denies that the universe is composed of intelligible "essences," the very abstractions that are said today to hold women, shackled by their essence, captive to men. But the consequence of denying essences is not entirely favorable to women because the identities we create to substitute for essences will be asserted through manliness, the specialty of men. James's pragmatism is a tough-minded use of reason. It deliberately creates chaos in which we have no assurance of getting our wishes and against which we must be tough-minded. This is the same chaos that Plato criticized in Homer and for the same reason as Plato's: to fashion what James calls "this moralistic and epic kind of a universe" and to set the stage for manly men.[14] A universe of that kind would be down home for Theodore Roosevelt.

William James was not a political man, nor was he a political philosopher, but Teddy Roosevelt with his effusions would have tested the calm of a Stoic. When Roosevelt praised the "strenuous life" James said that he was "still mentally in the Sturm und Drang period of early adolescence."[15] Surely there was something very boyish about Roosevelt's manliness, but Teddy would not have been fazed by a rebuke of this sort from a grown-up. Although he took James's course when he was at Harvard, he was not a disciple of James, who might have fallen into the category of "educated men of weak fibre" whom Roosevelt was pleased to excoriate.[16] The point of James's criticism was his distaste for the Spanish-American War, which tasted so good to Roosevelt. Yet the two agreed on manliness. Roosevelt, had he taken note of pragmatism, would have been happy to begin from James's notion of "tough-minded."

Roosevelt's first thought would have been to make James's tough-minded philosophers tougher by emphasizing determination and willpower over opinions about the universe. "In this life we get nothing save by effort," he said, dismissing God and nature by which we have the faculties that make possible our kind of effort.[17] Roosevelt was a sickly, asthmatic child who, by the advice of his father and with constant exercise, made himself fit not only for survival but for feats of manly aggression. His father's advice had been to lengthen the reach of his mind by strengthening his body; he said that Teddy should *make* his body by the effort of his will.[18] You cannot improve your mind by sheer willpower, I would say, but a strong body might indeed permit your mind to work longer, unless exercising your body gives you ambitions that distract your mind. But Roosevelt did just that. He went in for boxing, a skill that enabled him to knock people around, that must have fed his love of rivalry, and that could easily have encouraged him to exaggerate the power of willpower. He spoke frequently of "character," but by this he meant just one character, the energetic character, forgetting other forms of determination to set one's own course in life. He concentrated not on the mind but on the instrument of the mind.

Today, following James and TR, we are in the habit of calling someone tough-minded if he looks at things empirically — meaning not wishing them to be better than they are — and weak-minded if he reasons or rationalizes things as he wants them to be. Of course, if temperament controls the mind (as James argued), you are more in control when you are tough than when you are tender or weak or wishful; so under that condition the advantage goes to manliness. It also goes to men rather than women because willpower in this view requires a stronger, more athletic body. The women boxers we see nowadays show how far we should agree with Teddy on this point — I leave it to you.

Thus, according to TR, manliness is in the main a construction, an individual construction of one's own willpower. To make the construction a man should engage in "the manly art of self-defense" against other men (which is a closer moral equivalent to war than is James's community service), but he should also seek encounters with nature in the form of dangerous animals.

He must hunt. Teddy bears got their nickname from all the bears he shot, all the cubs he made orphans. He went to the Wild West, became a cowboy by impressing the other cowboys, a loner among loners certified with their stamp of approval.[19] Thus does the individual construction become social: after you have proved yourself. The theorists who say manliness is a social construction often give the impression that there's nothing to it; society waves a wand and a nerd is made manly. No, it takes effort to become manly, as Teddy Roosevelt says. The more manliness is constructed, the more effort it takes. The more we admire effort like TR's rather than the beautiful natures and noble ease of Homer's Achilles and Hemingway's old man, the more we admire willpower manliness and the more we depend on it.

Roosevelt's willpower manliness made him a man, but a man with boyish exuberance. Somehow the passage from boy to man in his case was not quite complete. What is the difference between a boy and a man? If we consult the maxim "never send a boy to do a man's job," the difference may be considerable. A boy, it would seem, is not up to a man's job because of incompetence due mainly to his irresponsibility. Boys are self-absorbed and absorbed with one another; they have trouble giving their attention to adult, manly tasks. Girls, however, are more oriented to the adult world, to the opinion it might hold of them, to the demands it puts on them.[20] Girls do not need to make an effort to become women. Boys need to wrench themselves from their friends and their gangs, perhaps in a formal rite. The Jewish boy in his Bar Mitzvah says "now I am a man." Willpower manliness is a stage but not the whole of manliness.

Willpower manliness can appear to have an air of desperation or can be said to be desperate underneath despite an air of confidence on the surface. Some would interpret TR's manliness as too emphatic to be true because true manliness has more quiet in its confidence, less stridency in its assertiveness. I can agree with this criticism if it is applied to TR, but if it is extended to all manliness, I disagree. These critics claim that all manliness is fundamentally fear or anxiety felt by men who think they do not measure up to what society expects of them. Manliness is desperate, superficial confidence covering up anxiety; the confidence of manly men is false. And to be specific, when the manly reject the unmanly as effeminate, they are really afraid of their own latent homosexuality.

Whoa! Don't go so deep. Apparent confidence, one might say for starters, is real confidence if it can be sustained despite one's fears. Even if some unknown future disaster is impending, we can be confident by relying on what we can know. Yet if all we know is based on social construction, meaning that all we know is contingently based on how society is now — and so manliness is impermanent and will pass away in the gender-neutral society — then it is reasonable to feel anxiety instead of confidence. And it might be reasonable to cover up one's anxiety with loud bluffing, like TR, because some kind of society is better than nothing. Perhaps the gender-neutral society needs its own bluffers too, counter-Teddies to defend it against its own contingency. For since gender neutrality is a social construction like any other, and not founded in human nature, the possibility of return to patriarchy is quite open.[21] But if there is such a thing as cosmic order, otherwise known as *nature,* a real basis for confidence exists and can be relied on.

For all that TR may have absorbed from Charles Darwin and William James against the reliability and reassurance that nature might provide to human designs, he was certainly, we would say today, an environmentalist. He believed as we do that nature left alone is valuable to humans. He believed in willpower, or as we say, social construction; and he also believed in a nature that deserves to be preserved despite our willpower. He did not use the neutral word "environment," an evasion that does not disclose what the environment surrounds or in what measure it nurtures or harms what it surrounds. He liked to speak of "the Strenuous Life" lived outdoors and testing oneself in situations of challenge and risk. Whereas environmentalists today do their best to exclude human intervention in nature — "nature" for them means what is nonhuman — and thus to confine human beings to the role of concerned and caring observers, Roosevelt wanted us to live with nature and react to it. He loved birds but he didn't object to shooting them. We should, within limits, be hunters, for hunting adds "no small value to the national character."[22] Nature does need to be protected from depletion, and there must be game wardens, "men of courage, resolution and hardihood" — not lecturers full of moral urgency passing out lists of small prohibitions as one meets in the national parks today.[23] Roosevelt's program of conservation was like William James's moral equivalent of war, quite contrary to environmentalism today, which desires universal peace, seeks no moral equivalent of war, and on its fringe (did you know that TR invented the phrase "lunatic fringe"?) wants to extend the welfare state from needy humans to all the presumed unfortunates of subhuman nature.

"Conservation" is for the purpose of conserving nature, which is for the purpose of conserving manliness. Manliness wants risk, not comfort and convenience. Roosevelt had his own, brazenly exclusive moralism; he liked being "in cowboy land" because it enabled him to "get into the mind and soul of the average American of the right type."[24] His democracy satisfies not merely the average American but one *of the right type.* "Life is a great adventure, and the worst of all fears is the fear of living."[25] Who would say now that visiting a national park is a great adventure? Yellowstone, where TR gave one of his most famous speeches in 1903, is now no more, perhaps less, an adventure than visiting Disneyland with its artificial thrills. Yellowstone, he said, would ensure to future generations "much of the old-time pleasure of the hardy life of the wilderness and of the hunter in the wilderness . . . kept for all who have the love of adventure and the hardihood to take advantage of it."[26] To challenge the manliness of average Americans of the right type, nature is not chaotic but scenic. To gaze on it is wondrous or sublime; nature does not coddle you but it is not an abyss you must leap across. Roosevelt was tough-minded but not a nihilist because being tough-minded requires that you have the right degree of challenge, enough to give you a charge but well short of inducing despair.

The manly reaction to the great outdoors that Roosevelt expected was not to live the life of a woodsman, but to seek positive responsibility for society. His own trip to the Wild West did not make him a loner but enabled him to become one of the cowboys and then prompted him to return East with energy refreshed. The question arises again: which is more manly, to be alone and self-sufficient or to be responsible and political? One might make the case that a scholar like William James, however incapable of boxing and hunting, is more manly by himself than is TR with his need to be admired and elected to office by average people of the right sort. In a notable chapter of his *Autobiography,* entitled "Outdoors and Indoors," Roosevelt says that love of books and love of outdoors go hand in hand, both being loners' occupations and neither requiring wealth.[27] He himself loved both, but he seems to regard them as preparation for politics rather than attractive mainly for themselves.

Roosevelt is at his most emphatic in urging a man to enter politics. Not for him a bland, mollycoddle word like our "participation." Finding no positive term strong enough to please him, he repeats negative verbs, his favorites being "shirk" and "shrink," to show his contempt for those who abstain from politics. To be efficient and practical a man must ready himself "to meet men of far lower ideals than his own" and not be content "to associate merely with cultivated, refined men of high ideals and sincere purpose to do right." Politics is struggle, and "it is sheer unmanliness and cowardice to shrink from the contest."[28] (You see what I mean about *shrink*; and note how vices are magnified with *sheer* in front of them. Not for TR the use of *weasel words,* another phrase he coined or made his own.) Here is where the professors like William James go wrong; they consort with one another, cherish their ideals, and shirk their duty to join the actual battle that is less pleasant than discussion with friends over tea. The tough-minded manly man not only accepts pain but actually does his best to avoid pleasure. Yet isn't manliness for all its risks and trials pleasant for the manly man? And not only at the end of the day? Roosevelt wants his manly man in politics to accommodate himself to the rough and coarse and the selfish, and this would seem to compromise rather than fulfill his manliness by making it depend on success in his relations with others beneath himself. He might become a team player or an organization man, hardly roles for a manly man. So we must not forget the manly loner and the argument to be made on his behalf. The loner would be contemptuous of bookish professors, but he shares with them a taste for solitude.

We must not leave Roosevelt in a situation he would hate—indecisively ambivalent. He would insist on the superiority of manly responsibility to manly aloofness, of which one sign is his attitude toward women. As if speaking closer to today, he declares that "women [must be put] on a footing of complete and entire equal rights with men," including "the right to enter any profession she desires on the same terms as a man." Yet normally, he adds, "the woman must remain the housemother, the homekeeper, and the man must remain the breadwinner." That is because we must not live in a regime of rights abstracted from the performance of duty with "indulgence in vapid ease."[29] In effect, women are not equal to men according to TR, but both above and below them. Women receive the bread won for them by men and delivered to them with gallantry. But they are models of effeminacy, the very thing a man must avoid.[30]

Roosevelt's remarks on American motherhood tell us something about the preference of the manly man for duty over virtue. Impelled by the self-drama of manliness, which posits risk and challenge at every turn, Roosevelt turns away from the American, constitutional notion of rights to embrace a sterner "sense of duty" that appears more Germanic and Kantian. Even virtue might be too undemanding for him, for the virtuous person finds virtue to be pleasantly harmonious with his inclination, does not worry about his willpower, and does not struggle to be good. Roosevelt does speak of manly virtues, but these are habits of the zestful performance of duty. Duty gives shape to willpower, directing and checking it; and society — not the loner — defines duty.

Roosevelt's manliness appears also in his advocacy of equality of opportunity, a phrase he and his friend Herbert J. Croly were perhaps the first to use.[31] Today "equality of opportunity" is a conservative slogan opposed to the liberals' "equality of result." One might think that conservatives with their slogan are harking back, as they often do, to the founders of liberalism; but the formula does not appear in the theories of such men as John Locke, John Stuart Mill, or the American founding fathers. For TR, equal opportunity is not the passive policy of a neutral government that watches benignly over the rivalry of talented people as they compete to succeed. Nor is it like the mixture of hard work and shrewd manipulation set forth in Benjamin Franklin's *Autobiography* by which an individual can rise to public esteem without challenging society's prejudices.[32] Neither is it Thomas Jefferson's "aristocracy of talents," which assumes that in a free country talent will find the means to propel itself to the top.[33] Instead, equal opportunity shows both concern for virtue and affirmative action by government. It requires that individuals accept a duty to grasp opportunity and to go as far as they can; lack of interest in success — goofing off on long vacations, relaxing in early retirement, or indulging in refined leisure of any sort — is not an option. And equal opportunity results from the use of government to equalize opportunity by making things harder for the rich (with a graduated income tax and an inheritance tax) and thus easier for the poor. But Roosevelt would not use government to reduce the effort required of the poor. They should be manly too. Manliness is preferable to any life of ease or riskless routine.

Let us not overlook the politics of Roosevelt's manliness. He was a great one for the assertiveness of executive power. His notion of the president's duty was not bound to actions authorized in the actual words of the Constitution. In a notable exchange with his Republican rival William Howard Taft, who held that belief, Roosevelt declared that the president is "the steward of the people, bound actively and affirmatively to do all he could for the people, and not to content himself with the negative merit of keeping his talents undamaged in a napkin."[34] The American founders made an executive power strong enough to stand up to popular opinion and to withstand the temptation to seek popularity, but progressives like Roosevelt and Woodrow Wilson made the president into a "leader" — that is, on occasion a follower — of public opinion. Roosevelt, for all his promotion of positive merit (in which he borrows words of the Bible), is still a steward — and how manly is that?[35] Who is more manly: George Washington, a man of dignity not to be trifled with, or Teddy Roosevelt, steward of the people, who sees humiliating constraint in the Constitution but not in popular favor? Here we detect a soft core to TR's blustering, outer toughness.

The same can be said of Roosevelt's imperialism. TR was no "chicken hawk," no armchair, theoretical imperialist whose main concern is with the *ist* or *ism* at the end of the word, and whose only action is egging others on. Quite the contrary! Having got himself named assistant secretary of the navy by President William McKinley in 1897, he was in office when the U.S. battleship *Maine* was blown up in the harbor of Havana in February 1898. But of course he was not the secretary of the navy. So he waited ten days until his boss took the afternoon off for a massage; then, having been routinely designated acting secretary, TR sprang into action — summoning experts, sending instructions around the world for the navy to be ready for war, ordering supplies and ammunition, and requesting authorization from Congress for unlimited recruitment of seamen. In four hours he created momentum toward war that neither the president nor his hapless superior could stem. After war was declared on April 19, Roosevelt, his alacrity now red-hot zeal, was offered command of a cavalry troop to be formed of frontiersmen, dubbed by him "Rough Riders." He declined the command for lack of experience but took second-in-command as being an office he knew how to work from. In short order, Roosevelt formed the troop consisting of cowboys leavened with polo players, having them ready by the end of May. Thus he gained the double glory with the double virtue that Machiavelli says is due to the captain who trains his army before he conquers the enemy.[36] Not content with this, he rushed into action contrary to the example of Machiavelli, himself always a behind-the-lines commander. At considerable personal risk, TR led his troops in the famous charge up San Juan Hill, and when he reached the top, shot and killed one of the enemy. After the action he was recommended for the Congressional Medal of Honor, America's highest decoration for bravery in battle. When he did not receive the medal, he was not too proud to lobby for it, anxious as he was to prevent the War Department from doing an injustice.[37]

In all this Roosevelt grasped his opportunities, or as we would say in his spirit, faced his responsibilities. Responsibilities as we use the word often attach to an office, and they might seem to be particular to it — whether president, assistant secretary, or a nonpolitical office, such as parent. But TR's willpower manliness looks at the office as an excuse for action rather than the source of a duty imposed on the officeholder. It was manly of TR to seek the office, which he did eagerly rather than dutifully. Yet we cannot overlook the fact that taking on a responsibility is — nonetheless for its enthusiasm — accepting a duty. And it is a duty to those less competent and willful than oneself, hence a compromise of one's own freedom and independence. Roosevelt's stress on willpower retains the ambivalence we have seen in defining the manly man as either a loner or a take-charge guy. It takes willpower to withdraw as well as to commit oneself; either way could be condemned or praised as willful. To be sure, TR tries to make it appear that one who shirks or shrinks from his responsibility lacks the willpower of a man, but that is not necessarily so. Even in the form of an opportunity, responsibility is a constraint. It is a self-constraint perhaps, yet still a constraint.

Pragmatism is an idea with this same ambivalence, as we have seen in the dichotomy between the tough-minded who want to be assertive and the tender-minded who want to fit in. These two contrary temperaments reflect two moods in the use of the word. In American English *pragmatism* means *getting it done* ("let's be pragmatic"), implying active energy, and *taking satisfaction in less* ("you have to be pragmatic"), implying a degree of resignation. To be pragmatic is optimism that our problems can be solved, but how can we solve them, given the doubt we are taught by pragmatism in the efficacy of reason? Reason, we recall, is disdained by pragmatism as the tender wish that things will somehow fit together on their own. Progress under pragmatism requires an addition of willpower, of manly assertiveness, to reason so that reason, in the form of science, does not construct a boring, peaceable civilization that appeals only to mollycoddles and fails to meet the ambition of humans who want dignity more than peace. Pragmatism is an outgrowth of liberalism, but the opposition within pragmatism between tender and tough endangers liberal progress. The trouble is that the manliness needed to express confidence depends on doubt of reason, yet reason is the source of our confidence in better things to come. When you add manliness to reason so as to make reason more capable, you also subtract from the capability of reason. The danger to progress is that manliness, instead of endorsing reason, will get the better of reason.

We can see the opposition of manliness and science in two genres of nineteenth- and early twentieth-century literature: the literature celebrating imperialism and the literature doubting the goodness of science. The opposition between manliness and science, regarded apprehensively by writers in these two genres, will introduce us to the manly nihilism of Nietzsche, who welcomes, revels in, the mutual incitement of manliness and unreason.

Let us glance first at the work of H. Rider Haggard, Edgar Rice Burroughs, and Rudyard Kipling. All three celebrate imperialism by showing the superiority of Western civilization over the native tribes it rules, but at the same time, contrary to what we expect with our anticolonial sympathies, they show admiration for the manly qualities of those defeated and dominated. Manliness in these writers has become *primitive* — attractive but out of the reach of civilization in their time. Today we do not claim to have civilization but only a civilization, a "culture." We have become so doubtful of civilization as never to use "civilized" in contrast with "primitive," which we replace with "less developed." As a result, we lose sight of primitive manliness; it is swallowed up in the vague blob out of which society develops, and there is nothing we see to lament its loss. In the confusion of our moral neutrality and our eager sympathy, we are more oblivious of the virtue of the colonials than were their oppressors. We are also more pleased with being *developed* than we used to be when we thought ourselves *civilized*.

H. Rider Haggard's adventure story *King Solomon's Mines* (1885) is dedicated by the narrator to "all the big and little boys who read it." Three manly white Englishmen — apparently grown up — go to Africa to seek a fabulous diamond mine and while there encounter black Africans as manly as they among a people where manliness is much more at home than in the white man's civilization. It is a black man, the servant Umbopa, who certifies that his master, Sir Henry Curtis, is a man: "We are men, thou and I."[38] He refers to the fact that both are big men, for size is part of manliness. (You might see a small manly man, but you would wish him to be bigger.) While the white men hunt elephants for recreation, the natives hunt for food and do not kill for fun.[39] Manliness is their way of life, not a relief from it. Later, Umbopa turns out to be Ignosi, the lawful king of the Kukuanas (a fictive tribe), and he is compared to a Greek hero out of Homer, the purest man of the best poet in white civilization.[40] "You white men are so fond of toys and money," says Umbopa, referring to their unmanly love of diamonds.[41] When he becomes king, he plans to prevent his kingdom from trading with them, for their civilization would contaminate his people's manliness. For Haggard, the native blacks of his day are the standard of manliness.

Manliness is presented as a simple quality without frills or civilized refinement; the man is like a boy, and he wants action and raw meat (or a "simple meal" of roasted giraffe marrow).[42] But manliness is shown in the excitement of adventure, and here complication enters. Haggard's novel, though not great literature, is more thoughtful than it appears. It is aware that manliness seeks adventure and that the adventure needs to be beheld, narrated. Haggard puts the narrator into his tale; he knows better than the scientists we have studied who cannot factor themselves into their study of manliness. His narrator, Allan Quatermain, accompanies the two other manly heroes and tells the story. As the narrator vouches for the events he witnesses and experiences, the fictional adventure becomes a nonfictional report. Quatermain claims to tell the adventure of simple men in the "plain language" of truth, as if he were a scientist or historian; but of course he is not. Nor is he simply a "gentleman," for in the first chapter he asks a theoretical question a gentleman would never ask, "What is a gentleman?" Unlike a gentleman, Quatermain is interested in money; he bargains for his fee as guide, and at the story's end, after the party has found the diamonds, he makes sure, in the confusion of escape, that some of them are brought home.[43] Whereas Sir Henry would allow no living man to call him a coward, Quatermain does not mind calling himself "a bit of a coward."[44] He is prudent, and it is his curiosity that enables the party to escape from the cave where the diamonds were hidden. He has a "detestable habit of thinking" that takes him beyond manliness (in the service of manliness).

Umbopa, the manly black, has a despairing metaphysics of manliness, and at one point he exclaims over the origin of mankind: "Out of the dark we came, into the dark we go. . . . Life is nothing. Life is all."[45] This sounds like manly nihilism, a construction of chaos to make men the only source of meaning. But Quatermain's story—the plot of the novel—moves very differently, from the light of civilization to the daylight of the African sun to the dark of the cave where the diamonds are, and then back to the light outside and a return to England.[46] An adventure does not end up in the dark! It is not a voyage to the end of the night. Quatermain corrects Umbopa's inadequate thinking. Life is neither nothing nor all; the "elements of life" are immortal, but individual life is not. From these elements individual men must make their own lives, and these lives will end. Quatermain is "fatalistic," as he says, but not nihilistic, and so he goes on the adventure (while making sure he is well paid) even though he is not adventurous. His fatalism tells him that life is not determined by human beings but by a divine power humans cannot control. Life not being secure, it makes no sense to pursue security; hence the policy of accepting risk is reasonable. Manliness is reasonable. "Reasonable" does not mean calculated. Manly men do not calculate the risk in the hope of controlling for it, as do insurance companies. Like Umbopa, manly men plunge ahead and do not reason out their manliness, but the reasoning can be done for them by the narrator or the novelist. In H. Rider Haggard we get an elementary metaphysics of manliness based on the nature of human life and developed through the duality of being manly and serving as the herald and interpreter of manliness. What are women, we might wonder. "Women are women, all the world over," says Quatermain.[47] They are the same everywhere, but men, manly men, differ. By seeking risk, manly men welcome the accidents that make for human individuality and diversity.[48] Even though manly men are a universal type, they are responsible for varieties of types like Englishmen and Kekuanas.

Tarzan's author does not trouble us with deep thoughts. In Tarzan we see the assertiveness of man over beast and man over woman. Who can forget the manly assurance of Tarzan in the Johnny Weismuller film when he declares to Jane Porter: "Me Tarzan, You Jane!" This makes Tarzan seem a little dim, but in the book (*Tarzan of the Apes,* 1912) by Edgar Rice Burroughs, Tarzan is shown to be intelligent in impressive ways. He learns to swim after jumping into water to escape a lion.[49] He learns to read when confronted with a book.[50] He learns how to use a knife in the middle of a fight with an ape and discovers the half nelson while wrestling with another ape.[51] He learns French in about a week in order to converse with a Frenchman.[52] His desire to learn is greater than his desire for revenge and greater than his desire to rule.[53] But by the use of his reason he gained revenge and became King of the Apes, even though he was smaller and weaker than they. Rather than reveal, like Rider Haggard, the narration or the philosophical reasoning that accompanies and underlies manliness, and that manly men need but do not have, Burroughs shows us the "presence of mind" that is compatible with manliness and that manly men need and have.[54] This sort of reason distinguishes men from apes in the very practical ways that would enable a man to kill apes and rule them. Tarzan is, of course, just a story about a mythical man testing the difference between man and beast — not so practical but illustrative. In real life today manly knowledge enables a man, not to be Tarzan, but to act effectively in an emergency and to fix things and solve problems without professional help.

Human reason makes a "vast difference" even in a story designed to bring out the closeness of men to apes.[55] It's difficult to count Burroughs as a Darwinian. Where are the gradual steps that could make intelligible the "descent" or rather the ascent of man from his forebears? The behavior, however, that most distinguishes men from apes has to do with protection of females. When Tarzan fell in love with Jane, he did not reason but knew that "she was created to be protected."[56] Male apes might want to protect females, but only as their own property and as a sign of their dominance. When Tarzan first fights to save Jane from an ape, he carries her off "like the primeval man who had fought for her and won her." But then, in his desire to please her and be worthy of her love, he makes the transition from "savage ape-man" to "polished gentleman."[57] His heredity as the scion of an English aristocrat takes over from his upbringing as an ape. At the end, it is true, Tarzan leaves Jane in Wisconsin to return to his home or habitat in Africa. (Wisconsin? Burroughs was an American who wanted Tarzan to have a nobler inheritance than is available to Americans.) But however much a "wild beast at heart," he leaves her in accordance with the code of a gentleman, abandoning her to her fiancé—his inferior—and telling her a noble lie when the truth would have destroyed her happiness.[58] Perhaps telling the noble lie did not destroy *his* happiness . . . but telling the truth would have done so. Tarzan's manly prudence becomes the instrument of his manly protectiveness. Although reason and love are not consistent, both are distinctively human and thus involved with each other.

Rudyard Kipling, who coined the phrase "the white man's burden," is the very voice of imperialism and of the manliness that goes with it. The poem that features the phrase was written on the occasion of the Spanish-American War in 1898 to congratulate Teddy Roosevelt and the United States on its first act of civilized maturity, an act of imperialism. Today "the white man's burden" is used as shorthand for the thoroughly unjustified way that masters seek to justify themselves, and it is invoked only to be dismissed. But a brief look at this very politically incorrect writer will show us something more about the mixture of reason and unreason in manliness, about the *excess* at the heart of manliness.

Kipling in contrast to Haggard and Burroughs writes about India as well as Africa. His *Jungle Book* (1894) and its sequel feature "the law of the jungle" in India, though of course it refers not just to India but to all nature.[59] Now what is the law of the jungle? To us now, it means the law of those who reject human law and obedience to law in favor of "might makes right" or "get the other fellow before he gets you"; the law of the jungle is imperialism. This is not at all the meaning that Kipling gives to the phrase he invented. For him, both the law of the jungle and imperialism are better than we think, and they are not the same. The law of the jungle is for the beasts, not for men, and it sets limits on the exploitation of one's greater strength. This law holds sway in conditions more difficult than Thomas Hobbes's "state of nature" because the jungle contains predators who eat what they kill. Thus they have to kill in order to live, by contrast with human beings in the state of nature who can live in peace if they consent to government. The law of the jungle distributes game equitably according to demand or need. Enforcing moderation, it precisely denies that each is only for himself and it appeals to a common good, if you can imagine it, of those who are required by their nature to eat one another. Thus it contradicts Spinoza's law of "might makes right" in which the big fish eat the little fish; they do that, but only according to need. The law of the jungle does not merely replicate what the beasts do; it holds them to a higher standard. It must therefore be taught, as it is by the wise old bear Baloo.

Where is manliness in this law? The law of the jungle does not hold for human beings, who are above beasts, and it enjoins the beasts never to kill man. Man has fearsome powers of wisdom and fire over beasts. All beasts fear fire, which perhaps represents the Promethean gift of technology. With human wisdom comes human folly, both of which are characterized by excess over simple need. Man wants to know more than he needs to know, and this unnecessary desire can lead him to folly. In the *Jungle Book,* human folly is represented in the aimless chatter of monkeys who think that because they live in the tops of trees they have a better view than animals like old Baloo, who sensibly keep their focus on the ground in front of them and do not meddle in the affairs of others. There is something assertive, which means manly, in both wisdom and folly; and manliness in the sense of asserting what goes beyond need specifically defines humans. The law of the jungle does not apply to humans because it forbids excess whereas humanity is excess rather than necessity or Darwinian survival. Human law, the law of civilization, can at best constrain or manage excess, for men will insist on freedom and they will always resist the single command that sums up the law of the jungle — Obey![60]

Manly or human excess is expressed in civilization, a mixture of wisdom and folly that transcends bare needs and embodies answers to big questions that do not need to be asked. But civilization is not only the West, as with Haggard and Burroughs; it is divided into East and West. Kipling's most famous book, *Kim,* presents the attractions of East and West in the Lama who leads Kim to purification and the British colonel who educates him for the Great Game of politics. We all know that "East is East and West is West, and never the twain shall meet"; so we know that the deepest opposition is not between civilization and savagery but within civilization.[61] Although the civilizations represent forms of manly assertiveness and can therefore never meet, still, as Kipling says in the same poem, the difference is overcome on the level of individuals "when two strong men stand face to face." And we remember the avowal of the British soldier over the body of the Indian boy who died to succor him: "You're a better man than I am, Gunga Din!"[62] The West is superior to the East in technology, organization, and desire for power — and occasionally in responsibility (the white man's burden) — but not in everything. Manliness is essentially individual, and Kipling's over-quoted poem "If" speaks to the individual who has the will to "hold on" and concludes that if he does, "You'll be a man, my son!"

Kipling, like Haggard and Burroughs, is not a devoted Darwinian. In company with Darwin, he looks at men in the light of beasts; but his conclusions are different. Insofar as the law of the jungle is Kipling's lesson to man, it is to pay more attention to what distinguishes men from beasts than to the similarities. Men are essentially excessive in their desires, beasts not. Both need to be ruled by moderation, but moderation is much more difficult to get from men, who with their manliness are given to excess. Moderation, in any case, is not consistent with Darwin's evolution, which requires for the sake of the common as well as the individual good that the weak not survive. The law of the jungle explicitly (as opposed to Darwin) takes for granted the existence of the species as species, each with its own rights despite the need to kill. In the *Just So Stories,* Kipling tells moral fables about the origin of the species — "how the leopard got his spots" — rather than presuppose, as does Darwin, that the species evolve gradually. In Kipling's time and in ours, the resistance to Darwin's theory is as remarkable as its influence. In Kipling's time Darwin had such influence that his theory, an instance of science, stood for science generally.

The novels of imperialism we have examined disclose surprising doubts about the superiority of civilization based on science. Two other novels of this time, one by Robert Louis Stevenson and one by Mark Twain, raise the direct question of how science and manliness are related. The problem is that science seems to be both unmanly and manly. Science seems to unman men by ministering to our fears and to our desire for security. The social influence, the political consequence of science can be seen in its support of the middle class, characterized, as Hegel said, by fear of death—as opposed to the nobility, which is always raring to fight. Yet science also seems manly in the intrepidity of its advance, or should we say its reckless charge, into the unknown. So Darwin, on one hand, defines man as seeking survival (unmanly) and, on the other, leaves man undefined while evolving into God knows what sort of future (manly). Science supports bourgeois regularity but also inspires antibourgeois nihilism.

Stevenson's *The Strange Case of Dr. Jekyll and Mr. Hyde* (1886) reminds us of Mary Shelley's romantic masterpiece *Frankenstein* (1818), for both are stories about the scientific creation of human beings, Dr. Jekyll of Mr. Hyde and Frankenstein of his monster. But Frankenstein wants to create an artificial life instead of having a natural child, while Dr. Jekyll experiments on himself—as it were dissecting himself—with a laboratory analysis out of which comes his evil half, Mr. Hyde.[63] He becomes a "case," a strange case, for his lawyer Mr. Utterson, a modest middle-class man who follows the case through with mixed curiosity and reluctance.[64] Dr. Jekyll himself is a man of science with a number of degrees and honors signified in the initials that follow his name, but he surpasses normal science, venturing into the realm of what ordinary practitioners consider to be "unscientific balderdash."[65] He wants to know the difference between good and evil, a thing that we all want and need to know but that science shies away from. To learn this he is willing to take the great risk of experimenting on himself. He believes that man is not a unity, being not one but two, half good, half evil, a conclusion Frankenstein reached only after creating his monster.

In an act of scientific reduction, Dr. Jekyll takes a potion that separates out the evil in him, forming a new being: Mr. Hyde. From the moment we see Mr. Hyde everybody regards him with loathing but has difficulty in describing him exactly. Only Stevenson, the author and not a scientist, describes him surely and confidently.[66] Dr. Jekyll in his simple-minded behavioral science wants his outside to conform to his inside. Unlike the average everyday scientist, he cannot simply ignore the entangled ambivalence of good and evil, and in his manly way he takes the bull by the horns and tries to wrench good and evil apart. The pure made-in-the-laboratory evil of Mr. Hyde creates pure terror for those who look upon him. Because he cannot tolerate the undependability of human courage in facing the choice of good and evil, Dr. Jekyll experiments with a scientific solution that will proceed from the separation of the two elements of man. This was the first step toward the reconstruction of man that Frankenstein neglected to take. But Dr. Jekyll does not succeed; he fails to complete the separation. Mr. Hyde is perfect evil, but Dr. Jekyll remains torn between good and evil, aghast at the result of his experiment but tempted to continue it. Mr. Hyde, it turns out, is unaware of Dr. Jekyll's good, but Dr. Jekyll is painfully aware of Mr. Hyde's evil. Dr. Jekyll concludes that his experiment had not only been a crime; "it had been a tragic folly."[67]

In telling the story, Stevenson helped to create the modern horror story (now horror film) that attempts to excel tragedy by displaying a hero who is within the bounds of respectability and without a tragic flaw. Dr. Jekyll did not achieve that ambition; he did not excel tragedy. He committed the tragic folly of trying to abolish tragedy, and *this*—his susceptibility to tragedy—was his tragic flaw. The heavy drama of Stevenson's story contrasts sharply with its description as a "case," a mundane scientific case from which all personal interest has been removed. Stevenson poeticizes science so as to make it both more interesting and more true.

Dr. Jekyll in his self-hatred sounds like Achilles and complains of his sufferings: "I could not think that this earth contained a place for sufferings and terrors so unmanning."[68] His experiment tests his manhood, his ability to stick with what he knows or thinks to be good, but at the same time it denies that such a quality is needed. All we need is the discernment of science to guide us to unqualified good and save us from evil. We do not need this third element, manliness. Dr. Jekyll does not understand the element of facing risk that supplied the motive for science and yet is endangered by science. Facing risk supplies the motive for science to go beyond the given and the received, but it is endangered when science shows that everything is under control and nothing is to be feared. Stevenson's lesson is that science is not beyond good and evil however much it tries to be.

Mark Twain's *A Connecticut Yankee in King Arthur's Court* (1889) is the work of a master analyst of democracy who has studied democratic manliness closely. Twain's wonderful book seems at first to locate manliness in King Arthur's court, a place totally foreign to Hank Morgan, the Yankee who is knocked out in a fight and wakes up in sixth-century Britain where knights are at the ready to "try a passage of arms" with one another in manly, feudal fashion. The contrast could not be greater between King Arthur's court—with its Round Table of knights fighting meaningless duels and then boasting to one another of these murderous adventures in childish, simple-hearted monologues, all the while bemused and misguided by the magic of Merlin—and the practical Yankee, who promises and performs real accomplishments, practices democracy and introduces a republic, substitutes the guidance of experts for the rhetoric of privileged windbags, and bases his innovations on applications of science. In his book Twain rewrites *Le morte d'Arthur,* the original story of Camelot presented in its own terms. We see Twain at the beginning receiving a stranger who proves to be Hank and who leaves him a journal, in fact a palimpsest of parchment on which Hank has written his account in such fashion that you can see some of the old writing behind Hank's.[69] This is a hint.

When Hank arrives in Camelot, he immediately loses a duel he unwittingly provoked and becomes a captive. He escapes prison and foils his enemy Merlin by knowing very fortunately that an eclipse will occur on the next day. Having exposed and bested Merlin, Hank vaults to power, becomes Arthur's "executive," and sets about establishing "a new deal" for the kingdom.[70] He rejects the principle of inheritance and introduces merit as the criterion of status, replacing the well-born nobles with experts of various kinds. Actually, the nobles are adapted to the new deal. Hank commercializes the aristocracy to the point that knights are seen walking around wearing signboards advertising soap, and at the end Sir Launcelot has become president of the stock exchange and the knights' Round Table is used "for business purposes" (perhaps made square because Sir Lancelot is able to corner the market for a stock).[71] A patent office is the first institution of the new deal, revealing Hank's understanding of the relation between science, commerce, and the middle class. But in the end his new deal is a colossal failure. The republic collapses in a war where 25,000 are killed, the monarchy returns, and the reactionary church takes over from the society of progress. Just as in *Dr. Jekyll and Mr. Hyde* only on a larger scale, the scientific principle proves unable to sustain itself socially and politically; the reason is its neglect of manliness.[72]

Hank thinks himself quite a man, and often says so, yet his new deal shows little reflection on what a man is. Vastly impressed with the differences between knight-errantry and his own innovative practicality, in the manly overconfidence of his superiority he does not see what he has in common with the knights. He does not notice, though it's obvious to a reader, that his whole adventure begins in Connecticut with a fight he gets into for no reason. When he wakes up in Camelot he is immediately assaulted — not for no reason but for an unspecified reason ("for land or lady or for . . .").[73] Nor is he much of a democrat, satisfied with equality. Already a "head superintendent" in Connecticut, his first thought on realizing he was in the sixth century was that with his superior knowledge he would "boss the whole country inside of three months."[74] And he does: though he does not supplant King Arthur, he says he has greater authority and becomes known as The Boss. He claims to be "elected by the nation" instead of ruling by inherited privilege, but in fact, he is not elected; he is guilty of many arbitrary and dishonest acts, and unlike Franklin Roosevelt's New Deal, Hank Morgan's is never submitted for popular consent. His ambition is as large as a knight's and more reckless because it is not controlled by any sense of honor. Unconscious of his own ambition, he does not recognize the rights of someone else's ambition, and thinking only of success, he does not hesitate to cheat and humiliate his fellows. Twain makes other points, too, behind Hank's back. Hank's use of science is no less deceptive and conniving than Merlin's use of magic. The picture of knights wearing signboards works two ways: is Twain ridiculing knights by showing them as sidewalk salesmen, or is he ridiculing salesmen by showing them to be knights?

Hank gets the better of a certain blacksmith, "a self-made man, you know. They know how to talk."[75] But a self-made man is just what Hank is and talking is what he does. When he gets to talking big, manly nihilism comes out. "There is no such thing as nature," he says; "what we call by that misleading name is merely heredity and training." In the procession of ancestors that stretches back a billion years, there is just "one microscopic atom in me that is truly *me.*" In denying the existence of nature he means that nothing has authority over him, a thought King Arthur would never have held. Having this thought does not, of course, prevent Hank from pretending to a virtue King Arthur would never claim: "And as for me, all that I think about in this plodding sad pilgrimage, this pathetic drift between the eternities, is to look out and live a pure and high and blameless life."[76] The scientific outlook that defines the Connecticut Yankee makes him see himself as one microscopic atom with a very big mouth. The more science diminishes man, the more it encourages manliness. Hank cannot see, therefore cannot admit, that the manhood he admires is at bottom aristocratic, that the meritocracy he establishes is another (and in some respects inferior) aristocracy, that his merit-inspired democracy is held together by honor, not by gain, and that in sum his new deal is not as new as he believes. Twain also points out to us that Hank as a cowboy in a rodeo is like a knight in the lists. And baseball played in armor is another convergence of democracy and aristocracy.[77] Manliness seeks honor for the individual man and, by implication, for the human race. Honor for the human race requires a special place for it in nature, contrary to Hank's effusion and to the scientific outlook he represents.

Criticism of the scientific outlook is the point of departure for Friedrich Nietzsche (1844–1900), who culminates the doubts we have collected. Nietzsche is *the* philosopher of manliness in modern times. He saw modern civilization in decline and made it seem that the only remedy was manliness resurgent and recreated. So powerful is his thought that it laid the basis, as we shall see, even for the feminism of our time. He raised the stakes by declaring science to be a promoter of nihilism, and then by formulating in response a manliness that surpassed in breadth and ambition all the examples we have given. Homer's Achilles and Hemingway's old man presuppose, if they do not take for granted, a natural order of rank in which their manliness makes sense and deserves respect. Nietzsche's superman does not. He creates, while in a sense presupposing, a rank order; he must occupy himself with the virtue of manliness from which he begins in such a way as to be his own poet and to show the way to poets; he is a philosopher and his manliness is mainly philosophic. Manliness for Nietzsche is both crude and refined; it is the warrior and the philosopher not merely admiring each other but sharing the same soul.

Like the pragmatists, Nietzsche is surely tough-minded, but unlike them he does not merely make concessions to the tender-minded (which for him would be slave morality); he thinks through the difference and the connection between the two tempers. And his will to power differs from Theodore Roosevelt's willpower in not requiring focus on what is urgent or learning to box or self-promotion. He did not waste time and effort in calling for manliness but surpassed Roosevelt in denouncing human, or modern, weakness. Roosevelt would have been shocked to hear that a man could argue that morality is the cause of weakness, that the alleged cause of human strength—human reason—could be implicated in human weakness. He would have had choice words for an obvious shirker like Nietzsche.[78] As for the five novelists of manliness we have visited in this chapter, Nietzsche would have appreciated their rebelliousness toward Darwin but concluded that they did not go far enough. Darwin himself did not go very far into the nihilism of his theory as he managed somehow to retain his credulous faith in the science that undermined the dignity of everything human, including science. Our novelists are more perceptive than Darwin and doubt the progress of science, but in comparison with Nietzsche they are, or would be in his view, too quick to believe that science or reason can be saved, its defects overcome. Haggard thinks that science can be rescued from routine with adventure. Burroughs thinks that primitive man can be made a gentleman and that gentlemen can be saved from being defined away as too primitive. Kipling thinks that manly excess is not obsolete, that the West can be balanced by the East. Stevenson thinks that when tragedy abandons greatness it can survive as horror. Twain thinks that through love the Connecticut Yankee can learn to live with the moral blindness of science.

For Nietzsche nihilism has arrived and manliness is all. What is nihilism? "Nothing is true, everything is permitted." I take that to be Nietzsche's definition, succinct and radical.[79] Since nothing can be said to be true, there is no standard by which any action could be forbidden. It seems as if, in Nietzsche's view, the lid is off; in modern times, any extreme action can be expected. But that is not what happens or what has happened, he believes.

The lid is on, not off. A great curtailment of human excellence, a great leveling of human attainment, has occurred. For if nothing is true, everything is equally valuable and nothing is worth striving or sacrificing for; nothing is worthy of human effort. How has this come about?

In his first book, *The Birth of Tragedy,* Nietzsche shows that the birth of tragedy in Aeschylus and the other Greek tragedians was followed almost immediately by its death in the philosophy of Socrates. Socrates invented rationalism as a way of life, says Nietzsche; he invented the "what is" question and went around posing it to those he met, requiring them to defend themselves by giving arguments on behalf of their assertions. The manly desire to win over your opponent must yield to the desire to learn, which can be fulfilled only if you follow the argument (the *logos,* meaning also speech or reason) rather than maintaining that you are right regardless.[80] It is better to be refuted than to win, Socrates said to the sophists (and to us as well), because he who refutes you does you a great benefit in bringing you closer to the truth.

Socrates' reliance on reason has very bad consequences for humanity, particularly for human life. Humanity is not to be found in reason but rather in the spark of life — the assertion of each man's life by that man — that reason perversely tries to control and deny. To make the point, Nietzsche conflates Socrates' reason with Francis Bacon's science; he contends that classical rationalism intended for the *understanding* of things extends seamlessly into modern rationalism aimed at the *control* of things for the increase of human power. Theoretical man who believes that nature is comprehensible implies that knowledge is your guide and will make you, nay, all men happy — and thus paves the way for modern science and modern socialism. Socrates is directly responsible for Darwin and Marx. Marx said that philosophers had interpreted the world in various ways; the point, however, is to change it.[81] For Nietzsche, interpretation implies change and all philosophers, ancient and modern, are the same. Human control might seem in principle to divide human beings into controllers and controlled, as in Aldous Huxley's *Brave New World,* but Nietzsche sees that the controllers really belong to the controlled because controllers are control freaks who think for themselves along the same lines that they use to control others. All are *last men,* men who blink complacently and find nothing to be concerned about; the next stop in their history or evolution is subhumanity.

To remedy this revolting situation Nietzsche wants a rebirth of tragedy, perhaps, he thought for a time, a modern German version of tragedy in the music of Wagner. If we recall the passage in Plato's *Republic* where Socrates seems scandalized by the bad example set by the behavior of the gods displayed in Homer's *Iliad,* we can see that Nietzsche wants to revive for our time the warring gods that Socrates declared impermissible.[82] Let 'em rip! Warring gods will reintroduce drama and value to us, give us a problem, confront us with a task—the monumental task of rescuing mankind from the last men.

The rescue comes from Nietzsche's version of manliness, which is truthfulness. Reason, he thought, must be subordinated to life, and truth is less interesting than the pursuit of truth. In this he differs from Socrates. For Nietzsche, the pursuit of truth proceeds historically by stages, while for Socrates (who also made a theme of the life of the philosopher), truth comes out of opinion. Coming out of opinion, but never severing its connection to it, truth for Socrates is inseparable from irony; if you speak the truth you must practice irony and take care for others' opinions. But for Nietzsche truth is expressed in truthfulness, not ironically. The life devoted to truthfulness goes through a stage of self-denial as opposed to the self-awareness characteristic of irony. That is why Socrates in his moderation is always deliberately not quite saying what he means, and Nietzsche is always not meaning everything he says but speaking boldly and notably as if he were wisecracking without restraint even though he knows he will be misunderstood by most people. It isn't that Nietzsche doesn't care for "most people"; on the contrary, he wants to effect a great improvement in mankind, including most people. But he doesn't think he needs to consult them. They are last men, the problem not the solution.

Let's see how Nietzsche's notion of truthfulness emerges, and departs, from ordinary manliness. Nietzsche shares the appreciation of war and the warrior in TR and the various promoters of manliness we have been considering.[83] In contrast to Roosevelt, he was not steward of the people (or of anything else), but it's also true that he did not actually go to war. If it's true, as Nietzsche said, that "a good war hallows any cause" rather than the reverse, then the means take precedence over the end. Or the apparent end becomes victory followed by victory, endlessly, in order to produce manly virtue, the true end. Manliness loses the aspect of protectiveness; the manly man is no longer a guardian as in Plato's *Republic*. The natural primacy of peace as the goal of war, the satisfying victory that does not require another victory, is lost to view. Or let's say that in Nietzsche's new concept manliness is sublimated — the low is made high, made sublime. In praising warriors Nietzsche says, "And if you cannot be saints of knowledge, at least be its warriors." Warriors are the "companions and forerunners" of the saints.[84] What warriors do is not to protect the peace but to replace it with war, and the unattractive features of warriors, their shameless hatred and envy, are preferred to their protectiveness and are swept up — recycled! — in the new virtue that Nietzsche formulates to appropriate and transform manliness. To this new virtue, manliness is not a means but a companion and forerunner, as Nietzsche says. Still, if knowledge is what he wants, war is not the end.[85]

The new virtue is honesty in a new sense of truthfulness (*Redlichkeit*).[86] Nietzsche heralds it as the latest and the youngest virtue; he does not claim to have invented it. This is not the old-fashioned, common-sense honesty of telling the truth as opposed to boasting or covering up, which is one of Aristotle's moral virtues.[87] It has always been a difficulty in the moral virtue of honesty that you have to know the truth in order to tell it. Those who excel in telling the truth often have modest capacities and don't always excel in knowing the truth. Nietzsche's honest fellow is required to find the truth in order to tell it. Because finding the truth takes an effort of will, truthfulness in this new, philosophic sense is manliness carried to its greatest heights, but for that reason no longer truly manliness. It is manliness asked to do something beyond its capacity, which is to be philosophy. The warrior traits that Nietzsche patronizes and that manly men might warily appreciate in his account are transformed. The warrior is compelled to turn on himself and make war within his own soul; there is a ladder to climb. He goes through historical stages (that are also psychological), particularly the stage of slave morality in which he denies himself and his manliness.

True manliness in Nietzsche's famous account (in the *Genealogy of Morals*) survives and absorbs the unmanliness of the slave. The manly man must see both sides, for human life, including his manliness, needs the tension of opposites. Slavish people like saints and scholars, whom manly men would rather not notice, suddenly come on the scene and appear more manly than warriors. They exult in their suffering and their self-denial; the saint for the sake of God, the scholar for the sake of scientific objectivity, both being cases of the "ascetic ideal." When the ascetic ideal is in turn affirmed, it is seen as self-creation in addition to self-denial. The self-denial is reinterpreted as self-improvement: "What does not kill me makes me stronger."[88] The goal of the superman — that's what he is — is to create the world before which he can kneel; the creator worships his own creature.[89] With a soul scarred and twisted from turning on itself, the manly man has become *interesting* in a way John Wayne would not have cared for. The "high points" of Nietzsche's high-class, warrior honesty are nothing like him but rather like Machiavelli, Jesuitism, Montaigne, and La Rochefoucauld.[90]

Although Nietzsche is the philosopher of perspective, he is not a relativist. He is the first philosopher to say that perspective is "the basic condition of all life."[91] Plato had said that man by nature lives shackled in a cave where he sees shadows of artifacts manipulated by human beings — a political kind of perspective; but there is a way out for a few philosophers who may be liberated. Nietzsche denies there is a way out and includes the philosophers within "all life," each form of which lives by its peculiar view of things. Yet he maintains that there is a "rank order" to things, a low and a high: for example, in manliness, the low hatred and the high generosity. The two are linked, not distinct; you cannot have one without the other. But this complication does not deny, rather it affirms, that one is low and the other high.[92] Scientific truth, trying to explain away the high, reduces the high to the low, the human to the animal as in Darwinism; but acquiring and adhering to such truth is manly not only for the individual but for the culture and even for all mankind.[93] It is good for us to think ill of ourselves. Thus science is unpretentious on behalf of mankind but in a manly, pretentious way; this is the wrenching complication to which Nietzsche compels manliness to conform. Looked at for content, science levels all things and contributes to relativism or nihilism, but with regard to its motive and its moral perspective, science is manliness. At one point Nietzsche thought science could be our savior against nihilism.[94]

Nietzsche wants us to stop here, but we today have taken a step beyond to unveil the *sensitive male,* the man whose manliness demands that he abandon manliness. For we mustn't suppose that any man finds it easy to be sensitive, or if perhaps there is one who does, we cannot allow him any merit. Instead of the feminist woman treated equally by the sensitive male, Nietzsche, for all his creativity, retains the traditional role of woman as companion to the manly man. Men must be manly in a terrific new way, women must stay as they are. "The true man wants two things, danger and play. For that reason he wants woman, as the most dangerous plaything."[95] Woman a dangerous plaything? How offensive! Yet the thought stands in the way of treating women as objects or as seekers of utility. Nietzsche is disgusted with the reduction of beauty and nobility to utility, and this causes him to throw himself into the lap of manliness and then, out of excessive zeal or ambition that is not manly, to revalue manly man into superman. Superman is manly man who does his own thinking, and his thinking is called a "redemption" of everything against him.[96] For this, superman needs manly man together with his opposite, the feminine — even (in Goethe's phrase) the eternal feminine.[97]

Nietzsche's project for the revival of tragedy needs a little comic relief, or levity, to balance the gravity of its creative mission. Although Nietzsche says a number of things about women that are wounding to women today, he is not a misogynist.[98] He likes women for their willingness as opposed to will; or in another formulation women will prefer, he says that a woman's intellect shows complete control and presence of mind, whereas a man has more temperament and passion.[99] Thus women are shallow and men are deep, provided that each is understood as a virtue.[100] Women, he thought, do not have the strength to will creatively on their own, but they are the recreation of warriors and through their wiles they spur men to greater strength. Women's honor is to love more than they are loved.

Nietzsche has a soft spot for women and their softness. He is opposed to women's rights and ridicules women's qualifications for manly jobs: "When a woman has scholarly inclinations there is usually something wrong with her sexually."[101] He means that whereas a scholar is notoriously absent-minded because of his ability to abstract himself from daily life, women are characterized by presence of mind. Presence of mind is the same attention to context that we have seen attributed to women by several authorities (though not by Edgar Rice Burroughs). It is by presence of mind that women deflate the pretensions of single-minded manly men, and perhaps it is the danger of deflation that Nietzsche has in mind when he says that woman is a dangerous plaything. Women are not needed to deflate men; science does that job too well already. There is little attention to the ridiculous in Nietzsche and not much for comedy to do except to provide relief (but not insight).[102] Imagine a Lois Lane who made fun, not just of Clark Kent, but of Superman. The comic book Superman is a moralized caricature of the real thing in Nietzsche. Comic Superman foils the schemes of evil men and saves women from peril, for he is definitely within and not beyond good and evil. This makes him an agent, not an overcomer, of nihilism — just another leveler, in fact. He may as well be a socialist!

Now for Nietzsche, do women with their presence of mind represent the force of morality? Morality is the worldly context demanding our attention, and women by reminding men of the context also remind them of their duties. But Nietzsche wants women who spur men on, like Lady Macbeth to her husband, as opposed to women who try to rein them in, like Tecmessa with Ajax. Nietzsche's commitment to super-manliness prevents him from endorsing the full extent of woman's traditional role. Just as Nietzsche's superman is not a guardian, so his woman is not a critic. She is secondary to her man in the sense of endorsing him and decorating his vicinity, providing "support" as we say, not in the sense of holding him to a standard.[103] Nietzsche's peculiar promotion of manliness leads him into injustice to women, for his willful philosopher cannot let go of tough-guy aggressive manliness even though he must transcend it. So his women resemble gangsters' molls.

It would seem that Nietzsche holds to the natural permanence of the sex difference, and perhaps he does. Or perhaps he thinks it is advisable to hold to the difference as if it were natural. But in one place he anticipates the gender-neutral society to come, he supposes "a few centuries" ahead: "women can through a few centuries of education be made into anything, even into men."[104] It can be done, but it isn't appropriate to do. In the transition lies the real trouble, Nietzsche says. Concerning marriage, the situation may be reversed. If wives traditionally were barely more than concubines, inducing men to seek intellectual companionship outside marriage, the new serious wives, with no time for fooling around, will induce men to seek concubines to serve as their dangerous playthings. Furthermore, men will be angry because the arts and sciences will be choked by "unheard-of dilettantism," politics will be more fantastic and partisan than ever, society will be in dissolution — all because women, "the custodians of ancient morality and custom," have become ridiculous to themselves. Once they let go of being guardians of morality and custom, where else will they find a comparable power? Nietzsche foresaw the gender-neutral society, but so far he seems to have overestimated the anger of men toward the new women.

Nietzsche seems to have underestimated the anger of men that would be directed against the civilization of the last men, however. If he were living in our time, looking back on the twentieth century, he would not be complaining that manly men became too soft. He was too brilliant to read Plato carefully, and his understanding of pity is inferior to Plato's. Nietzsche believes that pity is the defect of soul that deprives modern men of the ability to judge others and leaves them soft and weak, in fact pitiable. But Plato shows that pity for others easily transforms itself into pity for oneself, a self-centered, self-dramatizing pity that causes one to be hard to others.[105] When pity is called for, who deserves it more than yourself? We in our time are familiar with self-styled victims who do not cower in fear of further blows but go on the attack. It is justice, not pity, that makes the gentleman. If you believe you can afford to do justice to others, if you consider you have from some extrahuman source a margin of safety, then you will be not soft but gentle.

Although Nietzsche himself would never have been a Nazi, his influence helped create what has been called "German nihilism," the principled rejection of a liberal-democratic civilization aiming at cosmopolitan, utilitarian peace.[106] German nihilism in action at its worst was Hitlerism, and Hitler deliberately incited a low, worse-than-vulgar manliness with no finer features and no restraint, a manliness that was nothing but manliness. He himself was manly, he thought, and he compared his domination of the masses to a man's domination over a woman, the stronger exercising his natural right over the weaker as well as the weaker offering a willing and proud submission. Both the masses and women prefer to yield to those who care nothing for their preference or consent.[107] The Nietzschean philosophic superstructure of manliness, the entire struggle to create a superman, is lacking in Hitlerism, which produced nothing more interesting than militaristic manliness convinced of its rectitude but vicious and servile in fact. Nazi manliness claimed the sanction of nature, which permits everything, for its ambition to cleanse mankind by the murder of all Jews. Nature is understood in vaguely Darwinian terms as demanding the triumph of the strong over the weak for the betterment of the species; but the strong are a race (a people with a culture) within the species that must keep itself pure and unmixed—a notion not in Darwin. "Mankind has grown strong in eternal struggles and it will only perish in perpetual peace."[108] For the perverted virtue Hitler wanted to justify, he needed never-ending war and he started a world war. It would be hard to say whether the war was begun in order to purify the species or the species purified so as to have a war, but my guess is the latter.

A similar though somewhat concealed manliness appears in communism under the jargon of "revolutionary consciousness" and "struggle for peace." As opposed to the Nazis, the communists were more certain that history was on their side, but their hatred just as much as that of the Nazis required militant action, and they would never have been content merely to let the inevitable occur even if it meant victory. When we plumb the depths of human malice we find a version of manliness in its company and at its service, that is true. Yet the problem is not manliness but the liberation of malice from the confines of morality in order to go "beyond good and evil."

Manliness must stay within "the confines of morality." But what are they? Posed like this, the problem is to apply good and evil to manliness and not allow manliness to escape into immorality. Theodore Roosevelt was manly in a moral way, Hitler in an immoral way. This simple view of the matter is not wrong, but the full truth is not so simple. Roosevelt and Hitler share a certain moralism, Roosevelt's mostly benign and Hitler's altogether monstrous. Moralism is morality carried too far, and TR's willpower manliness propelled him into acts of reckless imprudence done not only with manly readiness but also in order to be manly. Hitler, for his part, did not reject morality; he made a virtue of warlike manliness. His horrifying immorality was neither soft like a pleasure lover's nor acquisitive like a gangster's, as he and his doctrine strongly rejected both pleasure and gain and called for great personal sacrifice. His immorality took the form of fervent moralism, exceeding the bounds that one can and should expect human beings to be responsible for. The Third Reich project for purging humanity of inferior races was manliness run amok, using vicious means to an impossible end. Manliness before a background of nihilism is too serious, sometimes much too serious, about itself and issues in moralism.

Moralism is a vice we have suffered from greatly in our time, but since it is close to what we consider the virtue of idealism, we have not reflected on it much. Without loosing a tirade, let it be said that moralism is a consequence of nihilism and a close companion of exaggerated manliness. Nihilism says that nothing is true. This means that the world has no intelligible structure of its own; it is an "all" of particular motions rather than a whole with parts. There is no nature, in the sense of the Socratic tradition, composed of discrete, knowable natures, like the nature of a human being, a chimp, and so on. Not having any meaning outside human beings or even in human nature to appeal to, human beings have to make their own meaning. This takes a terrific, superhuman (the superman!) effort of manliness as the means and results in moralism as the end. Plain old morality is content to work with human nature, aware that human nature is composed of body and soul, and that our bodies prevent our souls from being as noble and rational as our souls would like. For example, fear for our bodies intrudes upon the calm of our souls, forcing us to control that fear with the virtue of courage or manliness. That sort of morality—what Aristotle called moral virtue—recognizing the division in human nature between low and high elements, holds virtues that mediate between them. Those virtues call the attention of the soul to the needs of the body and of the body to the wishes of the soul; they enable divided beings to function, in the best case the high element ruling the low.

But if you say there is no high and low, hence no human nature, the task of morality is very much enlarged. If human beings are to have goals and go someplace, they must create the high out of the low or, what is the same thing, out of neutral and indifferent matter. When you first hear of Darwin's theory you might wonder about the moral consequences: will this mean that human beings, since they are no better than brutes, will be encouraged to forget morality and behave like brutes? The answer is worse than you suppose. It is that human beings may think it their moral duty to behave like brutes. Nietzsche foresaw this very well when he said, "Man would rather will nothingness than not will."[109] That is, of course, a statement about human nature and its perverseness. It implies that the low and the high are permanent elements in man and that if the low does not serve the high, the high will serve the low.

The dissolution of man under nihilism does not do away with manliness but, on the contrary, intensifies it. Nietzsche's "last man" is man without manliness, a "dwarf animal" with no desire or ambition. The task is to redeem him and save mankind. Because there is nothing special about the last man, no nature of man with which to protect and revive him, we human beings are under the necessity of creating ourselves. The task demands all the more effort as we have no guide in performing it, no inclination to aid us in self-assertion. Yet in fact one easily sees that under nihilism human nature continues and still serves as a standard for human conduct, despite the denials one hears of both propositions. Darwin's theory by destroying the specialness of human beings denies that nature can be a standard for them; "nature" is merely what evolves by chance and thus has no authority for us humans. This very denial makes nature into a standard for us in the phrase "survival of the fittest"—first a description of what happens, then a prescription for how men should behave.

All of what is called "social Darwinism" uses nature, even and precisely when it is rendered meaningless, as the standard for meaning in our lives. This does not mean that all those who took account of Darwin's theory adopted a moral standard of brutish survival. None of those we have considered took their notions of manliness to this extreme. James's pragmatism made concessions to the tender-minded; Roosevelt had a strong sense of political responsibility; Haggard made an adventure out of nihilism; Burroughs showed the superiority of man to the ape; Kipling made a point of the difference between human law and the law of the jungle; Stevenson made a moral lesson out of the scientist's hubris; and Twain made fun of the rational Yankee's crazy manliness. Here is a heartening variety of responses to the same question of how to live in the face of nihilism. We do not have to surrender our manliness nor do we have to surrender to it. We seem still to have a number of choices. One of them—not a surprise to Nietzsche—turned out to be, at our end of the twentieth century, a claim to manliness by women.

Chapter Five

Womanly Nihilism

In the 1970s manly nihilism came to American women. It did not come directly from Nietzsche, who, though not a woman-hater, was hardly a friend of feminism. It had to come indirectly through Simone de Beauvoir and others who inspired the women's movement. Nietzsche was on the right, and he looked for manliness exclusively in males; but strangely enough these seemingly fatal mistakes did not condemn him. They could be shrugged off as inessential. The women's movement, never fussy or fastidious, took ideas from other men who were not favorable to the cause of women (or otherwise misbehaved with women) — not just Nietzsche but also Marx, Freud, Sartre, Lacan, Foucault.

What interested these women in Nietzsche was the nihilism he proclaimed as fact — God is dead — and the possibility of creating a new order in its place. Nihilism, or the disappearance of nature, represented opportunity, and it should of course be applied to the sexes, as Nietzsche had failed to do. Male/female was not a distinction society needs to respect; it could be female/male, for a start. New identities could be constructed in place of old-fashioned, worn-out natures and a new rank-order installed. Here was the manliness of the women's movement, appropriated from the high priest of manly nihilism and used against his arrogant chauvinism. The feminists were so assertive as to conceive, announce, and establish a new definition of woman and, somewhat incidentally, of man. The new definitions were in a sense nondefinitions — no more than possible identities — so as to help create the new gender-neutral society.

What was womanly in the woman's movement? It was in the manner of this accomplishment, which did *not* come from Nietzsche. The revolution was done by "raising consciousness," a new method of political promotion borrowed from business psychology. This generation of feminists did not go to the streets, as their sisters had in the campaign for women's suffrage. They did not flaunt their virtue or appeal to the conscience of society. Working through language, they just asked men and other women why it is natural to use "he" instead of "she" to refer, for example, to a doctor. Isn't this bias in favor of the male sex? And the males nodded dumbly in agreement. "Why didn't we think of this? From now on, we must be a little more sensitive." This was enough; no heavy argumentation was required.

It was not that the feminist women wanted equality for its own sake, an equal sharing of the burdens of society, for example. They wanted equality for the sake of independence or autonomy. And they wanted independence not for its own sake but specifically *from* what they had previously depended on. They wanted independence from morality, which kept them in subordination to men under the yoke of the "double standard"; and from nature, giving them wombs, compelling them to be mothers, which kept them subordinate to men; and — is the point coming into view? — from men. In order to be free of men, these women wanted to change morality and deny nature. No longer were women destined through reproduction and child rearing to serve the common good and the future of the species. Women could be as irresponsible as men and leave those vital matters to someone else. The feminist women wanted independence from men in order to be as independent as men. The women's movement is a vindication of manliness as representing the height of human attainment, provided, of course, that manliness be separated from males. As the sign of separation, the word *manliness* should be repressed. The thing, however, is all around us: only differently in the two sexes.

I am looking at feminism as if manliness were still alive, thriving in the gender-neutral society where it is most denied. Let us give feminism closer attention in its own terms.[1]

Why nihilism, you will object. Isn't that going too far? Feminists today do not believe that nothing is true, everything is permitted. They believe that women are truly equal to men and, therefore, that oppression of women by men should not be permitted.[2] Actually, however, those two propositions can be found in nineteenth-century women's movements. (The word *femi-nism* came into vogue about 1913, but I will use it to refer to earlier partisans of women's equality.)[3] But they do not capture the novelty of our feminism or the radicalism of the idea behind the gender-neutral society. If we con-sider two leaders of women's movements of the earlier period, two great dif-ferences between their notions and recent feminism come to view: earlier leaders argue for women's morality, and they do not argue against sex roles (though clearly they want to loosen them).

Mary Wollstonecraft published her book *A Vindication of the Rights of Woman* in 1792 during the time of enthusiasm for the French Revolution, when she hoped her arguments would be opportune. Her arguments op-posed the opinions of Jean-Jacques Rousseau, to some degree the philoso-pher of the Revolution, who saw men and women as separate creatures with different rights. Wollstonecraft is not sure that women are exactly equal to men, women having less bodily strength, but the two sexes have the same virtues and women deserve to have "more equality."[4] Women should be freed from the tyranny of having to live in subjection to social opinion and reputation, the fate that Rousseau advocated for women, for this subjection kept them artificially ignorant and encouraged them in various feminine vices, such as to be irrationally religious, sentimental, fond of dress, always agreeable, and cunning.[5] Like some other feminists, Wollstonecraft was harder on women than on men. Yet one virtue, modesty, is a feminine virtue and also the sum of "private virtue." Modesty features chastity, and Woll-stonecraft unhappily made a point of it: "to render the human body and mind more perfect, chastity must more universally prevail." In her own life, love proved more powerful than chastity. When her lapse from chastity be-came known, after her emphatic declarations in this book, she was ridiculed and her arguments unjustly discredited. It is not mere gallantry to say that there was nobility in her concern for men as well as women. Men should be taught "not only to respect modesty in women but to acquire it themselves."[6] Teaching modesty to men is not an item in today's feminist agenda, unless sensitivity to women counts as modesty. It also has to be said that Wollstone-craft did not have a program for making men modest. She thought that if women were more knowing than they are, and were freed of subordination to men, men would listen to them. She did not consider that if women were more knowing, they might be less modest.[7]

Why should a woman be more knowing? "For it would be as wise to expect corn from tares, or figs from thistles, as that a foolish ignorant woman should be a good mother," says Wollstonecraft.[8] Sexual distinctions at present are coercive and arbitrary, but as women's rights come to be respected, "the sexes will fall into their proper places."[9] So the sexes have *proper places,* the second contrast to our feminism, which denies any such places.

If we turn to the American Elizabeth Cady Stanton (1815–1902), the difference is not so clear but still visible. Stanton hails the accomplishments of women who have entered the professions and looks forward to more such progress in all occupations. Yet many of her efforts were directed at correcting the legal inequality of wives, and she took it for granted that "nature has made the mother the guardian of the child."[10] The attitude of modern feminism, we shall see, is hostile to nature and insists on the social construction of sex roles not only in the past, as Wollstonecraft and Stanton maintain, but also for the future. Modern feminists on the whole take a baleful view of motherhood as a trap nature sets for unwary women, to be entered into not automatically or dutifully but only by somewhat defiant choice.

Women at present, Stanton says, are "mere echoes of men. . . . The true woman is as yet a dream of the future."[11] The true woman is not a social construction but the correction of a social misconstruction, "in violation of every law of their being," a state in which men are allowed to be more selfish, and women more selfless, than they truly are. "The same code of morals" should apply to men and women, thus producing a "new code of morals" — the old one made equal.[12] Stanton thought that woman's moral power would exert itself through the ballot box and produce moral reforms, such as those women were already pursuing in movements to abolish slavery and for temperance.

Early feminism had the high moral purpose of creating equality between the sexes by raising men to the moral level of women. It was "the new power destined to redeem the world."[13] Nothing like this can be heard in today's feminism; it wants to create equality by lowering women's morality to the level of men's. It claims the privileges of men, which amount to exemptions from morality, and it does so under the names of "autonomy" and "agency." Stanton makes no appeal to these ideas. She authored the famous Declaration of Sentiments at Seneca Falls in 1848, a sort of copy of the Declaration of Independence that accepted its authority and justified women's rights by the same appeal made in that document to the laws of nature and of nature's God.[14] A comparable declaration founding the National Organization of Women in 1966, while referring to the worldwide movement for human rights, offers no ground for women's rights and merely asserts that "the time has come to move beyond the abstract argument . . . over the status and special nature of women."

Wollstonecraft and Stanton differ markedly from our feminism by standing for the greater morality of women and accepting women's special place in the home. These two differences are related and should not be quickly dismissed as dead and gone. They imply that women should not be independent of men but should serve as their moral teachers and homemakers. And yet the early feminists had a hankering for independence. In 1892 Stanton gave a speech chiding women for their tendency to lean on a man. Although women "prefer to lean," she said, each must "make the voyage of life alone."[15] Is this good advice, or could it be better for women to lean on a man?

To help us answer the question, let us look quickly at Oscar Wilde's play on the subject, *An Ideal Husband* (1895). In the play, Lady Chiltern is said to make an ideal of her husband, Sir Robert, a politician on the rise — "the error all women commit," says he. She cannot believe he would have gained his position by fraud, as turns out to be the case. When she finds out, the question becomes, will she stand by her man? Lord Goring, a philosopher-dandy, manages with his considerable agility to extricate her and her husband from the situation. He persuades her that moral principle needs to be tempered by the forgiveness of love and at the same time to be given energy by ambition. Lady Chiltern should not forswear her husband for the early crime that made his career possible, and Sir Robert should not resign from politics from shame because his wife has found him out.[16] Both her love and his ambition must inevitably compromise principle, but neither is possible without principle.

What interests us is that the problem of moral fidelity is shown in the roles of the two sexes. Moral fidelity in the play means not sexual fidelity but fidelity to moral principle in politics. Lady Chiltern has more principle but less ambition than her husband, yet her principle is not abstract because it centers on her hopes for her husband. Her ambition is his, but because it is wrapped up in him, she is not conscious of it as hers. It is not ambition for mere success; she needs to believe that he is morally pure or at least defensibly moral. At the end Lord Goring says, "women are not meant to judge us [men] but to forgive us." But a woman necessarily judges a man through the ideal she makes of him; her very partiality makes her want him to *deserve* to succeed. In the action of the play Lord Goring, philosopher though he may be, gets married to a perky young woman (Mabel Chiltern) who will judge him (despite her denials), and his love compels him to depend on her. Mabel is not ambitious, and she chooses the philosopher knowing that his interests are "domestic."

In both marriages the two sexes are mutually dependent, not alone — much less autonomous. Both sexes have to do with morality, men by advancing "upon lines of intellect" and women maintaining morality by "revolving in curves of emotions." Both sexes use reason, but men abstractly (intellect) and women particularly by fastening on the men in their lives (curves of emotions). Wilde's play is an essay in the difference between moralism (the "high moral tone" taught by "German philosophy") and morality. Men and women have diverse inclinations, or the same inclinations, such as ambition, which they feel in diverse ways; but they do not normally follow them to extremes because they fall in love with — the opposite sex. They also make mistakes in following their inclinations and need to have them pointed out by careful observers like Lord Goring and Oscar Wilde. We note the kinship between women and philosophers in three things: careful observing, being withdrawn from the public into domesticity, and furthering their ambition indirectly by leaning on others. Wilde could have learned this from Aristotle, or perhaps he thought it up for himself.

Henry James's *The Bostonians* (1886) answers Wilde's question and also deals directly with feminism. The novel portrays a struggle for the affections of a young woman, Verena Tarrant, between Olive Chancellor, a feminist who is called a "nihilist" at the beginning of the story, and Basil Ransom, an "intense conservative." Olive advances the feminist thesis that women can live their lives without incurring obligations to men and can cling to "a great, vivifying, redemptory idea without the help of a man."[17] The idea is of course women's rights, but rights are not enough and perhaps not even justified if women cannot vindicate them on their own. Whether women can advance an idea without a man was the point at issue in Wilde's play. Basil, a southerner coming to Boston to visit his cousin Olive, quickly learns to detest the views she is teaching to Verena; he thinks that women are inferior to men, particularly for public and civic uses.[18] Saving Verena from feminism becomes a challenge to his "manhood," and this is what he does; he wins the contest with Olive and at the end of the novel takes Verena away from a public speech supporting feminism that she is about to give and marries her.[19]

Basil says early on that one can't sympathize with both sides, but that is what *The Bostonians* does.[20] Today we might think that James takes the man's side entirely, but it would be better to say that, unlike us, he takes it into consideration. He also depicts the failure of a woman (Olive) to govern a woman, her protégée Verena. In both regards, his novel seems outdated, as we in the gender-neutral society have moved past the debate between "sides," and we do not care for a conclusion that cannot be right. But let us not be impatient with Henry James, for what he says helps to identify our difficulties and his sympathies cannot be inferred from the victory of Basil. In the famous ending of the novel, Verena says she is glad but is actually in tears, "not the last she was destined to shed," the author pronounces. Her marriage promises to be unhappy, she resentful and he dominating. Can we see what will go wrong? We have to try to discern what "unsuspected truth" lies in each of the two sides and why it cannot be seen by the other.[21] In a sense one can sympathize with both sides, for James does this and invites us to join him in the use of what he calls moral imagination. But though one might imagine, one cannot *take* both sides, and thus James chooses Basil over Olive while handing Basil, and us, the prospect of an unhappy marriage.

With the action of the novel James says that unhappy marriage is better than the feminist idea of women's governing the world without men. What is responsible for a result so generally unfortunate and affecting? In the novel Basil is "a representative of his sex," not the only one; but he is the only one on show. The feminist cause, however, is represented by several

women, "the Bostonians," so that James can display its variety and consequences. There are: Mrs. Farrinder, a matron majestic in aspect, the teacher
and leader of the movement; Miss Birdseye, the venerable abolitionist and
credulous all-around reformer; Olive Chancellor, spinster, and noble, an-
guished mentor of Verena; Dr. Mary Prance, a doctor and successful feminist in practice; and Verena Tarrant, not so devoted a feminist as Olive but a
better speaker and more effective popularizer. To make the case for feminism, Verena says that women are superior in morality to men; they are not
selfish but generous and full of heart. Women are the part of humanity that
is for all—here Verena echoes Praxagora in the *Congresswomen*—yet women
are the very part that is excluded from the government of all. "A new moral
tone" can be established that brings peace and reason and excludes "brute force
and sordid rivalry." Yet instead women suffer from the "cruelty of man . . .
his immemorial injustice," from "the great masculine conspiracy."[22]

Somehow the generosity of women issues in a complaint about the suffering of women that fills women with resentment against men.[23] This is not
a desirable new moral tone. Olive, for all her elevation of purpose, was filled
with "silent rage" over "the usual things of life" that remind her of men's
iniquity. Thus, while speaking of humanity, feminists are in fact devoted to
the "universal sisterhood" and have no way to include in their vision men as
they are or might be.[24] The suffering they complain of confirms their weakness more than it recommends any competence, and in the midst of Verena's
claim that women are the heart of humanity, she overlooks her own remark
that men do not have "the same quick sight as women."[25] James indicates
that women's generosity works in private and in particular, but not when it
goes public. Universalized in democratic America, and transformed into political action and oratory, the insightful virtue women have loses its accuracy
and intelligence and becomes coarse, inconsistent, stultified, and ineffective.
In *The Bostonians* we see Verena orating when she should be conversing.[26]
These lady humanitarians would be better off as provincials, as Bostonians.

Basil Ransom, no humanitarian, says to Verena "my interest is in my own
sex," which is being feminized. He grounds his case against feminism on the
fact that men are the "stronger race"; this is decisive for him.[27] Having a
share of southern chivalry, he believes that women's rights consist in a standing claim to the generosity of the stronger race but no more. Men's gen-

erosity is more forceful and dependable than women's because it is based on strength rather than weakness. Men are aware that in order to be generous it is necessary first to take care of yourself. Men are also better equipped to operate in public, where appearances matter. So we see that chivalry is a show of male pride, whereas women's generosity in the relief of suffering is quiet and unassuming (not passive). Basil felt he could not marry Verena until he could provide decently for her, doubtless a point of false pride, James the narrator tells us. He also tells us there is a "thread of moral tinsel" in the idea of southern chivalry, and we see worse than tinsel in what Basil does to Verena at the end. Basil carries her off, declaring "she's all mine!"[28] Men don't say this today but they haven't stopped feeling it. Their offer of provision has the character of possessiveness that does not stop at sexual chastity. Basil is perfectly capable of falling in love with Verena while despising her ideas, but Verena cannot do the same. She knows that when she marries Basil she is renouncing her feminism and embracing his ideas: this is the cause of her tears.

Feminists as Henry James presents them do not know how to deal with men. Olive Chancellor isolates herself from them. She does not marry and she tries to keep Verena from marrying, sensing that if she does she will be lost to the cause. "No man that I have ever seen cares a straw in his heart for what we are trying to accomplish." Olive adds that there are men who pretend to care for women's rights, "but they are not really men."[29] Perhaps she refers to Mrs. Farrinder's ineffectual husband. Verena, on the other hand, surrenders to men — to her man. She resembles moderate women of our day who do not dislike men, as opposed to the radicals who like to attack men. Another possibility can be seen in the person of Dr. Mary Prance, who as a "lady-doctor" was independent but not active in public. "Whatever might become of the movement at large, Dr. Prance's own little revolution was a success."[30] She succeeded by not caring about the movement at large. "Having as many rights as she had time for," she was in the habit of forgetting that she was a woman, and in this she resembles many successful professional women of our time. In James's view, women are more moral than men, but their morality is corrupted by "ideas" that universalize their perceptions and intuitions and, like a grainy photo enlargement, cause them to lose their fine subtlety. The worst of these ideas is feminism because it deprives women of their self-awareness. Hence James agrees with Oscar Wilde that in public a woman needs a man to lean on. We do not agree with him, but this does not prevent him from knowing us well.[31]

Yet is it not an unacceptable affront to the dignity of Lady Chiltern and Verena Tarrant that they must give over their public voice to a man? Oscar Wilde and Henry James offer what may appear to be a successful riposte to nineteenth-century feminism as we have sampled it. They say that women cannot govern on their own. Elizabeth Cady Stanton had said that women do not need a man to lean on, but in fact they do. If women are to sustain morality, they must do so from their private roles as wives and mothers and not from the lecture platform. For morality is, in effect, *women's* morality. You can give it a fancy definition that seems, or is designed to seem, gender-neutral, but morality is women's in a double sense: it is women above others whom it protects and it is up to women to enforce it. Women enforce morality by criticizing men, not men in general but *particular* men, the ones they know and love; and they have access to particular men only in private. The price for a woman of reducing domination by *her* man is to forbear from a general, public attack on male domination. For the general attack is bound to fail, and it will draw her attention from the particular effort of taming that might succeed. There is a difference between universal pacifism and peacemaking in the home, even though the former is but a generalization of the latter. And in forbearing from a general challenge to men, a woman in effect leans on her man. She is not a mere dependent because she gains the right to criticize him, which is often done fairly well. But to be effective, the criticism must come from within the household. Hence the link between morality and women's acceptance of sex roles that we see dramatized by critics of feminism, such as Wilde and James, and also admitted by early feminists, such as Wollstonecraft and Stanton.

The problem for feminism, if it wants to escape that criticism, then becomes quite clear. It must counter these critics and find a way to avoid leaning on a man. This is what feminism proceeded to do under the influence of Simone de Beauvoir.

Beauvoir's famous, founding book, published in France in 1949 and translated for America in 1953, was called *The Second Sex*.[32] From the title alone you see that the book is a complaint against male domination in general, and when you open it, you find it hostile to sex roles and to motherhood.[33] Here is a pronounced contrast to the writings of Wollstonecraft and Stanton, in which we see the desire for women's independence compromised by respect for women's nature as previously known. Beauvoir is much more radical; she shares the desire but as far as possible rejects all compromise. In rejecting the tradition of inequality for women, she does not avail herself of the shelter of liberalism, as did Wollstonecraft and Stanton by relying on the rights of man (whether from the French Declaration of Rights or the American Declaration of Independence). Beauvoir does not demand women's rights but depends instead on a difficult mixture of "historical materialism" and existentialist choice. Her book ends with a quotation from Karl Marx affirming the brotherhood of men and women in a new realm of liberty in the communist utopia.

In the spirit of Marxism, Beauvoir dwells on the material condition that makes it possible to sweep away the remnants of sexism found in earlier feminism; this is contraception or birth control.[34] It is clear enough without reference to Marxism that contraception makes motherhood a matter of choice and opens the possibility of greater sexual liberty to women. But contraception does not require women to esteem motherhood less or to select the possibility of greater sexual liberty that (capitalist) technology provides by entering the workforce. Nor does contraception require the use of abortion as a fail-safe device in case the pill doesn't work. One could accept contraception but draw the line at abortion, believing that it is one thing to prevent conception and another to eliminate it. Thus the difference between Beauvoir and the earlier feminists is not just the advance of technology; it is a difference in ideas. Beauvoir argues that women should not esteem motherhood as much as they have, that greater sexual liberty is not just a possibility but a good thing, and that abortions should not be done reluctantly or regretted. Her argument has been accepted by almost all feminists today, who honor the early feminists but do not take their thought seriously, either overlooking the key differences between their feminism and ours or rejecting them as obviously outdated.[35] But we will learn more if we look for the reasons given by Beauvoir that account for those differences.

The Second Sex begins very theoretically on its first page with an attack on the notion that a woman might be a "Platonic essence." It's not that the "eternal feminine" has been got wrong but that there is nothing permanently feminine. Wollstonecraft and Stanton were content to say that men had mistaken and underestimated the nature of women, but Beauvoir goes further, arguing that any fixed nature of women is bound to be mistaken. As her first page attacks essences, so the first chapter denies the so-called data of biology. Women are not bent out of their natural shape by conventions, but conventions are all we can have because women have no natural shape. Hitherto women have been defined by men; henceforth they must be defined by women. Why? Because women, being human, have the power to define. To be human is to be transcendent over nature, to redefine what is given, to act freely and with sovereign power. Thus, it is not quite that nature does not exist; rather, nature, which is fixed, is not friendly or hospitable to humanity or human freedom. Unlike Darwin, Beauvoir does not deny that there is "animal nature," an expression she uses repeatedly. Animal nature is what is given to us, and what is given has nothing of us, nothing human in it. Women have been forced to live at the level of animal nature in *immanence,* and at present the only human world is "a man's world."[36]

Beauvoir is opposed to essences, but apparently there is an essential distinction in her thought between transcendence and immanence. What is transcendent resists the dictates of nature; thus, it is transcendent to risk one's life, to be a warrior. It is also transcendent to be creative, to be able to make objects like an artisan (this is called objectifying your will in the external world). And to think noninstrumentally, to be able to forget yourself like artists and philosophers, is transcendental. Immanence, on the other hand, is a life enslaved to nature, reproducing the species rather than advancing it through technology. Seeking pleasure is immanent, as is living for no principled end, for one cannot be transcendent except by acting for the sake of an idea.[37] Transcendence has a basis in biology because in reproduction the male leaves the scene, often quite soon, whereas the human female is stuck with hosting the product for nine months, from which one might infer, as does Aristotle, that there is something natural about transcendence.[38] But for Beauvoir true, transcendent transcendence is based on an idea and is above biology. She says in a phrase become famous: "One is not born, but becomes, a woman."[39] In this statement she seems both to know, and not to know, what a woman is. At the end of her book she says that woman has a situation rather than an essence, and her future remains "largely open."[40]

"Transcendence" appears to be Beauvoir's gender-neutral term for manliness, a self-assertion by means of self-dramatization against a backdrop of chaos. Perhaps "chaos" is not quite right, since Beauvoir does speak of animal nature and does allow differences in men and women in that regard. Even though there are no essences, not everything is social construction. But in her view nature does not allow for the truly human, for human excellence. Nature is more a challenge to us than an endorsement of our good, still less our comfort. Transcendence is all the more impressive, and transcendent, as it is unsupported by anything immanent in nature that is given to us. One could even wonder whether the immanent is posited as unhelpful—for Beauvoir does not investigate the matter—just so that we don't have to be grateful for any blessings we may have received.

Womanly nihilism is the repetition and the culmination of manly nihilism. To repeat Nietzsche's formulation: men—and now this includes women—would rather will nothingness than not will. Willing nothingness is a reasonable description of seeking transcendence without knowing, or rather without wanting to know, what the transcendent is. Beauvoir says that woman has no "mysterious essence" but has a "largely open" future. Now, what is the meaning of "largely open" if not unknown or mysterious? That's why I call our feminism nihilism.

Actually Beauvoir and feminists today have something more definite in mind than transcendence, and that is independence. But independence to do what, and to live how? It could be that women's independence consists in doing the same things as before but now freely and without compulsion. Tocqueville says, "in America the independence of woman is irretrievably lost within the bonds of marriage." Yet he thinks it makes a great difference that a woman chooses marriage and "freely places herself in the yoke on her own."[41] This is not what Beauvoir has in mind "concretely," as she says. Although she makes some provision for women's traditional proclivities, it is not enough for her that women merely return to the old family routine with a fresh spirit, using the "manly reason" and "virile energy" that Tocqueville saw in American women more than a century before. The life of independence will be a new one, outside the family in one way or another. *One way or another.* One way is apparently that women will get jobs, for Beauvoir says vaguely that women's liberation requires that the "economic evolution of women's condition be accomplished."[42] Yet she goes on to discuss not the economic evolution but women's narcissism, women's love, and women's mysticism while still enslaved to immanence.

The strangest feature of *The Second Sex* is its almost complete failure to discuss women's jobs and its almost total preoccupation with *another way* of escaping the family — sex. Nowadays, with a view to the gender-neutral society, one might think that feminist independence is mainly about the jobs that free them from dependence on men. To be specific, feminists want women to have jobs in the professions; and to be still more specific, in the academic profession, where one can be aloof from men and devote oneself to the study of the destiny of woman. Why is it, then, that today's feminism invests so much of women's independence in sexual liberation? Men could not be so free for sex these days unless women were looking for the very same thing. To see why women might do this, let us turn to what Beauvoir expects from sex.

Beauvoir's book, to repeat, concentrates on sex. It has chapters on sexual initiation, on the lesbian, and on prostitutes. The last chapter on the "independent woman," displaying the model for the future, is mostly about sex and has only a little on reconciling family and career, the most practical concern. How can one get independence from sex, you are wondering. Beauvoir thinks that it is the passivity of a woman in the act of sex that renders her an erotic object to men and also to herself, thus preventing her from becoming an independent subject.[43] So it is in sex, not in women's weakness or man's aggression — hardly mentioned by Beauvoir — that she finds the primary cause of women's oppression.

Being passive in sex is "required by society," says Beauvoir. But though being a sex object is oppressive, it seems to be more natural for a woman than a man.[44] A woman's eroticism has a "peculiar nature" that urges her toward monogamy, it is true. But Beauvoir says it does not destroy women's independence. Even within monogamy there is the possibility of "virile independence," by which she means adultery or open marriage.[45] Thus with "undemanding generosity" man and woman can live in "a condition of perfect equality" — a condition admittedly rare but nonetheless an example to all. Being two autonomous individuals, they cannot quite be called a couple, but they live together, mostly.

Yet Beauvoir in her womanly realism appears to accept, without saying so, that the second sex will always be second. For though a man can be human (that is, transcendent) without ceasing to be a male, a woman cannot be. To realize her femininity she must be an object, which is to say she must renounce being a subject. The emancipated woman, therefore, suffers a conflict between her sex and her humanity. Her humanity requires her to be complete, which includes her dependent sexuality; she cannot renounce her sexuality without renouncing her humanity.[46] One could add that the conflict in the condition — or nature? — of a woman comes to sight especially in the emancipated woman like Beauvoir herself who cannot blame society for its oppression. And if women are conflicted, men too will be affected by having to deal with them. What man wants a monogamous woman on his hands — who also thinks she is full of virile independence? What woman wants an asserted equality that devalues woman's femininity as "immanent" and then doesn't deliver the equality of transcendence that it promises? In this situation of never-ending alienation it seems that certain rules of sexual morality will still be required and that autonomy is not all it's cracked up to be. Have we strayed beyond Beauvoir's book? No, she led us there by virtue of the honesty and experience that give a tinge of realism to her overblown philosophy of transcendence.

Let's return to the question of women's leaning on men for their ideas. Beauvoir is an intelligent writer who merits our careful attention, but she is not a great thinker, and she leans on great thinkers, who were males. Anyone, male or female, who is not a great thinker leans on great thinkers. All our ideas come from them (usually through lesser intermediaries like Beauvoir), and if any human beings are truly autonomous, it is they. The feminism that Beauvoir influenced derived from Marx and Nietzsche, a strange combination of left and right that flourished in France after World War II and then in America. Another prominent instance of that combination was Jean-Paul Sartre, Beauvoir's life companion in her sense of a very honest but not very strictly monogamous relationship.[47]

Marx contributed the thought that human alienation could be ended only by abolishing the division of labor, because specializing in one kind of work leaves a person narrow and incomplete. Division of labor arises from the production of material things, and Marx devoted most of his life to the study of economics, which would reveal that capitalism would necessarily collapse into a communist utopia where the division of labor had been abolished. Under communism a person could fish without being a fisherman and do many other things without devotion to any one thing, including the economics that Marx was forced to focus on. Sounds great! But what about sex roles? Marx admitted that they would have to go too, and it's easy to see why. Particularly if production is the core of humanity, the division of labor in reproducing human beings leaves each of the sexes lacking in the experience of the other, hence alienated from full humanity. Men need to learn how hard, women how easy, reproduction can be. Economics, it seems, would have to be extended or transformed into biology to make possible sex changes that would allow an alternation or combination of male-female experiences. In our century we know that this is not altogether science fiction, that there are people who want and are able to choose their sex.[48] (They do so, however, to specialize and not to be everything.) The idea of a society without roles comes from Marx.

Nietzsche, as we have seen, supplies the idea that sex is power (in which he is joined by Freud). To love is to exude power onto an object, a "sex object," the Other of which Beauvoir complained in discussing copulation. In this view, the lover has power and spends it on his beloved, as a male spends his semen. This is a masculine view of sex, according to which love goes from high to low, the lover being superior to the beloved. Opposing it is a view we shall study in Plato, in which sex is not power but attraction, not from high to low but from low to high, the beloved being superior. Love is a dependency, even an enslavement. This view of love, the true one, is hardly ever discussed by feminists, but one sees the effect of it in their distrust of love when felt by women. A woman in love justifies and invites the oppression of the man she loves by giving him power over herself: better to have the "autonomy" of an open marriage with many lovers, or homosexuality, or — well, not celibacy.

Now, how do we match the autonomy of Nietzsche on the right with what seems to be its opposite on the left, Marx's communism? Very easily. The ideal of communism, "the free development of all," has as its condition "the free development of each," and the communist utopia is really an individualist utopia in which, every individual having what he needs, none depends on another.[49] Communist solidarity, like feminist sisterhood, exists in the movement, to be sure, but this is mutual dependency only on the way to abolishing itself. Neither Marx nor Nietzsche had any use for morality, especially sexual morality, in the enforcement of which they might have looked to women. On this important matter, Beauvoir and her feminists followed Marx and Nietzsche, not Wollstonecraft and Stanton. Marx and Nietzsche in their diverse ways very conveniently made morality unnecessary. Either morality is mere ideology that echoes economic class relations (Marx) or it is an exercise of power that oppresses the strong (Nietzsche). Yes, for Nietzsche, *the strong* are oppressed. This antidemocratic possibility has not gained entry into feminism, for feminism does not appreciate the power over stronger men that women lose when they let go the authority and superiority that come with the guardianship of morality. It is difficult for them to carry on the pleasurable duty of henpecking if all they can say to a husband is "treat me equally." He can answer by asking why he should do so if he is stronger.

These were the thinkers Simone de Beauvoir depended on, and to them we could add her friend Jean-Paul Sartre, whose work can be seen in hers.[50] Did Beauvoir lean on Sartre? However she may otherwise have behaved toward him, she was not entirely submissive in ideas. She had her own voice and she found it on one occasion that deserves to be inscribed in the annals of womanly reproach to men. The "interview" between these two enduring companions took place in 1975 and was printed as a dialogue between them under the title "I would like to interrogate you on the question of women."[51] To begin, Beauvoir gets Sartre to admit the oppression of women, a fact that he, life-long surveyor of oppression, had overlooked until that moment. He had seen only particular cases of women put upon by men. It was true that he considered himself superior to women, but then he thought himself superior to many men, too. After this disclosure Sartre accuses himself of male chauvinism (*machisme*), though Beauvoir declares that he has always treated her as an equal. She then asks him how the struggle of women relates to the class struggle, and he makes an important point: women are not a class. As we have seen in discussing Marx, the end of the class struggle, and the liberation of the proletariat, do not bring the liberation of women. Half the human race is omitted by the merely economic argument of Marx. Women's liberation must be accepted in its "specificity," which according to Beauvoir requires that one look at myth about women.[52]

Although Beauvoir says her method is "historical materialism," it is not Marxist; she looks at the biology of women's bodies, at the psychology arising from them, and at the anthropology of myths about them. And she does this with a view to creating new "concepts" for the undefined future. Except politically, she and the feminism she made are closer to Nietzsche than to Marx. Why did she stay on the left? So as not to surrender to or "lean on" men as Nietzsche and all the other triumphant men on the right insisted. She would not have had as easy a time with Nietzsche as with her man Sartre. And Sartre was not to every modern woman's taste. In this wonderfully revealing short interview he says he approves of the feminist struggle but cannot contain a certain comic sexism. In pondering the sexual difference, as if for the first time, he arrives at all the stereotypes and gives them high-flown expression. He says that when conversing with women, he lets them suppose they are equal to him, but of course "it is I who took the lead in the conversation. I took the lead because I had decided to take the lead." Beauvoir finds a certain *machisme* in this, but neither of them stops to consider where manliness fits in the combination of Marxism and existentialism that they espouse. But isn't it true that in order to be tough-minded, as both consider themselves to be, you have to be tough or depend on someone who is tough? It doesn't seem that you can think yourself into being tough. But perhaps we should not be too quick to deny that manliness is teachable.

Beauvoir taught the notion of transcendence, a kind of manliness, to other feminists who passed it on to the women's movement, where transcendence became a political goal and achievement. Let us track Beauvoir's influence in the construction of the gender-neutral society, the society, as we now see, in which women can be independent. Beauvoir's influence is greater with radical feminists than with their more moderate sisters. What is radical feminism and what is moderate? A radical feminist attacks the family; a moderate one accepts it (though probably doesn't defend it). I will use this simple criterion to navigate through the diverse world of feminism. According to this criterion, Betty Friedan's book, *The Feminine Mystique* (1963), which preceded the radical feminist books we will assess, presents fairly moderate feminism. A quick look at moderate feminism will reveal the greater depth of the radicals closer to Beauvoir.

However diverse, all feminism today is looking for ways to keep women independent of men. The main way, one might think, is for women to pursue careers. Having a career lets a woman achieve economic independence from her husband so that she can leave him or survive being deserted by him. Even if she remains married, her contribution to the family treasury changes the terms of marriage, giving her equality or more equality than she would have if she depended entirely on her husband's pay. The importance of women's careers seems to be confirmed by the massive shift in recent decades of women into the workforce. Feminism could have advocated this change and facilitated it by addressing some of the difficulties women would face when as wives they went to work. Who would take care of the children? Who would make the meals?[53] How could a wife get her husband to do 50 percent of the housework? How could she make up for the loss of pride he might feel from no longer providing for her? These questions were barely asked, let alone answered, even by moderate feminists. Women were to be protected at work by laws on sexual harassment, and their children were to be provided with government-subsidized day care. In both of these programs proposed by feminists, government substitutes for husbands and women are induced to put their trust in impersonal bureaucracy rather than in a man who loves them. Both are designed to make it easier for her to work, not to combine career and family. Both, in fact, facilitate divorce as much as marriage. Neither requires that women come to terms with sexual difference, or, which is our topic, with *manliness*.

Moderate feminists, then, do not speak practically about careers. But the radical feminists hardly say anything at all about careers; their preoccupation is with sexual liberation as opposed to sex. If they had wanted lots of sex, one could call it an obsession. But they are interested in liberation, a release of power or "empowerment," as we say, not in sex. As with Beauvoir, the radical feminists want to annul the passivity of the female and to avoid the condition of sex object. Sex they would do dutifully for the sake of the whole movement, perhaps, but as women they show themselves to be very unerotic. Not for either desire or love are they preoccupied with sex. It is actually for the sake of—prepare for a surprise—*morality*. Sexual liberation will make them, and everyone else, more authentically human.

The radical feminist morality rejects the "bourgeois" morality so prominent in previous feminism. Consider three important feminist books published in 1970: Germaine Greer's *The Female Eunuch*, Kate Millett's *Sexual Politics*, and Shulamith Firestone's *The Dialectic of Sex*. These authors show the logic of transcendence, learned from Beauvoir, in their promotion of sex.

Germaine Greer sprinkles her text with highlighted quotations of Mary Wollstonecraft, whom she admires, but none of them have to do with the chastity Wollstonecraft so insisted on. Greer begins her book by disparaging the "old suffragettes" as "genteel middle-class ladies."[54] Kate Millett, in her discussion of the "sexual revolution" from 1830 to 1930, dismisses the morality espoused by feminists in that time as "naïve optimism"—as if one could raise boys to be as "pure" as girls. She declares herself in favor of "sexual freedom" for women and espouses a sexual revolution whose goal would be "a permissive single standard of sexual freedom." She does not say what, if anything, would not be permitted. Her target is the double standard of sexual morality that permits, or more readily excuses, transgressions by men as contrasted to those by women.[55] Shulamith Firestone notes the kinship between feminism and Freud and approves Freud's understanding of sexual morality as repression and not elevation. But she observes that the sexual revolution of the sixties, welcomed by men, was a snare for women who believed that men had just now learned to appreciate them for their intellect and other fine qualities. Yet she, too, wants a "more natural polymorphous sexuality" that includes no restraint that she cares to name.[56]

None of our three revolutionaries has any criticism to make of male behavior in sex or proposes any standard to which men should be held.[57] Their concern is only for women; and not only should women not be required to be more moral than men, but it is carelessly implied that men too should be liberated from the lesser standard traditionally imposed on them. It seems that abandoning the double standard in sexual morality means abandoning *any* standard. These women do not worry about violence in sex, and they do not refer to the respect in which one should hold one's partner (points that would be made soon enough in the light of reason and experience). Their point is sexual liberation *from* morality, not with it. But we do not have far to look for the transcendent morality that demands liberation from morality.

It used to be said that motherhood and apple pie were the two things exempt from public criticism in the United States. No longer! The list is down to apple pie, and even that is the pie your mother made. In Millett's book, "holy motherhood" is presented sarcastically as a feature of Hitler's Germany; in Greer's, motherhood is derided as imitating mother ducks who "act as instinctive creatures, servants of the species." (Note Beauvoir's notion of womanly immanence in this accusation.) Ms. Firestone, a deeper thinker, quotes Beauvoir in order to argue that women's reproductive biology, and not the social construction of patriarchy, is the cause of women's oppression.[58] You can't blame men; it's nature that's at fault. But did not nature give men aggressive biology to complement women's reproductive biology? Don't we have to deal with men's manliness as well as with women's femininity? Firestone, together with other feminists, has her eye more on the disadvantages of women (as she thinks them) than on the advantages of men (as she also thinks them). She is not so unfriendly to aggressiveness or so disdainful of men for showing it as one might expect.

With dislike of motherhood goes rejection of domesticity. Firestone does not care for housework, which she calls "domestic chores." She hopes that a larger household with a dozen or so members would eliminate the waste and repetition of the nuclear family without sacrificing intimacy.[59] With other feminists she assumes that the household is within, or constitutes, the realm of necessity as distinct from the realm of freedom. It is "domestic slavery," as Engels said. Well, let us not be romantic about making the beds, cooking the meals, and so on. But the feminists make no room for the pride of a woman in good housekeeping, which if they noticed they would dismiss as a delusion. Yet if you add decorating and adornment to housekeeping, the result can be a delight to the eye and the soul. Women seem to desire more than men to make a nest and to take responsibility for making it. To do this, they sometimes need the help of their men, and they nag them responsibly and more or less charmingly according to their skill. The situation is quite different from a negotiated fifty-fifty split of odious tasks in the workplace, for the necessities of housework are alleviated and dignified by the consciousness that they are done, spontaneously by women and with a reminder by men, out of love.

These radical feminists do not care much for love, however. Women as of now, they believe, are liable to fall in love and to be carried away by romantic delusions about successful (read *manly*) men who are stronger and taller than they. To address this susceptibility, Greer has a chapter in *The Female Eunuch* in which she considers romance from the man's point of view. "Many a young man trying to make out with his girl has been surprised at her raptness and elation, only to find himself lumbered with an unwanted intense relationship which is compulsorily sexless."[60] Poor fellow! Greer's feminism will be good for him as well as for the women she liberates for unencumbered sex. Or have I got it turned around? Perhaps unencumbered sex is good because it liberates from love.

Shulamith Firestone says that love is "the pivot of women's oppression today." She believes that love in its simple, unromantic sense is acceptable; true love — love between two equals — would be a mutual exchange of vulnerability so that neither party could be hurt. She exposes the fact that falling in love is taking a risk, giving a hostage to fortune; and the solution is for both parties to open themselves totally to the other (assuming that both are equally vulnerable).[61] Total risk is your insurance against risk. But typically, today "true love" is idealization of one party by another, a corruption reflecting an unequal balance of power. Now it might seem that when a woman's lover idealizes her, an inferior woman could become equal to a superior man. In this way chivalrous romance would at least counteract if not overcome the oppression of patriarchy, and the legendary indirect rule of women over stronger men would be vindicated. In general, the phenomenon of wrapping a man around your little finger is underestimated or dismissed by feminism, but Ms. Firestone has an answer for the difficulty. A woman idealized by a man lives a lie, she says: "her life is a hell." Either she is anxious that her man will find her out and see that she is inferior, or she lives the lie successfully and feels inauthentic.[62]

Firestone is not satisfied with this discussion of love, however, as it still focuses on love between two parties. Such a focus she calls "the sex privatization of women," a process by which men conceal their predatory, contemptuous disregard for any difference between one woman and another and feign fidelity to one supposedly lucky member of the class of women.[63] She proposes doing away with "sex privatization" both as pretense and as fact so that women can be as forward, even as predatory, as men and neither sex will have to pretend otherwise. There will be households still, but they will not be formed of families. They will have about ten members and last for about ten years, thus preventing "family chauvinism" (no family reunions! no genealogies!) while providing intimacy and care for the children that Firestone hopes will be reproduced artificially.[64] This would be a household of in-laws without the "natural" ties that bring on inequalities of power. Firestone has no serious objection to the way men behave and greatly exaggerates when she implies that no man is ever a gentleman. But the exaggeration gives her a model for women: imitate men at their worst.

Of course, men at their worst, as Firestone conceives them, are not really at their worst. Somehow her men are led by sexual appetite alone and do not commit acts of violence against women. Perhaps they do not need to if women do not feel any modesty and are never in a mood to resist. Resistance, after all, would imply that a woman is being choosy and is committing the error of "sex privatization." Later feminists certainly take notice of male violence and rail against rape, but that stance, while more realistic, doesn't solve the problem. To resist rape a woman needs more than martial arts and more than the police; she needs a certain ladylike modesty enabling her to take offense at unwanted encroachment. How dare you! But only a woman can be a lady, and the feminists have deconstructed "woman" because they think it is a product fashioned by men. According to them, being independent from men requires women to embrace the extreme of abandoning any difference between women and men. Becoming manlike is a strange way of proving you are independent of men (ladylike would seem to be a better way). But from the beginning, the desire for independence is compromised when you pursue it *with a view to men*. The desire to be independent of men leaves you still in the grip of men. This will show them! We'll refuse to be women. In response one may say that women and men have this in common — they are happier and more attractive when they live for the sake of something above themselves on which, in a sense, they depend. That something might be making a family together, a task that creates something independent. Being independent is not just sitting there without a commitment to other human beings but doing something with them so as to be entitled to the respect of leading a useful life.

Refusing to be women, our three feminists from 1970 therefore mount an attack on nature. Nature imprisons women in the home, gives them over to childbearing and child rearing, and makes them dependent on their husbands. Or is this "nature" in quotation marks a social construction imposed by men whose interest is to imprison women and then make them think that everything they are forced to do issues from their "nature"? Here we have an interesting difference of opinion between Firestone and Millett (perhaps joined by Greer). Firestone really believes that nature made women distinct from men by giving women wombs. She doesn't blame men for this discrepancy. Since men weren't given wombs, it was reasonable and natural of them not to behave as if they had been given them. By this logic patriarchy is the work of nature, not by choice of men. Patriarchy can be overcome, Firestone asserts, only by conquering nature through artificial means of reproduction; she mentions (this is 1970) "some awesome implications" of cloning.[65]

Millett, by contrast, taking the side of John Stuart Mill, declares that "'nature' is preeminently a political gesture," by which she means artificially imposed. Thus for Millett, patriarchy could have been avoided and deserves to be blamed.[66] But if patriarchy could have been avoided, why is it universal? Why is there no example in history of a matriarchy or gender-neutral society to which we could have recourse to inspire and reassure us today? We would be on firmer ground in blaming men if we could be sure that patriarchy is not inevitable. As things are, it appears that men are always in the position of being able to make a "political gesture" by creating a "nature" in quotation marks that favors their domination. But if men always dominate, they must be stronger and more able to impose on others; their strength would have to come from something outside themselves, that is, from nature. Those who begin from "nature" are brought by this route back to nature. As we have seen, men have the power to assert, and those who have the power to assert their nature also have the power to remove the quotation marks that would call attention to their assertion and deny its naturalness. The feminists are right to allege that anyone who claims to act "by nature" is adding human imposition or "social construction" to nature, but they do not see or do not care to admit that the manly assertiveness responsible for social construction is also by nature. Of course, nature has its way whether we assert it or not, but it has its way differently if we do not assert it. Thus the gender-neutral society cannot destroy manliness, but it can repress it and confuse it.

Sigmund Freud was an important figure to the feminist three.[67] Complacent sexist though he was, he proved that the family, rent by the Oedipus complex, was, to say the least, naturally disharmonious. A family in which father and son compete for the love of mother can be held together only by a fierce repression that belies the innocence and the legitimacy of a family in the mode of Ozzie and Harriet. And the feminists liked the sexual primitiveness implied in this picture of the family, to say nothing of Freud's concentration on sex. Freud laid before them the notion of "polymorphous perversity," which was very much to their taste (or, as we shall see, very appealing to their sense of moral duty). Freud had coined the phrase in 1905, but it was updated for the benefit of the sexual revolution of the late sixties by Herbert Marcuse. For Freud, polymorphous perversity was the original, or primitive, or natural character of human sexuality, later channeled and repressed to make the family possible and human society livable. To call it "perversity" surely implies that it is against nature as well as inconvenient, but we can set that difficulty aside. In any case, what Freud presented as a problem our three feminists with the prompting of Marcuse declared to be the solution.[68]

The original human sexuality should be liberated rather than repressed, and polymorphous perversity should become the rule of civilized as well as primitive life. Again we see that feminism in its desire for independence surpasses the liberties that randy males had taken for themselves and for themselves only. "Polymorphous" goes well beyond (or is it only somewhat beyond?) the successive conquests of Don Giovanni, which, in order to be conquests, presuppose the modesty of women. The fun of sexual conquest, moreover, depends on its being a transgression of modesty and morality — a point that Freud understood well. But feminist sexuality is not fun and is not erotic. It is transgression *on principle*.

Germaine Greer says that her principle is the pleasure principle. Never mind that in Freud the pleasure principle is opposed to the reality principle (there's something unreal about pleasure). Now when you hear that someone holds the pleasure *principle,* you know that she doesn't care about pleasure. The pleasure principle is for someone who is really earnest about pleasure, which again means that she wants to be earnest rather than seek pleasure. When Greer tells us at the end of her book what really moves her, she says it's "the joy of struggle."[69] It's the joy of leading a revolution and transgressing the conventions of society that have held women down for millennia, coupled with the realization that there will be no pain and no punishment in the attempt. Of the three writers, Greer is the only one who seems to enjoy being naughty; Firestone and Millett enjoy being sober and responsible. All three share the combination of prudishness and licentiousness characteristic of radical feminism, as if the bodies of Casanova and de Sade had been invaded and captured by the spirit of Mary Wollstonecraft and Elizabeth Cady Stanton. They feel it is their duty to promote, if not to practice, polymorphous perversity, and to do so not for the fun of having sex but in pursuit of a new society of women liberated from sexual morality so as to be liberated from men. In this pursuit any definition of woman is abandoned or destroyed and replaced by a fierce determination not to be defined: traditional sexual morality falls before a new moralism demanding power and transcendence with no stated goal. This is why I have called feminism "nihilism." It says that being a woman is nothing definite and that the duty of women is to advance that nothingness as a cause. A certain nobility attaches to the cause even if we are not invited to say what it might be. But this is only because we think we know something of the definition of a woman — knowledge these feminists reject.

These three feminists are revolutionaries, but they are the first revolutionaries not to give a single thought to the use of violence. Jesus Christ was an unarmed prophet of peace, but his revolution was unpolitical and not of this world. These women want to change the world by introducing a new, very worldly independence to the lives of women. Having been oppressed for millennia by men, how do they expect to overthrow their oppressors? Especially when, for all the feminists know, men oppress women in accordance with their nature? Marx said that the bourgeoisie will not abdicate, that violent revolution by the proletariat is necessary. How do feminists conceive that men will not defend patriarchy? In fact, men did not defend it but instead of fighting amazingly surrendered almost to the last man. How this happened I do not want to say, but I do want to remark on the strategy and tactics of feminism. For in the manner of its attack on patriarchy we see why one can speak of *womanly* nihilism. The feminists knew more of the nature of woman than they cared to admit, and they relied on womanly devices.

Our three feminists never directly admit the weakness of women in relation to men. They do not face the facts that rape is done by men to women (and sometimes to other men), not by women to men; nor that one often hears complaints of wife-beating but seldom of husband-beating (it does occur). They do not explain why patriarchy held sway everywhere until now. In *Sexual Politics,* Kate Millett says that men have bigger muscles but that superior physical strength has no authority within civilization. Civilization! Two pages before, she said that all civilization has been oppressive patriarchy; now we see that patriarchy was not so bad after all.[70] Patriarchy either created or tolerated civilization, and civilization was very good for women because it nullified men's advantage in big muscles. In fact, men must not be so bad either because despite their advantage in bodily strength they consented to its being nullified — they abdicated. You could even say they behaved as gentlemen. Shulamith Firestone has a different view, but it comes to the same thing. She says that civilization relied on male supremacy to liberate human beings from their enslavement to biology, only to re-enslave women with romantic delusions.[71] In that case men were not such gentlemen and did not abdicate, but men are still responsible for liberating humanity from their own bigger muscles even if they took away liberty by foisting romantic love on unwilling women. (Yet isn't it better to be wooed insincerely than beaten up?) Firestone takes the acquisition of "culture" for granted; once it exists, feminists can work within it to transform it. As with Beauvoir, the proletarian revolution is the necessary though not sufficient condition of liberation. Yet if a violent male revolution is necessary to women's liberation, we have to conclude that women must depend on men for their liberation.

Anyone might object that men always depend on women, and particularly in the building of civilization. To advance that point, you have to accept the value of sex roles, which these feminists do not. As we see, they would rather have women stand for nothing than for something, because any quality or virtue is a prison for women and being nothing is liberation for them. Since these feminists take no account of men's greater strength, they also disregard the strength of women together with their contribution to civilization. In truth, strength comes in two kinds: men have greater force, women greater endurance. This great truth of common sense gets in the way of the nihilistic denial of sexual definition, so it must be ignored. In sum, it is clear that civilization is a boon to women. It greatly reduces the advantage of men's muscles and it validates the advantage women have over men in . . . we shall see in an instant. At least in the beginnings, civilization was built on slavery; that we must admit. Aristotle tells us, however, that one mark of civilization is to distinguish between slaves and women.[72]

Germaine Greer has the solution that will make possible a nonviolent revolution. "Women's weapons are traditionally their tongues," she says. She doesn't want women to be meek and guileful because that sort of dissimulation is slavery. Women who are free do not entreat, inveigle, or cozy up to you. They talk straight and tough, sprinkling their discourse with four-letter words for emphasis. In case of trouble with stronger males arising from this approach, like true revolutionaries they can always call the police. But wait! Greer had spoken out against a "masculine-feminine bipolarity" earlier in the book; what is this about women's traditional weapons?[73] In this implicit, grudging recognition of weakness, feminist nihilism becomes womanly. *Suaviter in modo, fortiter in re.* Manly in substance, feminism is womanly in manner. Rather than by violent revolution, feminism undertook to bring on the gender-neutral society by *raising consciousness.* Unlike the manly suffragettes, who broke the law and demonstrated scandalously in public places, the feminists, who in their writings dispensed with morality and claimed to be ready if not eager for polymorphous perversity in matters of sex, were so law-abiding in their behavior that none of them spent a moment in jail.

Raising consciousness was intended to make women and men aware of how much society is prejudiced against women. The prejudice is so powerful that it is barely noticed; it is embedded in our language and in the pronouns we use many times every day. To use "he" for the impersonal pronoun, for example, when referring to a doctor or lawyer, conveys the assumption that situations of power and authority are normally held by males. Raising consciousness by substituting gender-neutral pronouns would excite the ambition of women and induce men to welcome the change. It would make clear that doctor and lawyer are nouns equally available to women and men rather than presumed to be male. So the formula he/she was born, together with variations with the same aim, including the use of "she" as the impersonal pronoun, giving tit for tat and getting revenge for women after millennia of male oppression. This particular new convention was not imposed by the government (though the government soon adopted it) but was first insisted on by feminist copy editors at publishers (particularly university presses), subordinate employees whose job was to check copy for errors in spelling and grammar and who inserted gender-neutral pronouns on their own. By working through changes of language, feminists were able to correct social prejudice without having to demonstrate or even argue for reform. How could one answer them that the impersonal pronoun "he" did not favor men or that women were not equal to men?

Consciousness is a word used by Marx, and *consciousness-raising* is a compound of neo-Marxist origin that was apparently first used in 1969 in the *Red Stockings Manifesto*, coauthored by Shulamith Firestone when she helped found a radical feminist group in New York.[74] Although it is not used in the first edition of Betty Friedan's *The Feminine Mystique*, the term appeared in a later edition after it had worked its way not only into the mainstream of feminism but also into American public discourse. The term is a reminder that feminism came from the left and that it owed much to Marx's critique of liberalism; many of the early feminists considered themselves Marxists, and Friedan herself was either a communist or close to communists in the 1940s.[75] Marx's theory was directed above all against the division of labor, which he thought to be the source of all oppression; his associate Friedrich Engels extended Marx's theory to sex roles, concluding that under communism they would have to be abolished. Original Marxism argued, to be sure, that consciousness was determined by economic forces, but when events showed the economic argument to be implausible, neo-Marxism arose to say that consciousness might revolt by itself. (This was what Beauvoir was saying to Sartre in the interview discussed above.) The way to liberation that economics could not provide was open to psychology, and feminists turned gratefully to (male) psychologists. Friedan actually studied with two of the most important: Erik Erikson, who touted the concept of identity, and Kurt Lewin, who pushed sensitivity. Erikson, following Nietzsche, showed how identity could be both an individual and a social creation, but Lewin had an even greater success with the notion of sensitivity, to which we owe the Sensitive Male. The gender-neutral society is much indebted to post-Nietzschean psychology of this sort.

Sensitivity was a movement in social psychology that had some success after World War II in corporate management. Businessmen would get together to meet in a "T-Group" or "encounter group" where they would begin by disregarding all existing hierarchy among those present. They would then proceed democratically to make a new hierarchy or — surprise! — confirm the old one and in the process teach sensitivity to one another. To become sensitive meant to become aware of your tendency to throw your weight around and hurt other people, especially to hurt their feelings. Comment in T-Groups was supposed to be personal rather than abstract because abstractions give offense and reduce intimacy. "You're a fool!," for example, is the kind of abstract description that gives offense. When you have to respect personal feelings, however, those feelings become immune to moral judgment and do not have to face critical challenge — as they do when you are told to stop sniveling. Here we see a sudden access of democracy through the exposure and purging of aggressiveness, done by males to themselves as if they were too impatient to wait for the feminists to do it to them.

Sensitivity, like political correctness at the end of the century, was (and is) the insinuation of opinion into others without either argument or imposition. It is an effective rhetorical method traditionally used by women to deliver a surprised reproach: Tut, tut! With expressions such as "You just don't get it!" women can get what they want without having to ask for it directly, thus without asserting themselves. Applied to their careers, which are now part of their identities, women can have their merit recognized without having to call attention to it. That is why the heroes or heroines of feminism have not been great doers like Joan of Arc, Queen Elizabeth, or Catherine the Great. The mightiest woman of our time, Margaret Thatcher, is no model for feminists, partly because of her conservative opinions, of course, but also because her renowned insensitivity makes them uneasy. Feminists prefer to seek out and confer recognition on unnoticed women from the past; they favor obscure authors rather than great names like Jane Austen and Edith Wharton, who, having been noticed before feminism came on the scene, are somewhat tainted by association with corrupt patriarchy. By taking advantage of sensitivity, feminists ensure that their manly revolutionism has a feminine touch. Sensitivity, we note, has nothing to do with having sex but is intended to open the doors for women's ambition, not merely to let women pass through in the literal sense. Sensitivity is what has happened to gentlemanliness in our day.

Conscious that I have moved from speaking of three or four radical feminists to feminism in general, I would not want to leave the impression that I have given a complete picture of feminism. Beauvoir, Firestone, Greer, and Millett are only the original core of feminism, and feminism today has moved on to issues not raised by the pioneers. And we have not yet considered Betty Friedan, the first of the American pioneers, who was a moderate according to my rather desperate definition of not wanting to abolish the family. *The Feminine Mystique* came out ahead of the radical books that I have discussed above, and it had much greater influence. "I am still awed by the revolution that book helped spark," said Friedan with good reason twenty years later.[76]

Friedan's book starts with the "problem that has no name." But it turns out to have a name, boredom—the same problem known in another language as *ennui* that had been the accusation against the bourgeoisie throughout the nineteenth century. *Ennui* was what Emma Bovary suffered from, and it led her to adultery. But Friedan thinks that "sex-seeking" is still part of the feminine mystique in which women have been imprisoned in their relationship to a man; and besides, suburban adultery is not as exciting and unconventional as Madame Bovary's sad adventure. Unlike the radical feminists, Friedan does not dwell on sex. She wants to answer the voice within women that says, "I want something more than my husband and my children and my home."[77] This "something more" proves to be a job, or rather, "creative work of her own." Creative work enables a woman to sense her freedom or her autonomy, says Friedan at the end of her book.[78]

"Something more" is a moderate goal if it means recognizing that being a wife and mother in our time is no longer a full-time occupation and that being a male is no longer necessary for many professions and jobs. Without assailing all previous societies for having practiced and all previous thinkers for having countenanced patriarchal oppression, one could moderately call for an adjustment in favor of women to the new circumstances of life. Of course, there would be problems in making this adjustment, and feminist thought could address them by considering how women might combine job and family and how men might be persuaded to relax those demands of their manliness that seem to require them to resist such changes. For both points thoughtful deliberation is the key, not raising consciousness. None of this is to be found in *The Feminine Mystique*. The author is awed by the revolution her book made, but revolution is what she wanted. She wanted *autonomy* for women, for that is the word she used; and autonomy is not something more but something *other* than "my husband and my children and my home." Autonomy is not a policy of accommodating others but a demand that they adjust to my will, or to the will of all those who think like me.[79]

Friedan, by contrast to the more radical feminists, left husbands and children relatively unscathed, but she unloaded a bitter denunciation of the housewife—going so far as to call the American home a "comfortable concentration camp" and to compare housewives with its inmates. [80] This excess, later regretted, was not what most feminists felt or wanted to say, but it reveals a very immoderate cast of mind. Friedan also says that a woman is a "human being of limitless human potential, equal to man."[81] Here she flirts with nihilism, both affirming and denying an essence to human being. But the main point is to claim for women anything that men have. All womanly qualities are rejected in her attack on the feminine mystique, leaving only the desire to be autonomous, like a man. Anything characteristic of women, in which women might find comfort and take pride, is deliberately thrown overboard. No sort of femininity is proposed to take the place of the feminine mystique. Women are to find themselves by looking inward and seeing nothing valuable there but limitless potential, just as she supposes men do. Yet men who want to play with their lives as if they were supermen, or little toy figures of Nietzsche, have always had to face women as their critics. The trouble with feminist women is that they don't have wives to teach them sense. Their autonomy is not a substitute, much less a recipe for moderation.

Other feminist moves toward moderation can teach us something further about manliness. When women in their feminism try to be manly, they expose to view hidden preconditions of manliness that may be concealed by the familiarity of sex differences. Thus the radical feminists show what would be required in the way of independence to give women the lives of men. But when moderate feminists recoil from that picture they show what women, perhaps reasonably, dislike about manly independence. Is autonomy good for women? If not, is it such a good thing for anyone? Is identity? Is transcendence?

Naomi Wolf raises the question whether a woman's beauty gets in the way of her autonomy. Wolf is a feminist writer who made a name for herself with a book, *The Beauty Myth* (1991), that developed Friedan's notion of the feminine mystique. Beauty is a myth foisted on women by men, and women are much too impressed with it. Women shouldn't pride themselves on their beauty, shouldn't sacrifice for it, shouldn't allow themselves to be ranked by it. Beauty is a form of enslavement — that is, of course, to men. Here is a truth known to all beautiful women, hence to Ms. Wolf herself.[82] Beauty also enslaves women who wish they were beautiful. And it enslaves men who admire beautiful women and want to be attractive to them. Still, if you were a beautiful woman, would you trade your looks for autonomy? Wolf is known more recently, in the 2000 presidential campaign, for having advised Al Gore on how to be or appear more manly (more "Alpha male") and thus more attractive to voters who are not repelled by manliness. This was a notable concession on her part to the male side of the beauty myth, though in her advice to wear agreeable colors she may have been confusing sexy (trying to be attractive to women) with manly (not seeming to care about that).[83]

Wolf's doubts about feminist radicalism became evident in two books where she related her discoveries that polymorphous perversity was not so good and motherhood not so bad. In *Promiscuities* (1997), she retold stories of women who learned from their first sexual experiences not how polymorphous they might be but just how distinct they were from men. Wolf lamented the "silencing of the female first person sexual voice" and aimed to correct it in her book, but one wonders whether it is in the interest of women to blurt out their sexual voice and thus incite men to the aggression they are already too much in mind of.[84] Moderation in women seems to require the modesty they are inclined to anyway, but Wolf leaves that point to more conservative, antifeminist women.[85] Obviously at some point modesty has to yield, but without it there is no task for impetuosity and life diminishes into routine. When the feminists ask, "What is it about the word 'no' that you don't understand?" the answer is whether a woman is being modest.

One problem of women's autonomy is that women are the weaker sex. This is a hard thing to say, and not only in these days. Women are stronger in endurance than men and in whatever enables them to live longer, and many women have admirable strength of soul. These are not small advantages. But in strength of body most men are easily stronger than most women, as well as more aggressive. The difference remains despite the equalizing tendency of both technology and democracy, which diminish the importance of strength and aggression. When women drive cars and shoot guns, when everything conspires to equalize them with men, the fact that women remain weaker is all the more notable. No doubt, the "weaker sex" is a phrase better left to be understood than to be stated, still less repeated, for it is ungentlemanly to make a point of one's greater strength. Yet gentlemanliness would not be needed if there were no weaker sex. So let's tell the truth. Now that women are equal, they should be able to accept being told that they aren't, quite. Just how important this leftover fact is, is hard to say, except to remark that in everyday life it reinforces traditional courtesies and sex roles. A truly moderate, realistic feminism would confront this awkward reminder.

Besides being weaker than men's, women's bodies are made to attract and to please men. These facts, causing women to be in a sense subject to men, cannot help but affect women's autonomy. Feminists often avow their desire to secure control over their bodies. Hitherto, they say, women's bodies have been on call to men, all women have been prostitutes to men, an assertion some feminists would insist is not exaggerated. How can women have self-control (that is, moderation) if others — men — control the readiest and most needful thing to control, one's body? Polymorphous perversity, or promiscuity, is one answer because one can gain a measure of control of one's body by offering it freely to all. With many lovers, one has none or is subject to none, one hopes. Or is it nonsense to think that turmoil in one's sex life is independence? To be independent it seems that one must have some calm. Another answer is homosexuality, so that one gains control over one's body by keeping it away from men. Men bring anxiety and heartache, and their big muscles add to the problem by magnifying both their means and their presumption. Add to this the solid mahogany they often have instead of brains. Why then ask for trouble by sleeping with men? It's better to find some substitute. A third, more moderate solution is not to compete with men or to compete with them indirectly by not challenging them, not giving them notice of a threat. But this way, though effective, is an age-old, prefeminist maneuver that cedes formal sovereignty to the stronger sex and thus again feeds male presumption and confirms male authority.[86] It might be that women rather admire presumption and authority.

"Control over one's body" is a phrase often used to claim the right of abortion, an act that frees a woman from the troubles of giving birth and child rearing but does not save her from regret or from the risk of becoming callous if she should get in the habit of preferring her convenience to other, more valuable things. Autonomy sounds good when it is claimed for the sake of nobility, much less so when it is for convenience. To insist on keeping the right of abortion absolutely intact, with no concessions to reasonable doubt, betrays the presence of moralism in those who rail against that fault when they confront the other side of the debate. And there is a debate on abortion in which women should feel free to think for themselves — autonomously, if you like.

Can you be autonomous without having an identity? Or does having an identity cut down your options and cramp you too much? Let us turn now to identity, a notion that seems to contradict the characterization of "womanly nihilism." To have an identity means precisely that as a woman you are not nothing. You have rejected the womanly essence, the "eternal feminine," because it enslaves you to men. But you do not stop with rejection; you replace the essence allegedly created by nature and actually created by men with an identity you have created for yourself. Clearly it is not really an identity if it has no specific content. An identity of creativity or "choice," in which your main idea is to keep your options open without specifying what is to be created or chosen, simply repeats the negativity of rejecting the old essence. So again, if you hear the question "Is there anything about the word 'no' that you don't understand?" the answer is, "to what will you say 'yes'?" Under the old code, a woman turning down a man does not have to answer, but the new code does not permit such reticence.

In general, the answer we get from feminists comes from psychology, from the sort of psychology derived from Nietzsche, the big bad wolf standing behind feminism who said that psychology is the queen of the sciences.[87] Yet though derived from Nietzsche's heady "honesty," identity is a tame, routinized version for democracy's everydayness. An example is the "different voice" that Carol Gilligan, whom we now examine as a feminist, finds in women. In her book *In a Different Voice* (1982), she finds it not in a select few but in all of them. Working as an assistant to the psychologist Lawrence Kohlberg, Gilligan grew restive under his assumption that a healthy identity develops toward recognition of ever more universal rights.[88] This identity, she thought, was too abstract and too much suited to the abstractness of males. She began to see that women are relational rather than abstract; they find frightening the male insistence on rights with its corollary of noninterference with, unconcern for, others. Moreover, women relate to others without standing on ceremony or insisting on hierarchy; women are more democratic than men. But in this influential book men are never discussed!

Without saying so Gilligan returns to traditional sexism, but only to the female half of it. She criticizes the maleness of feminism and praises the womanliness of women but still manages to remain a feminist. Her definition of voice as "an intensely relational act" omits the male voice of assertion that we have studied (why can't you *relate* to someone by telling her what to do?). She contrasts the ways that women and men describe themselves without noting the obvious fact that the men she quotes are all boasting.[89] How can women do the jobs of men unless they are equally assertive? It seems doubtful that relational women will get to the top; they will likely remain stuck in the middle where their good humor and their talent can be exploited. To do better while remaining relational they would have to stop caring and start scheming. Gilligan illustrates the feminist tendency to claim equality on the ground that a woman can do anything a man can do and then, after equality is admitted, ask for special treatment because a woman is more vulnerable. She forgets that in demanding justice, a man might be asking for what is due to him because of his abilities. Still, let us not rely on harsh male logic, always so self-serving. It is well to treat women as women, and this includes recognizing their merit even when they don't boast about it. But let women be grateful for the generosity of this justice when they see it. They do thank you for it in their terms: "you are very *supportive*." This is not the sort of praise a gentleman likes to hear, but it is better than being denounced for sexism. If Carol Gilligan is right about women, feminism needs more revision than she has given it. Perhaps women shouldn't be quite so ambitious as the radical feminists want them to be? That is what their "identity" according to Gilligan tells them.

"The elusive mystery of women's development lies in its recognition of the continuing importance of attachment," according to Gilligan.[90] Where, then, is the idea of transcendence—a kind of *detachment*—said to be the human idea and the goal of liberated women by Simone de Beauvoir? Gilligan, though a professor, is not nearly as theoretical as the elite of academic feminists who transcend the crowd of ordinary women by the thoughts they think and the words they invent. To be sure, the academic feminists base their psycho-philosophical theories on the work of two men particularly, Jacques Lacan and Michel Foucault. Both were French, and they provided sophisticated simplification of the thoughts of great minds (such as Nietzsche and Heidegger) for the use of academic disciplines. Difficult thoughts were brought down to the level where common professors could handle them, and the reduction was disguised by processing it in heavy jargon. Lacan, for his part, made sense of Freud for the feminists by expressing his thought in the theory of language. He wrote an influential article entitled "The Signification of the Phallus." The phallus is a "signifier."[91] It signifies both demand (or power) and desire (or lack); here Lacan does his best to bring eros or attraction back to sex. But his best is not very good if only because reading his prose is not an experience with beauty.

While Lacan helped out the feminists with Freud, Michel Foucault translated Nietzsche for them into a theory they believed they could use.[92] Foucault took from Nietzsche the idea that knowledge is a form of power ("will to power") rather than the result of a simple desire or yearning to know.[93] Foucault easily found the power of knowledge in the ambition of modern science to bring rational control, especially "discipline," to human affairs. He studied the forerunners of today's social science in the eighteenth and nineteenth centuries and applied his insight to the "disciplinary system" enforced on sexuality so as to make sex more sensible and suitable for the bourgeoisie. He looked not at the central organs of society but at its "capillaries," where he discovered that the vaunted personal liberty of bourgeois liberalism was, in fact, social enforcement of exclusion and "marginality." Its purpose was to create "docile and useful bodies." To counter the rational disciplining of society, or perhaps just to expose it so that others might counter it, Foucault developed not a science of his own but an "antiscience" or "genealogy" (Nietzsche's term) that would substitute "discursive" talk for scientific rigor. A discursive genealogy of social power would avoid any judgment of what is essential, for seeking the essence of things causes science to be "totalizing," overbearing, and tyrannical at the expense of groups (such as homosexuals) it relegates to the margin of society. Foucault focused on the naïve, non-scientific discourse of resistance among the marginalized.[94]

All this was a sublime revelation to feminists. The only difficulty was that for some reason Foucault himself—like Marx, Nietzsche, Sartre, and Lacan—had not applied his analysis to women. Overlooking the fact that power was masculine, Foucault had accepted the essentialized domination of men and unfortunately marginalized women. He could be hoist on his own petard, and he was. He of all people should have known that masculinist power has always subjugated women "through their bodies," but his own essential nature held him in its surprisingly tenacious grasp. Subjugation through their bodies refers to women's natural weakness relative to men, to the mutual natural attraction of men and women, and to the function of reproduction that naturally occupies women more than men. Canceling all that subjugation requires overcoming the relevant powers of nature or, in sum (and for the sake of being sure), denying nature. This denial, we have seen, is what is meant by nihilism.

If women are not defined in some fixed respects by nature, then women are either what they make of themselves or what they are made by others, either creators or creatures. We are back to the distinction set forth by Beauvoir between transcendence, making yourself, and immanence, being made by others—which means by your context and inheritance. The distinction is embodied in an excellent debate held in 1990 between two feminist professors, Seyla Benhabib and Judith Butler.[95] Their exchange brings out the difficulty of a woman's wanting to be transcendent and at the same time refusing any natural essence of womanhood. Beauvoir tried to do both, but Benhabib and Butler together show why this is not possible. Each of them takes hold of one point and lets the other drop, Benhabib standing for transcendence and Butler representing contextuality.

Benhabib, closer to the old left, wants to criticize the traditional role of women, and believing that if you criticize you must be above what you criticize, she thinks that women must elevate themselves to improve their situation. To do this they need a strong sense of subject or self with the power to reform. The trouble is that having a self means having an essence that limits what you can do with your self, all the more if it's a strong self. You might, for example, have a strong self irresistibly drawn to your children. Butler for her part does not care to be stuck with a definition, which she regards à la Foucault as a "ruse of power." She is in the fancy postmodern left and believes in infinite openness with no exclusions or "binary" (either-or) definitions. The advantage to this position is that a woman, now undefined, can move into anything, since nothing is regarded as unwomanly. The drawback is that she is then defined by her situation, "constituted by her positions," not by herself. Her definition having been deconstructed, her context moves in and takes her over.[96] Her husband and the children won't let her go. By being infinitely open she is perfectly flexible and therefore has no resistance to outside imposition. When a woman lives beyond definition she has nothing of her self to insist on, and she becomes the very sort of passive patsy feminists abhor. Well, she can insist on her tenure: postmodernism is nihilism for professors.

So it's damned if you do and damned if you don't: this is the failure of womanly nihilism. If you have an identity, you cannot do everything; if you can do everything, you have no identity. But let us not drop womanly nihilism altogether. There is something reasonable in a woman's reluctance to be defined, and that is her desire these days to "have it all." To be specific, having it all is having both career and family and not being confined to one of them. Having a family will naturally be more demanding for a woman than a man so that less is left for her career. But as a man shares in the desire for a family, so a woman shares in public ambition. She may have less ambition or a different ambition, but being a political animal like a man, she too likes to rule, if in her way. So too—and I am speaking as always "for the most part"—she can be defined in her way. Her definition is less abstract than a man's just as her life is less abstracting, more rounded, and more attentive to the world around her. She is distinctive by not always striving to be distinctive.

Feminism prompts us to a further reflection more friendly to it. Feminism wants transcendence over previous definitions of womanhood. This is what it learned from Simone de Beauvoir, who learned transcendence from Nietzsche. But it wants transcendence for the sake of independence, and the trouble is that the two are not consistent. Independence means that you are satisfied with yourself; transcendence means that you are not. In relations between the sexes independence means that you do not need the other sex because you do not want to be dependent on it; transcendence means that you do need it because you want more than your own sex. Feminism is not to be blamed for this inconsistency. Not only feminists but all human beings want both completion and incompletion in this way. Homosexuals would admit that society depends, and so they depend, on heterosexuals. It's the utopian fervor of feminism that brings out the difficulty, which is otherwise concealed by the complacency of convention. Certainly manly men are both disdainful of women and chivalrous to them without reflecting on the problem. And the gender-neutral society does not know whether to ignore the sexual difference (independence) or abolish it (transcendence). So let us think again about the sex roles.

To be of one sex makes you partisan for your sex but also makes you yearn for the other sex. A profession or occupation is in a sense complete, and there is nothing about the role of carpenter or professor that makes the one yearn to be or be with the other. Sex is different because the two sexes are inclined, for the most part, to each other. Neither sex finds satisfaction only in itself but only or mainly in the other; this is a desire for transcendence of oneself. Now what is the character of the transcendence? Is it a desire to make our humanity universal so that the sexes are at last equal? So says the liberal doctrine of the "rights of man," which despite its somewhat sexist language holds the promise of sexual equality. Notwithstanding the scorn of feminists for sexist liberals, it is to liberals rather than Nietzsche that feminists are indebted for the idea of equality that is their fundamental premise.

Or is transcendence the desire for a more perfect humanity rising above the limitations of the sexes and combining their excellences? This would be a vertical transcendence as opposed to the horizontal liberal transcendence, and we find it in the classical philosophers. Plato and Aristotle have much more to say about men and women than do the liberals, for whom the sexual difference is something of an embarrassment. We will turn to the two kinds of transcendence in the next two chapters, beginning with the liberals who are closer to us.

The revolution that made the gender-neutral society was not led by liberals but by women of the left, inspired as I have argued, by a womanly nihilism. Their heroine was Simone de Beauvoir, and behind her, Marx and Nietzsche. The feminists discussed in chapter 5 — Firestone, Greer, Millett, and Friedan — were highly critical of liberals and of liberal principles as well. Although the women's movement followed close upon the civil rights movement, it took a very different path. Civil rights leaders in the 1960s, above all Martin Luther King, called on America to be true to itself, to live by the principles it had long proclaimed, and to cease the hypocrisy of talking one way and acting another.

The feminists did no such thing. Although of course they denounced male hypocrisy, they did not take liberal principles for a measure. Liberal principles were inherently faulty and inevitably hypocritical because they were formal. Liberal principles gave everyone a formal right to equality but deliberately refrained from examining whether formal equality was made actual. Under formal, liberal equality, the feminists said, women were at an actual disadvantage. For one seemingly small example, the use of sexist pronouns giving preference to males subtly conveys the secondary status of women and betrays their supposedly equal right of free speech.

In so arguing, feminists were echoing a long-standing complaint against liberal formalism, perhaps stated best in Karl Marx's *On the Jewish Question* (1844), that the unlovely informal practices of liberalism cancel out its published principles. Another way to put the objection is to say that in liberal society, the public, the sphere of the formal, is in fact governed by the private sphere so that the public promise of equality is betrayed. "The personal is the political" is the feminist formula for that point: women have been confined and oppressed by the liberal distinction between personal or private and political or public, which was intended for concealment and fraud. Moreover, the formula suggests, the way to reform is by the same route as the betrayal—by politicizing the personal, but now in reverse, in favor of the gender-neutral society, for the purpose of ending oppression. Martin Luther King did not resort to this Marxist argument. Although black Americans were in fact subject to intimidation, he spoke up all the more, vindicating his own equality and American liberalism at the same time. But King was a man. Still, his example suggests that the women's movement could have used liberal principles if it had wished. The liberal principles of Hamilton and Tocqueville (mentioned in chapter 1), giving rights to "each individual," were there to be exercised by a women's movement content to follow the example of the civil rights movement. Nor did women face the sort of intimidation that blacks claiming their civil rights overcame. It is as if the manly men were ready to abandon the quality they had insisted on for millennia, or longer, when urgently requested to do so. Manliness, the assertive quality, shrank to nothing in its own defense.

Thinking over why this might have happened, I settle on the character of liberalism in its generic sense, the dominant opinion of our age. As opposed to *being* manly, a *defense* of manliness requires that a man look a woman in the eye and tell her that she is inferior in certain important respects. Men cannot do that today. Men today believe in the equality of men that is the basis, and lately also the goal, of liberalism. Feminism won its easy victory because it was able to appeal to the liberal principle of equality and demand that equality for males be made actual for women too. Though liberalism was more opposed, even reviled, than appealed to by the women's movement, it was the cause of its easy victory. Americans were ready to give justice for women—the *liberal* of equality—and did not much care that the advocates for women spoke more of power than justice, more of sex than career, more of autonomy than happiness.

In the Declaration of Independence we find the "rights of man" stated as the basis of government and society. This is sexist language now, but clearly *man* in this phrase meant human being to the American founders, not males only, just as it included blacks as well as whites.[1] The universal meaning of "rights of man" gave and gives liberalism its mighty, expansive influence in the world.[2] Yet there is truth in the criticism that liberalism was meant mainly (not exclusively) for males. Liberalism was indeed not as gender-neutral as advertised. What does liberalism have to say about manliness, given its formal theme of humanity? We know that in the parallel case of the Marxist critique of liberal formalism, made on behalf of the proletariat, liberalism has a ready response as if anticipating that it might be made. In the matter of property, liberalism promises increase for everyone if not equality, and it defends the formalism of property rights and the distinction between public and private as necessary to limited government. Government would have to be an unlimited force, as we observed in communist totalitarianism, if its task were to create equality in property. Is there a comparable defense for manliness against the gender-neutral critique? What good does manliness do for liberty and equality?

In this chapter we shall have a look at a series of liberal philosophers to see what each makes of the relation between liberty and manliness. As citizens of a liberal democracy, our horizon is bounded by the liberal tradition we live in. But within that tradition there are several possibilities from which to choose, and we need to be aware of them to see what is more and less available to us. But before we survey these possible choices, we need a general sketch of how liberalism relates to manliness.

In liberalism there are love of liberty and desire for security. The two are linked because they are necessary for each other. Nobody wants liberty without security, which is chaos ("the war of all against all," said Thomas Hobbes), and nobody wants security without liberty, which is slavery. But, though necessary to each other, these are two distinct notions that might easily conflict. If we look at them from the aspect of manliness, they *necessarily* conflict.

The love of liberty will keep you from ever accepting slavery, even though subjection to a conqueror might save your life. Love of liberty is not calculated; it may not be in your interest, as interest is usually calculated; and on occasion it requires risking your life. Desire for security, in contrast, might prompt you to settle for slavery as better than death; it is therefore always calculated in terms of self-interest, and it is risk-averse. These differences add up to a contradiction from the aspect of manliness. For liberty, manliness is a necessity; for security, manliness is the main obstacle. In the life of a liberal society, the man who loves liberty is a hero who risked his life to become the father of his country like George Washington, whereas the person who fears death and wants to live in secure comfort is a nameless businessman or his spouse. A businessman is one who both discounts risk, looking for the sure thing, and takes a risk, betting that he will succeed. When risk-taking predominates, we call that man an entrepreneur or a capitalist, one who makes a name for himself like Henry Ford. The nameless characters who desire security are, you can see, closer to the gender-neutral society, in which nobody, or everybody, makes a name for himself or herself. The gender-neutral society is not friendly toward risky activity, even on behalf of liberty, that might give advantage to manly men as risk-takers and thus upset the balance of the sexes on which it depends (but on which, with typical liberal formalism, it pretends not to depend). Our main goal is to find out more about manliness from the aspect of liberalism, but we can also learn more about the liberalism we breathe every day from the aspect of manliness.

Thomas Hobbes (1588–1679) was a kind of liberal, though we would not recognize him as such today because he was opposed to self-government and favored monarchy. But by conceiving the idea that rights come before duties, he laid the foundation for liberalism. All liberal democracies today, though drawing different political conclusions from Hobbes's formulation, are indebted to him for the foundation. And manliness, identified by Hobbes as the toughest enemy of human rights, must be dealt with when a free society based on rights is constructed. If only the feminists had paid attention to Hobbes, they might have seen the danger that manliness poses to the peace of a free society. They would then have been better able to assess the costs and difficulties of suppressing manliness.

In Hobbes's thought, manliness is nowhere and yet everywhere. Nowhere (in his mature thought) does Hobbes praise manliness or even describe it. In the *Leviathan* (1651), Hobbes pointedly omits courage, the virtue of manliness in premodern thought, from a list of the virtues.[3] What is manliness, essentially, for Hobbes? It is not a virtue but a passion, a passion for preeminence that he calls vain-glory, or vanity. It is appetite but not for any particular thing, thus a generalized appetite that compels men to aggression.

We see now that the scientists (discussed in chapter 2) who identified manliness as aggression rather than confidence were unconscious disciples of Hobbes. If this passion were confident, it would not be vain; yet after making this distinction, Hobbes abandons it in effect when he says: "I put for a generall inclination of all mankind a perpetual and restlesse desire of power after power."[4] Such an inclination is necessarily in vain. It is not mere animal aggression but the human desire for precedence over other humans, a desire for superiority. Life is a race that "we must suppose to have no other goal, nor other garland, but being foremost."[5] The race is a competition especially as to who is more *intelligent*.[6] Precisely in their most rational feature humans are the most competitive. Overflowing with overconfidence, they boast that they know more than anyone else and therefore should be allowed to master others less fit to rule. We see that this competition is not innocent diversion as when "fierce competitors" play tennis but something more serious and dangerous. Play, indeed, is not harmless but a symptom of the fact that life is a race in which the object is not to reach a goal but to finish first. In Hobbes's thought, manly confidence that you can reach your goal is replaced by the passion for superiority, which, because it is infinite, has to be anxious.

We all know individuals more or less of this type, but why does Hobbes say that *everyone* is like this? Here lies the conceit or conception that lays the foundation for liberalism. Hobbes debunks the claimed superiority of humans over one another, calling it vanity; and yet he also flaunts that punctured vanity as the very proof of equality. He supposes that in a state of nature before society exists there would necessarily arise a situation in which everyone would be the enemy of everyone and thus compelled, even if possessing an even temper and an amicable penchant toward his fellows, to regard them as competitors without limit to the extreme of death. Everyone in the state of nature is compelled to live at the manly extreme, and this is why manliness itself becomes lost to sight in Hobbes's system. When manliness becomes the natural state of man, one no longer cares about manly men in particular, or about the differences between manly and unmanly men, or between men and women. In the state of nature all human differences are swallowed up by the universal necessity of behaving at the extreme of manliness. So as not to rest his argument merely on the nature of the male,

Hobbes generalizes male manliness to sexless vain-glory and then obscures even this by excusing vain-glory as perfectly rational in the situation he describes. There will be some who have a passion for eminence and enjoy conquest, but since one cannot tell who they are, and since one can suffer as much from a rival's modest defense as from his aggression, one has a right of anticipation valid against everyone and not merely against the overmanly. So the distinction between female and male or between the moderate and dominators is, on one hand, effaced and, on the other, resolved as if everyone were a dominator.[7]

Universal manliness is invisible as to what it is in particular. Hobbes's state of nature is as gender-neutral as our society today wants to be but only because there is no rational alternative to extreme manliness. The reason for Hobbes's conceptual leap is to teach everyone, but especially the manly, a lesson. First Hobbes narrows all social ills to a single problem, the inability to identify a sovereign who will make decisions all will agree to. The substance of controversies will always be disputable, especially religious controversy in which the various parties claim knowledge of God's will. In view of the religious wars of his time, which bring the vanity of human pretensions to a focus, Hobbes narrows the goal to peace. Peace is peace at any cost so that any form of peace is justice. Then he sees to it that everyone, through experience of the state of nature or, more likely, imagining it, will be disposed to peace. Each individual, required to be assertive in the state of nature, will receive a cold bath of truth in the fear of violent death. In the state of nature each individual is subject to sudden, unforeseen attack from everyone else, and each can imagine that this attack might happen. Recognizing how vulnerable he or she is, each will be willing to agree to the rule of a sovereign who will decide controversies for all.

The necessary fear is not merely fear of death in a general sense of revealing the fragility of life, but fear of unforeseen death at the hands of another human being, a violent death that causes each individual to abandon his overconfident dreams of glory and triumph over rivals. Only the fear of violent death addresses the problem arising from competitive manliness and forces manly men — now all of us — to become sociable or, as we say, *sensitive*. With the concept of the state of nature, Hobbes transforms human psychology from extreme manliness to extreme femininity, and without naming the qualities of either sex. He lays the foundation for liberalism by uniting liberty and security, each at its furthest extreme. The liberty to do *anything* to triumph over a rival—what Hobbes calls natural right—is joined to the security of establishing a sovereign who will be obeyed in *any* circumstance—what he calls natural law. The fact that the problem is resolved in the extreme case for both liberty and security ensures that all lesser cases are included in the solution, and nothing is left to chance. If you have a right in the extreme case to kill your parents, then what lesser right will be denied to you? And if you have a duty to kill them if the sovereign commands it, your obedience also extends to anything less (though not to kill yourself, which according to Hobbes is more grave than killing your parents).

Anticipating your violent death by a violent chance encounter puts you in the frame of mind to want to avoid all such chances. Being in the right frame of mind is a moral as well as an intellectual duty, according to Hobbes. You reach this frame of mind through fear, not through shame. When you feel shame you keep your pretensions intact; you are ashamed only because you know you could have done better. So Hobbes substitutes fear for shame.[8] You *ought* to be more afraid than proud, he says; not only do you show yourself wise when you tremble, but you also become a better person, more honest with yourself because you have given up your pretensions. Honest! Does this ring a bell? Hobbes has come upon the virtue of intellectual honesty that Nietzsche two hundred years later wrongly supposed was new and that the feminists picked up for their purposes. The difference is that for Hobbes honesty arises from fear, whereas for Nietzsche and for the feminists honesty is still vanity, now dressed up as "will to power" or "autonomy."

The desire to leave nothing to chance accounts for the formalism of Hobbes's theory and of the liberalism he founds. They give each individual rights and duties—the rights always prior to the duties—that he will probably never use, never perform, like the right to make millions of dollars and the duty to invest it well. The purpose is to ready society for any eventuality, however remote, like a male nurse or a woman president. A liberal in the style fashioned by Hobbes has the mentality of a lawyer or an insurance agent, always focused on the unlikely and the unexpected. Necessarily this liberal can be distracted from the normal and probable occurrences of life and may begin to think that anything is possible in his own case. Others, however, should be content with what they can normally expect in their situations. While inflating his own possibilities, the liberal tends to willful complacency in regard to others; he is ruled by his dreams, they by the realities of life. Liberal formalism is subject to biased interpretation in one's own favor.

Society's unfortunates are included in the guarantee of a formal right but nothing need be done to actualize that right. When women rose in revolt against sexism, they protested the complacency characteristic of liberalism in regard to the less fortunate. They took up against the false promise of a guaranteed formal right they believed they would never be able to exercise in fact. This was the response of the women's movement to liberalism's implied promise of a gender-neutral society that was formally possible but, because of the complacent sexism of liberals, could probably never become actual. When the feminists rose up against the exclusion of women, liberalism became the victim of its own half-hearted manly protectiveness that promises but fails to deliver. How could it object to women who decided, improbably but legitimately, that they were no longer satisfied with their traditional roles? Yet, as noted above, liberalism got no credit from feminists either for the promise on which it was obliged to deliver or for the good will it has shown. The credit went to disciples of Nietzsche, enemy of liberalism.

The conceptual leap in Hobbes's state of nature was the work of his science, the new political science he said he began. This new, modern science enables Hobbes to be quite ambivalent in his attitude toward manliness. In the state of nature everyone has the right to be a manly aggressor against everyone, but in civil society (or Commonwealth, Hobbes calls it) everyone has the duty, having signed away this right, to forget his manliness and become sociable, or sensitive, or relational, or unmanly. In Hobbes's theory just as in the gender-neutral society everyone has a formal right to be manly, but in fact manliness must be suppressed. Modern science itself shows this ambivalence. The individual scientist, humble and modest, waits until all the facts are collected and takes care never to force the evidence, take a risk on what he may find, or assert more than he knows as the manly man might do. Yet science as a whole, as an enterprise, is as proud as the scientist is humble. We often see scientists abandon their ordinary scientific caution when discussing the prospects of all science.

The manliness of political science is much more evident than that of natural science. Natural science does not have to oppose common opinion (or not to the same degree), as, for example, advanced mathematics has nothing against ordinary counting. But political science must take on the willful, errant, and vengeful opinions of vain and boastful men, encouraged in their foolishness by philosophers and clerics, in sum "the Kingdom of Darkness."[9] Hobbes's political science is itself manly because it teaches men how to stand up to the chaos that is nature and tame it, subjecting it to reason through the construction of a peaceable society. Hobbes entitled his mature work *Leviathan,* borrowing from the Bible the name of a "King of the Proud"; but he also called the Leviathan a "Mortall god."[10] His state is a proud creation with the function of taming the proud.

We recall that Plato complained of Homer for making his hero Achilles too manly when he set Achilles' virtue against the chaos of Hades. Plato noticed that manly men dramatize their actions as if they were the center of the universe. Their assertiveness is necessary to the meaning in our tenuous lives, which would otherwise sink into insignificance or oblivion. Poets such as Homer celebrate a manly Achilles because they accept his boastful inflation of a petty quarrel, however unreasonable, as the only way to sustain human dignity. But Plato the philosopher discovered nature, an orderly cosmos that supplies meaning and dignity without poetic or heroic boasting. In the interest of justice, Plato corrected the overwrought contrast of heroic virtue contending with arbitrary gods and chaos; with his political science he introduced a simple theology of rational gods that would not aggravate human disputes and justify exaggerated, heroic manliness. The manly men in Plato's best city became tamed guardians of philosophy.

Hobbes with his political science also opposes overambitious manliness, but he does it differently. He opposes manliness by having it support sovereignty, not philosophy, and by means of equality, not an ordered nature. He believed that Plato failed to tame manliness. With his imagined dignity, Plato merely endorsed with reason and philosophy what Homer had magnified with poetry. So instead of taming manliness, Hobbes tries to quell it. And in order to quell it he first exaggerates it. Hobbes recreates Homer's chaotic Hades and calls it the state of nature. He puts himself in Achilles' stead and dramatizes manliness against the backdrop of chaos, the better to suppress it. Representing the cause of science, Hobbes permits himself an exuberance that is suppressed in the work of the typical scientist; he writes a wonderful, sarcastic rhetoric and shows himself not so much a manly fellow as an impudent boy. One wonders if there is something not quite grown up, a failure to accept tragedy, in the progressive manliness of modern science.

In Hobbes one sees a terrific counteraction between the natural and the civil that gives his thought its characteristic power and paradox: war in nature versus peace in civil society. These two extremes supply the drama needed for manliness in which humanity is saved from chaos by heroic exertion: Hobbes the political scientist saves us from the terrors of the state of nature. Yet, of course, peace in civil society, even though artificially constructed, is also based on nature, the naturally stronger passion of fear and the laws of nature inclining men to peace.[11] So the drama of counteraction is within nature, and all the trouble that nature sets for us must be settled with its aid. In Hobbes's scheme, the invention or authorization of sovereignty (by which the dominators are replaced by covenanted authority) permits nature to be set against itself as man's natural vanity is overcome by his natural fear.[12] Human reason cannot by itself moderate human vanity; indeed, reason on its own or in company with our imagination puffs up our ambitions. But when nature makes us fear for our survival, our reason gathers strength and gets us to be moderate. All of Hobbes's effort goes into the construction and support of sovereignty, the government that makes peace and civilization possible. His argument, his rhetoric, his characteristic devices cooperate in the work and converge on the goal of quelling the uppity self-congratulation of human beings. And this vanity, though attributed to all, is promoted and defended by manly males, the dominators — who are, in fact, not so much the warriors (in the state of nature) as the boastful orators (in civil society).[13] Hobbes's manly effort has for its purpose the quelling of manliness; men will be free when they learn to think only of their security. The standard by which politics is to be judged is neither opinion nor reason but success in bringing peace. In quelling manliness, Hobbes vindicates the manly attitude of disdain for pretty speeches and right reason.

Hobbes might be called the first liberal because he invented the notion of a state of nature in which men have rights prior to their duties. But it is better to reserve that honor for John Locke and consider Hobbes a part-time proto-liberal because his system discourages the spirited defense of liberty that characterizes the true liberal. His liberty is the "liberty of subjects," and although this liberty includes various manly and revolutionary liberties of liberalism — to buy; to sell; to contract; to choose one's own abode, one's own diet, one's own trade; and to educate one's children as one sees fit — still they are presented as allowed by the sovereign when he omits to regulate them.[14] Hobbes does not praise vigilance in support of liberties or initiative in exploiting them. He disapproves above all of resistance to government, which he constantly denounces and which he forecloses by arranging that every apparent appeal against sovereignty lead right back to it.[15]

Because subjects of the sovereign get their liberties from him, they must always be on the watch to be sure that what they want to do is legal. Besides this wariness, Hobbes fashions moral virtues that work against the natural presumptuousness of man. He insists that right comes before merit, that no man has a right to office or wealth because of his merit; he cannot claim with assertive manliness in the manner of Achilles that his merit deserves recognition. On the contrary, he deserves something only if he has a right to it, that is, a right by contract.[16] All the virtues by which one might claim to be deserving — above all, those that might make one deserving of rule — are routed by Hobbes through the absolute sovereign that is necessary to repress such claims. Your virtues by themselves do you no good; they must be recognized by the sovereign; and if he fails to see them, you have no claim of justice against him. Placing justice ahead of merit, Hobbes sets virtue against virtue.[17] Virtue for him is justice, and justice, or natural law, is set the task of disciplining the other virtues to keep them quiet and make them serve peace. The nineteen laws of nature given in the *Leviathan* are intended to instruct men in sociability and are particularly directed against pride or magnanimity, the crown of the Aristotelian moral virtues. As noted above, courage is omitted.[18] Anything that might give a handle to manliness at its highest or lowest is held down or pushed out.

All in all, Hobbes deserves the mantle no one has yet awarded him of having created the sensitive male. For the sensitive male is one who follows Hobbes's advice to *lay down his right*.[19] Feminist commentators have not praised Hobbes for this foundational command, partly because of the want of apology in his tone, partly because it is not to women as such that the

Hobbesian male is to be sensitive.[20] Certain asides of Hobbes, such as that "men are naturally fitter than women for actions of labor and danger," disclose that he was more wary of men than favorable to women.[21] But the main point is that being more naturally fit in these ways, as men may be, is not a title to rule. Women are naturally equal to men, meaning equal in the state of nature, substantially equal, equal in the ability to kill. Women may not kill as often or as easily as men, but to establish a threat one example is enough, and one can readily imagine a Salome finding a way to catch a man off guard.

Ambivalent as Hobbes may be, he is mainly against manliness. Two fellow or rival liberals, Spinoza and Locke, are more favorable to it. Let us first briefly consider Baruch Spinoza (1632–77), a philosopher less studied for his politics than are Hobbes and Locke. Spinoza's politics is based on his equation of might and right, a famous formula lacking the moral and rhetorical appeal of the "rights of man" in mainstream liberal philosophers. It seems to offer nothing to the weak and unfortunate or to their advocates. Yet Spinoza does offer a defense of liberal democracy by contrast to Hobbes and Locke, and he is always worth visiting for the sake of the example he gives of his own *fortitudo,* the virtue he describes that comes closest to manliness. To this one may add his refreshing lack of sentimentality.

We may begin from the difference between Hobbes and Spinoza over self-preservation, the goal of man for both. For Hobbes, self-preservation is what reason, prompted by fear, tells us to do. Fear makes us honest and honesty makes us accept the — unmanly — truth about ourselves so that we abandon our vain hopes for precedence and settle for security. For Spinoza, however, self-preservation requires just what Hobbes is willing to forsake — a manly strength of character (*fortitudo*) that gives us determination to stick to our will and not falter in vacillation of mind between fear and hope. Strength of character, though aided by fear and (to a lesser extent) hope, might seem to be above the passions and, though rational, beneath reason, though Spinoza does not say this. Strength of character is akin to what Descartes called "generosity," or strength of soul. It arises from Spinoza's practical recognition that Hobbes's reliance on fear, "the passion to be reckoned upon," is bound to be in vain because fear is not reliable but inconstant.

A power of the spirit or mind (*animus*) is needed to fortify the will, to give it "tenacity" in holding to one's own advantage and "nobility" when it aims at others' advantage. Thus Hobbes's reliance on fear is inadequate because fear is too selfish as well as inconstant.[22] Spinoza expects from self-preservation precisely the moral qualities of tenacity and nobility that appear to demand not putting self-preservation first. So described, strength of character might seem to be a very useful resource for our gender-neutral ideal today, as it is clear that many women without great strength of body possess admirable strength of character.

Spinoza does not grasp this opportunity to make liberalism genuinely neutral to differences of sex. Far from it, with the maniacal realism that distinguishes his political thought, he insists on the supremacy of males. In his *Short Treatise* he describes fortitude as "manly" — which might be extended by courtesy to women.[23] But in the *Political Treatise* he shows plainly that the rights of man are, in politics, the rights of males. Explaining at the very end of the work why citizens of a democracy should be males, he answers an objection that it might be by convention and not by nature that women are excluded. He says that by consulting experience one sees that women are excluded by their natural weakness relative to men. If nature had made women equal to men, there would be societies in which women were equal to men or women rule men, but none have been found. Spinoza concludes that one is fully entitled to affirm that women are weaker by nature, and therefore, by the equation might = right, women have no natural right to be equal to men, much less rule them. Not satisfied with this enormity of sexism, he adds that when one considers human passions, it is not even by merit that men rule women. Rather, men rule women by right because they love them out of lust, because they judge their ability and wisdom by their beauty, and because they get angry when women show any sort of love to others, "and so forth."[24] It is actually through the stupid superficiality of men, which Spinoza does not bother to describe completely, that society would be harmed by allowing women to govern equally. Lustful masculinity is irrational, but it is powerful and must be compromised with or surrendered to. Here is a man willing to look women in the eye and tell them what they deserve.

This is the extreme of Spinoza's argument but not the whole of it. He also finds a more positive contribution to social peace in male anger. The rights of man are the rights of males because rights must be vindicated; they must be claimed and defended. Because your right extends only as far as your power, if you do not have the power to make your right actual, you do not have the right. Politically, Spinoza sees that the necessity to defend rights requires an armed multitude capable of objecting indignantly to oppression by rulers. His politics is much more democratic than Hobbes's, as Hobbes preferred the greater quiet of monarchy in which orators would be stilled. Spinoza believed that even in monarchy the indignation of an armed multitude would be a vital and healthy force. It is true that the multitude needs to be taught obedience, and taught in part by fear, but as peace is not just the absence of war, so obedience is not just sluggishness or apathy. It requires a steadfast will (*constans voluntas*) or strength of character in the people.[25] In Spinoza's thought we see the manly assertiveness discussed in chapter 3, just as irrational as male aggressiveness but more to be admired. Spinoza is the liberal who does not abide by liberal formalism, and when he speaks of the rights of man he offers no universal promissory note to those who simply want to be given their rights. Everything you want you must get by yourself. To him it is no objection that the weak are denied their rights, and he welcomes the irrationality of manliness. Philosophers can get their tenacity and nobility from reason and do not need manliness; politics consists in rational compromise with irrationality. A philosopher might take women seriously, it is implied, but not women who want to be in politics—unless to his surprise he should find them there.

John Locke (1632–1704) is a philosopher more clearly liberal than Hobbes in two ways. Beginning from the premise of the state of nature that Hobbes introduced—a debt he took pains to conceal—Locke avoided Hobbes's harsh and paradoxical political conclusions requiring absolute sovereignty and sociable "subjects." Locke laid down the outline of limited constitutional government that encourages a manly vigilance in politics and that has endured to our time; also to our purpose, he found a social role for manliness. As opposed to Hobbes, he sought to incorporate in civil society some of the independent spirit of men in the state of nature. Locke did not set natural and social man against each other as Hobbes did, the one self-seeking and domineering, the other peaceable and accommodating. For Locke, social virtue is, or needs to be, more resistant than pliable. He believed that civil society must be a free society and that a free society must be sustained by lovers of freedom. For the sake of freedom he allowed more to manliness than did Hobbes: free and manly go together like soul and body, mutually supportive and fit for each other.

Locke brought into civil society the manliness that was active in Hobbes's state of nature and latent under Hobbes's sovereign. The sovereign's subject, as noted above, is made over to be sociable, but within himself he is still full of fight. He considers himself the equal of anyone else just as he did in the state of nature. In that state human beings are equal because no one has a valid claim to rule anyone else, but Hobbes could not quite bring himself to say that men are equal in fact. What makes them equal is that each, in the vanity of his pretensions, *considers himself* equal to everyone else. When men consider themselves equal it may be politically wise to accept their self-assessments. This was Locke's judgment (as well as Spinoza's). Rather than cool down human vanity, Locke put it to work. To fix the character of a free people, it might be said that he resorted to Machiavelli (without, of course, naming him). Machiavelli had said that men in society are divided into two "humors," a princely one that craves domination and a popular one that does not wish to be commanded.[26] Locke selects the popular humor to characterize the behavior of a free people. He wants government to be sustained not by the virtues it promotes (as did Plato and Aristotle), nor by principles of subjection (as Hobbes), but by *hostility to government.* Government is to be obeyed in a spirit of unfriendly regard, the very spirit that makes government difficult to sustain. Precisely the intractability of the human will—its urge to say no to authority—makes government both difficult and necessary. Then why not appeal to a healthy dislike of dominion in order to counter the desire on the part of "princes" to dominate?

In the *Two Treatises of Government* (1690), still the greatest philosophical statement of the liberalism by which we live, Locke lays down constitutional forms that depend on, and at the same time nourish, manliness in a free people. He speaks of the forms and not of manliness, but the forms, we see, will work only when served with a manly spirit. His argument for free government is based on self-preservation, which he interprets in a mode lying between Hobbes's quelling of pride and Spinoza's endorsement of pride. In

Locke's argument, self-preservation is defined in the law of nature as both right and duty, the right to put one's own life first yet the duty to preserve the rest of mankind. Both right and duty imply that all are equal. Yet Locke begins his work in a spirit that differs from his argument: "Slavery is so vile and miserable an Estate of Man, and so directly opposite to the generous Temper and Courage of our Nation; that 'tis hardly to be conceived, that an *Englishman,* much less a *Gentleman,* should plead for't."[27] Slavery is vile and miserable, he says, not disadvantageous for one's preservation. And he appeals to the generous courage of Englishmen and gentlemen, not to the duty of human beings, to follow logic and extend the rights due to fellow humans. His rhetoric addresses a narrower audience than does his argument, perhaps because he needs to call upon more virtue and energy than reason alone can bring forth. The constitutional measures, so familiar to us, that Locke discloses toward the end of the work also depend on manliness rather than rational assent. Among them the separation of powers is designed to set "bounds" enabling the people to watch over the exercise of power by marking encroachments. The requirement of the rule of law posts notice that rulers themselves must live under the laws they lay down. The right of private property, defined as that which cannot be taken from you without your consent, provides a warning, when violated, that government has become despotic. Locke rejects a right of conquest unless the cause is just; and he denounces tyranny, urging that it be resisted. The resistance does not have to be merely verbal: "He therefore who may resist must be allowed to strike."[28] All these constitutional forms can be practiced only when they are exercised in an active spirit, and when so exercised, they cultivate a habit of activity. Locke does not believe that the people will overuse these forms, resist for slight cause, and readily descend into anarchy because he agrees with Machiavelli that the people are susceptible to fear and do not want the responsibility of ruling. But they don't mind resisting rule.

Locke's constitutionally limited government can thus be founded on the desire to limit government, in contrast to Hobbes's absolute sovereign who receives the just allegiance of submissive subjects. That desire must have a manly spirit of determination to stand up for one's rights, though Locke does not make a point of it. He does make a point of manliness quite at odds with Hobbes's sensitive male in his *Some Thoughts Concerning Education* (1693). This book of moral education was intended to form and guide the desire to limit government, replacing indoctrination in the opinions that will supposedly transform contentiousness into submission, in which Hobbes set such great store.[29] Locke produced this work on moral education for the purpose of forming the character of the young, a topic Hobbes did not undertake. He also wrote letters on toleration expressly denying to the magistrate sovereignty over doctrines to be taught. For him, character is more powerful than doctrine, a view that makes room for manliness.

In *Some Thoughts Concerning Education,* Locke exposes a universal love of dominion (in contrast to Machiavelli) that exists in children before they grow up and learn fear. He shows how to take the love of dominion that may be discerned in children from the day of birth and fashion it into self-mastery. Children must be treated with severity so as to prevent the self-pity that leads to "softness of mind." Such "effeminacy of spirit" may conceal a will to have one's humor obeyed.[30] At the same time, correction of the young must be mixed with dispassionate reasoning so that the child does not react with submission and impotent fear. Fear can be understood positively when it is seen as a pain or uneasiness similar to, or inseparable from, desire. "Fear is a passion that if rightly governed, has its use."[31] Self-preservation is not put to the purpose of making subjects tremble. Whereas Hobbes reckons on fear to quell fractious spirits, Locke uses it to shape them to manliness. For Locke praises a "manly air and assurance" that serves as "a fence . . . to virtue."[32]

The spirit of liberty can be sensed in the extremes of Locke's political thought, the state of nature and the breakdown of civil society resulting from tyranny. In the state of nature we see that spirit in the moralism of the power to punish (by which an action taken to preserve yourself is justified as duty to others); in the breakdown of civil society we see it in resistance against a miscreant government. Yet more important than the rights available in extreme circumstances is the everyday exercise of rights in liberal society. For Locke, the rights of man are not surreptitiously masculine; his politics is antipatriarchal in both theory and practice. The theory of contractual individualism includes women among the individuals, as one can see from Locke's practical endorsement of the right of women to divorce.[33]

But the exercise of rights requires a manly confidence in oneself that is neither dominion nor submission. To bring this character to a free people is the object of Locke's thoughts on education.

Yet Locke is an economist as well as an educator. He is the first philosopher to argue for the acquisition of property and the heaping up of money without limit, and this excess is justified by the consideration that he who works for more than he needs "does not lessen but increases the common stock of mankind." Locke recognizes and accepts that some men have a need for excess, for more than can be strictly described as required for self-preservation. He takes this need and channels it away from politics, where it might do harm, into economics, where it brings "increase" and "plenty." He says that God gave the world to "the use of the Industrious and Rational . . . not to the Fancy or Covetousness of the Quarrelsom and Contentious."[34] Manly competitors are diverted from politics to making money and to the bloodless killing of commerce. Manliness is still around, but it has been rationalized into socially useful industriousness that helps everyone while satisfying the desire to win. Locke's "gentleman" is on the way to becoming a businessman.

Nearly a century later, Edmund Burke (1729–99) calls more emphatically than Locke for manliness in the exercise of rights. It may seem strange to count Burke, known as the founder of conservatism, among the liberals, but since we want lovers of liberty and writers on manliness, let us not exclude him. Burke called himself a Whig, not a conservative, and in reference to the defining event of his time — the French Revolution — he took the name of "counterrevolutionary." Burke attacks the French Revolution for many things but most broadly for being inspired by a false notion of the rights of man. Rights of man are not to be rejected as such (and this might justify treating Burke as a liberal), but they must not be promoted abstractly, apart from their circumstances, thus claimed and awarded without regard to how they will be used. The abstract idea of the rights of man puts individual men in charge of their lives; they and none others decide how those rights will be exercised to preserve their lives, liberty, and property. In their abstract, universal form these rights are a free grant of power. Burke objects that when men lack the sense of responsibility to a power above themselves, they are easily overcome by vanity or self-pity and, unwilling to make demands on themselves, they come to prefer soft, liberal virtues.[35] To be manly is to be severe on oneself, hence not to feel free to set one's own standards or in the manner of Nietzsche to create one's own identity. To be sure, Nietzsche wanted severe men, but Burke in his political wisdom would have told him that severe men need to feel the presence of a power above themselves. As we have seen in commenting on Nietzsche, when the focus of pity shifts from others to oneself and one's class as victims, pity can be transformed into hard cruelty against the alleged oppressors. By this route the softer virtues can harden the heart to the suffering of enemies and produce the bloodthirsty "reign of virtue" by Robespierre.

Burke's lament on behalf of Marie Antoinette after she was assaulted (and before she was guillotined) by the revolutionaries is perhaps the most renowned statement of manliness in modern times. Burke would have thought, he says, to have seen "ten thousand swords" leap from their scabbards at this outrage: "But the age of chivalry is gone. That of sophisters, economists, and calculators, has succeeded; and the glory of Europe is extinguished for ever."[36] Chivalry had been "the nurse of manly sentiment and heroic enterprise" and had given a character to Europe that was lacking in Asia and possibly even in the "most brilliant periods of the antique world." The benefit was not so much to the women being protected as to the men doing the protecting. Chivalry "mitigated kings into companions, and raised private men to be fellows with kings." It made the powerful less fierce and inferiors less submissive. Burke says that we have seen the end of the age of chivalry, which is surely true, but this does not mean that we have seen the last of chivalry. The proof is that today one still hears the same lament frequently repeated.

Manliness is the remedy for both softness and hardness as it enables one to resist self-pity and at the same time to be protective of those who are in one's charge. For Burke, manliness is the virtue appropriate to the rule of gentlemen who have been bred in circumstances in which, elevated above the low necessities of making a living and habituated to command, they are free to take a broad view and to become more knowing of human weakness. One can also rise in rank in a manly way, without trickery, as in Burke's own case: "I had no arts but manly arts."[37] What a manly man does is open for all to see but is not determined by what everybody believes. In Burke, manliness becomes the circumstantial virtue of liberalism, the one that brings its universal benevolence into actual beneficence. Locke had introduced constitutional limitations into his political principles and had implied the usefulness of manliness in making them work. Burke goes further than Locke to embrace manliness as the chief political virtue, the support of the British constitution that he now presents, contrary to Locke, as the source and not merely an illustration of liberal principles. For this purpose manliness comes out more into the open.

Immanuel Kant (1724–1804) makes the same point in his own very different way. For him the rights of man are based on the duties of rational beings rather than arising from the prudence and manliness of British gentlemen ruling within the British constitution. Rational beings are required deliberately to rise above their circumstances, all of them, including their sex, as they legislate the moral law for themselves. Kant agrees that men need a power above themselves, but to respect their freedom, that power must come from themselves when they legislate the moral law for themselves. Ignoring not only transitory fact as it might influence us but all nature as it might determine us, men remake the world as a priori rationality would have it. They recreate and thereby take responsibility for nature, assuming the awesome task of divine creation.[38] That is the size of human ambition when it is guided and energized by Kant's morality.

Yet when morality comes to be realized, nature returns to accompany, and nag at, a priori rationality. The moral freedom that transcends circumstances turns out to require independence in one's circumstances, significantly the fact of being male. Male independence, resting on toughness, strength, and aggression, is the natural and political condition for executing the moral law. Women, Kant says, are unfit for citizenship, having been implanted by nature with fearfulness designed to keep the womb safe, so that they need the protection of males. This does not mean that women must be submissive, only that they must be modest. With their modesty women can manage the excessive, idealized desire of males in order to govern them.[39] Kant discloses these truths with what would seem to us the most casual and brutal sexism, as far as it could be from the seeming promise of liberation in his notion of the transcendental moral law. In the circumstances of freedom, the task of Burke's prudent gentlemen is given over to Kant's assertive males. Kant's a priori rationality cannot tolerate lesser forms of reason, such as prudence, which Kant despises as tainted with self-interest, but it will ally with sheer power as needed. Indeed, a priori rationality itself has something manly about it. While for Plato philosophy is an erotic attraction, for Kant it is a spirited overcoming of nature or a determined abstraction from it. But Kant cannot quite abstract from the human power to abstract, and would not that power also be manly?[40] Kant would appear to have reason to exclude women from philosophy, as from citizenship, insofar as philosophy requires a manly effort of the soul.

Like a knight coming to the aid of a struggling companion, G. W. F. Hegel (1770–1831) attempted to rescue Kant's transcendental freedom from being betrayed by the circumstances in which it would be applied. If I may be allowed a trendy word, Hegel *empowered* freedom so that it could develop out of circumstances instead of against them. Circumstances are baptized by Hegel with the name of History, in the course of which freedom emerges by stages and finally becomes actual and complete in a rational state. In the rational state at the "end of History" the twin goals of liberalism—liberty and security—are realized together and made inseparable.[41] No longer is it necessary to sacrifice one for the other. Man is revealed to be not an imperfect, yearning, erotic, or religious being but one who can take complete satisfaction in his humanity. In his philosophy the abstract formalism of liberal principles becomes concrete, and we learn what liberalism amounts to when realized. Is this good news for women? Hegel thinks so, but not in a manner to please women today. Unfortunately, reason in his presentation endorses not all the traditional legal inequalities imposed on women, but the essential stereotype in which the woman's place is in the home. It is no longer a stereotype, however, since for Hegel her place is the work of reason. This means that women as women are deprived of the work of making history, though they participate in history as human beings, once again leaning on men. Men for their part still depend on women, according to Hegel, in the traditional manner as keepers of the home, now conceptualized as the work of reason. After considering Hegel, we might conclude that the formalism of early liberalism looks better for women. In the liberalism of Hobbes and Locke women are lost to view as women because they share in the universal rights of man, but for that very reason could they not claim women's rights as human rights? Feminism perhaps erred in attacking the formalism of liberalism. Sometimes it is better not to be too concrete and to let the *impersonal* be the political.

Hegel's notion of recognition—this is where all the talk of "self" and "other" comes from—has influenced the feminists even though Hegel did not himself apply it to the liberation of women. This notion appeals to them because it answers their desire to create a new identity for women but to do so contextually without actual fighting.[42] Hegel's notion is explained in the famous section on lordship and bondage in the *Phenomenology of the Spirit* where he shows how the self comes to self-consciousness. Instead of beginning as equal in a state of nature, the self begins divided between the roles of lord and bondsman, and then it develops to self-consciousness as each self recognizes itself in the "other." In the process of "trial by death," the bondsman sees that the lord, apparently independent, actually depends on him, on his work. Through work, and not through courage, the fear of death characteristic of bourgeois society is overcome. This is perhaps a promising possibility for women even if the work of the bondsman is the imposing of form, or manufacture, rather than housework. Work does away with fear, courage deals with it; so work with its "feeling of absolute power" (compare Kant's divine creation) implies the elimination of superior force, while courage implies its presence. In early liberalism the ever-presence of nature suggests the need for something like manliness to cope with it, but with Hegel a more sober activity is more effectual: precisely bourgeois work overcomes the unmanliness of bourgeois fear. Thus recognition, for Hegel, means finding one's self in the other rather than above oneself in nature or in the supernatural.

To the feminists it is as if Hegel were saying that there is nothing to be afraid of; the "other" is another woman or a sensitive male; women don't need men. Nor do men need manliness at the end of history. Without sacrifice, difficulty, or any possibility of greatness, the rational state is all past and no future, no longer in a spirit or mood to assert itself. Hegel's insistence that liberalism's abstract principles be actualized, or made "concrete," deprived those principles of their power to inspire. To Nietzsche, denizens of the rational state seemed mediocre or worse, "last men" on the way to becoming subhuman. The American progressives, liberals who were closer to Hegel than to Nietzsche, did not think they lived in a rational state. They agreed with Hegel that liberalism must be concrete rather than formal, but they began as we have seen to promote and celebrate manliness as if they agreed with Nietzsche.

We must not overlook John Stuart Mill in our catalogue of liberals. Mill is much more like "liberals" as we know them today than any of his predecessors whom I have discussed, and his great work *On Liberty* (1859), often required reading at our universities, is read by many students with appreciation even though it is imposed on them for their own good, contrary to its main thesis. We will also look at Mill's essay *The Subjection of Women* (1869), which is not so popular despite the fact that it is "the only major work of feminist theory written by a man who is generally considered a great theorist."[43] In this work Mill argues forthrightly that women are equal to men, and not that their place is equal to man's but rather that man's place is theirs too. Liberalism's assertion that "all men are created equal" is made concrete but in such a way as to override, and not recognize, the sexual difference. For Mill, the liberal "rational state" is gender-neutral and does not continue and confirm traditional male dominance in public roles, as did Hegel. For that reason Mill avoids speaking of manliness, a word not to his taste; instead of analyzing manliness, he argues that treating women equally is in the interest of men. As with liberalism generally, however, in Mill's thought manliness is still present but keeps company with unmanliness.

Liberalism is unmanly in setting down self-preservation as the end of man, as do Hobbes and Locke. A man is not one who confines or devotes himself to preserving himself; something grander is needed in which he can take pride. But Mill sets aside the state of nature and begins from what is useful in society, particularly modern society, which despite its progress is still too much bound by custom and religion, too much under the sway of public opinion. Society needs reform in the direction of greater individuality, and individuality for Mill is a kind of gender-neutral manliness. An individual is one who cultivates his "character" out of an "energetic nature." He does it "in his own way," with "great energies guided by vigorous reason, and strong feelings strongly controlled by a conscientious will." His character will have ingredients of "pagan self-assertion" and "Christian self-denial"; on a lower level, it will be eccentric (for eccentricity is the attempt to be original in things that don't matter), on a higher level, it will be original. All this is manly, but called "energetic" to keep it from being the property of males.[44]

Mill's notion of individuality is protected by the famous "one simple rule" of *On Liberty* — and here it becomes unmanly. Mill's individual rules himself, but for the sake of *diversity* he is forbidden to *impose* his opinions on others. These are vital ideas in liberalism today, and they come from Mill. Mill's "one very simple principle" in *On Liberty* is that self-protection is the "sole end" for which mankind are justified in interfering with anyone's liberty; "his own good, either physical or moral" is not sufficient warrant.[45] Thus everyone (if mature and civilized) is allowed to rule himself but not allowed to rule others. Mill's cultivated individual, whom I call manly, cannot make a claim to rule others. He cannot assert himself in politics by taking responsibility for ruling others; he has the confidence of manliness but only in his own case. He is not a take-charge guy. Recall (from chapter 3) the connection in Aristotle between man's being a political animal and a rational animal: if someone gives a reason for his beliefs, that reason holds for others besides himself and becomes the basis for treating, or ruling, them in the same way. If eccentricity, for example, is a good thing for me, why is it not good for others like me? Thus eccentricity becomes a ruling principle in society. Mill's position that liberty demands forbearance from ruling others is open to an objection: if you can rule yourself, why not others? If you cannot rule others, why can you rule yourself?

Mill wants a gender-neutral manliness, but he wants it to stop short of politics and thus remain unassertive — or unmanly.[46] Rather than a free society comprising diverse claims to rule, Mill in his graduate-seminar liberalism wants diverse claims to *truth*. He would disapprove of a society of mere "free expression" such as we hear of today, in which free expression means self-display and letting off steam. His free society aims at something nobler, at truth.[47] He goes on to argue against *silencing* anyone; "all silencing of discussion is an assumption of infallibility."[48] Silencing is wrong because it means that you are not taking seriously the speaker's claim to speak the truth. Mill wants people to listen to one another, to consider one another's claim to truth, though not to rule. But if you consider a claim to truth, are you not assuming you either have the truth or can get it? Then one can pose the same objection as above: if you are capable of judging — if you are "infallible" — in your own case, why not with others? And if not with others, why with yourself? The combination of manly confidence and unmanly shrinking we see here is characteristic of liberalism because liberalism praises individuality and fears pride. John Stuart Mill and Theodore Roosevelt are liberals at the two extremes — the first a man who shrinks from imposing on you and the second a man who rushes in at the slightest excuse.

When Mill changes the subject of political, or social, discourse from ruling to truth, he prepares the gender-neutral society that he in effect proposes in *The Subjection of Women*. Not speaking of rule enables Mill to dismiss all previous human experience regarding differences between men and women; he says that since men have always been in charge, women have not had the chance to show what they can do. But why have men always been on top? It would seem to be a matter of greater strength and assertiveness combined, out of which men establish their claim to rule. This would be a difference of nature between men and women. As against this thought, Mill asserts that it is presumptuous to claim any such difference because the experience in its favor means nothing.[49] It might be better to agree that experience is not conclusive but add that it means something. If, contrary to experience, society were to try the experiment of equality for women as we are now, it would mean that society is allowing itself to be persuaded and willing to overlook the sex difference in strength and assertiveness. In Aristophanes' *The Assembly of Women*, the women pretended to be men; now, thanks to John Stuart Mill and others of his opinion, men were persuaded by women that past experience is no guide for the present. Partly out of guilt, partly out of gallantry, men abdicated without a fight. It is as if Mill were right that society is one big graduate seminar capable of being moved by philosophical argument rather than force.

Mill presents a more convincing argument for women's equality than one can find among the feminists. Instead of assuming that women are equal to men, he takes up the usual claims that they are not: that women are less original, less capable in politics, more nervous, less brainy, less eager for fame, more moral than men. He answers each of these reasonably and makes some important concessions to the view that sex differences are natural. He concedes that women, though capable, have not done as well as "the very highest rank" of men; that women are less original and less eager for fame; that women are quicker of apprehension and that "a woman seldom runs wild after an abstraction." But he says that society — that is, men — would be foolish not to see what women can do. Mill seems to assume that women will still "have the cares of a family," an occupation he calls the "superintendence of a household" requiring "incessant vigilance," and he does not demean as drudgery. He also says that in the new society women will still care for charity, for which "many of them are by nature admirably fitted."[50]

In sum, Mill provides a reasonable case for women's equality that ought to satisfy reasonable women. It is mostly about careers and occupations, and though it makes sensible concessions to the doubts of sensible men, it opens all doors to women and allows them to prove their merit wherever they can. It is not about sexual equality, and, like the case made by Wollstonecraft and Stanton, it does not attack motherhood and the family. It invites women to find out what they like, and it expects that society will benefit when they do. It is true that the "individuality" Mill promotes in *On Liberty* is probably less prized by women than by men, since most women are less standoffish than men and prefer, we know, to live in "contextuality." But both women and men might wonder whether persons with individuality, disinclined to impose on others, are sufficiently responsible to be manly. Mill himself was always full of advice, and we should give him credit for that. But at some point the need for action arrives. These difficulties in the ideal of individuality show that it is not easy to construct a truly gender-neutral virtue. However much liberty and security are necessary to each other, they are not the same; and the liberty that the manly stand up for is not the security that the unmanly wish to enjoy.

On the whole Mill's ideas are very promising to women, if not altogether to their taste (what can you expect from a man?). Yet what did the feminists do? They turned down this sensible, sensitive male — a wimp when you come down to it — and went mad for crazy, manly Friedrich Nietzsche. It was Nietzsche in drag, as Simone de Beauvoir, but Nietzsche it was. Nietzsche was the source of the *transcendent* in Beauvoir's lingo, the noble desire to rise above the immanent, the merely given that does not aim at what is grand or call for sacrifice or, as we like to say, commitment. Liberalism in the end lives in the given. For all its devotion to progress, it does not inspire greatness, or if it does — for example, the women's movement itself — it does not know how to understand greatness or has lost that understanding. It arrives at the equality of men and women by downsizing greatness to "individuality" and does not see what is lost. (This is somewhat unfair to Mill but not to liberals today.) So let us not lose sight of transcendence, but let us not confine transcendence to the will to power. Plato and Aristotle have yet to be consulted.

Chapter Seven

Manly Virtue

The gender-neutral society has for its goal the transcendence of gender or sex. Gender-neutral transcendence means that society as a whole and in all its members will not automatically give you a plus or a minus on account of your sex. The humanity we share in common will become the standard for behavior, enabling each of us to transcend his or her sex and live as much as possible without regard to sex. Of course everyone has a sex, so becoming neutral as to sex requires that we overcome our own sex. The gender-neutral society, though far advanced in aspiration, is not yet realized in fact. Hence it does not just sit still in equilibrium; it has, or needs, a tendency to repress the inclinations that belong to one's own sex, whether they are natural or merely historical and up to now. Now what idea does this tendency come from?

So far we have seen two ideas behind the impulse to transcend one's sex: the feminist idea (in chapter 5) and the liberal one (in chapter 6). The feminist idea, arising from behind the brow of Simone de Beauvoir, is based not on women but on humanity. The only true humanity, according to Beauvoir, so far exclusively male, is to transcend the given or the natural or the "immanent" in a manner I have called nihilist because it accepts no guide but will to power. In the feminist society there are no social roles. Roles would be replaced by individual identities, and the expectations or plain duties that go with roles would pass over to the penchants or temporary desires of individuals. There might be responsible individuals but there would be no responsibilities to be met regardless of one's likes or dislikes, except for one overriding responsibility in the new gender-neutral society. That responsibility is to challenge and do one's best to confuse and destroy social roles, and to do this a woman or a sensitive man must take every opportunity to attack the chauvinism of males, including those close to oneself, your husband for instance. This is the responsibility of relentlessly raising consciousness in every situation, on all sides, without hesitation or respect.

The more moderate liberal idea is also based on humanity, but with an abstraction from one's sex rather than repression. The abstraction creates a formal human being with rights that may or may not be exercised. If women want to vote, fine, let them vote. If they want to run for office, that's fine too. But it's also fine if on the whole they want to leave politics to men like John Stuart Mill who will take care of women's interests without making inconvenient or insensitive demands on women. (Could it be that the truly sensitive male is the one who, unlike some others you are thinking of, does his job and leaves you alone — except when you don't want to be alone?) Abstracting from one's sex does not compel you to construct your own identity; you can keep the one God gave you and use it to fill in the blank space left to define the liberal human being. If you want a role, then by Zeus it's yours. For reasons we have considered above, this liberal idea, available for at least a century and a half, did not become the feminist idea. But it is perhaps more influential now than original, radical feminism even though it is less powerful and less inspiring and not quite compatible with the gender-neutral society that all now say they desire.

A third idea of transcending one's sex, also not quite compatible with the gender-neutral society, is manly virtue, now to be explored.

What does it mean to say that manliness might be a *virtue?* To answer, I will refer back to Plato and Aristotle. My purpose is not to impress readers with textual interpretation, much less to support my speculations with their authority, long lost since the day when it was said that "Aristotle controls the university." "The writers of sound antiquity" (Burke's phrase) do not convince us today and we do not study them in school. But without making an impassioned plea, I remark that virtue has recently been making something of a comeback and that Plato and Aristotle have always been the master teachers of virtue. They have much to say about manliness as a possible virtue if only because the Greek society in which they lived, unlike ours today, bristled with manliness and thought it the main, or only, virtue. Plato and Aristotle speak without hesitation, though subtly too, of sex differences, and we do not have to go searching as we do among modern thinkers to find what they have to say. Virtue today is making a comeback because self-interest by itself does not seem to be an adequate motive and because abstract principle, the opposite of self-interest, seems too vague and lofty. Virtue is somewhere between these rather dull extremes. Now, of all the possible virtues, or parts of virtue, manliness seems most to illustrate virtue by not being either in one's interest (narrowly understood) or defined by principle. The question of manly virtue lies before us whether we want to study manliness or virtue.

What is the meaning of virtue? If we speak of manly virtue, it is clear that virtue means more than a woman's chastity, to which it is sometimes reduced today. But from that shriveled meaning we can infer that virtue belongs to something, like a woman or a man or a human being. In this virtue differs from Beauvoir's transcendence, which rises above something—toward what?—and from the abstract self of liberalism, which represents a common denominator of humanity and deliberately overlooks the highest there. Virtue being the virtue of something, that something needs to be defined. The definition is its nature, what it is when it is complete or perfect. That is why speaking of virtue is often called "perfectionism." A man's virtue is what the best man does; his perfection is the standard or guide for his virtue. Since human beings do not have instincts enabling and compelling them to be perfect (like the perfect jackass), virtue is reasoned, reflective, deliberate rather than spontaneous. Even when virtue is a habit (as Aristotle said of moral virtue), it needs the help of reason to gain control and to defend itself. In regard to human beings as opposed to other animals, what is natural is not what occurs instinctively or spontaneously.

Yet since the eighteenth century, "natural" has been taken to mean spontaneous, as in the "system of natural liberty" that was Adam Smith's term for the free market in which order results from everyone's acting on his own, spontaneously. So today in the evolutionary or sociobiological view of manliness, nature operates with its own laws, spontaneously, without regard or need for human reflection and direction. Spontaneous nature works for human beings in typically modern fashion through self-interest, a conceptual counterpart to animal instinct. Adam Smith can sit back and reflect that free spontaneity in markets is better than abusive interference with them, but the buyers and sellers he surveys do not need to think as he does; they merely follow the self-interest with which they are equipped by nature. But this picture is too simple because it neglects the higher part of human nature. If Adam Smith can think, why can't those whom he surveys do the same thing? It appears that Adam Smith wants others to think as he does or deliberately not think. He doesn't want thinking that leads to disagreement. He wants to simplify human nature by repressing the reasoning element, except for his own reasoning in favor of repressing reason. The Darwinian theory of evolution is another version of the same scheme of spontaneous nature, in which you have only to substitute the self-interested behavior of genes for the action of the market.

We need to move beyond the simplistic views that human nature does not exist, or that it does exist and is easy to discern. Human nature is complicated by its higher part, for by its very name a higher part implies a hierarchy. Let us propose that humans have a soul that rules the body, and within the soul some parts that derive from the body and some that do not. We do not have a simple "self" that emanates from the body, as in the notion of "self-interest." Since the higher part rules the lower passions and appetites, it does not ignore, eliminate, or repress them but controls them. The higher part is not a pure principle, for precisely when ruling, reason is affected by the character of what it rules: moderate ambition is still ambition for oneself, for example. The lower passions and appetites are, to be sure, spontaneous to some extent, but they can be controlled, and to control them is more natural than to set them free. A human being is most natural when at his best, in a hierarchy in which the higher rules the lower. Only thus is John Stuart Mill's individual truly an individual as opposed to an eccentric.

Thus human nature is both spontaneous and reflective. To be reflective in the truest sense is to reflect well, which few can manage, but all human beings can and do reflect with such partial success as gives them a direction, a penchant, a bias, a character of their own, however flawed or inconsistent. Because human nature is complicated, the notion of spontaneity becomes questionable. Anyone who watches women athletes on television, for example, becomes aware that they never spit, as male athletes always do to prime themselves or to punctuate an effective move. Since men in other occupations do not spit in such situations—I know professors don't—the practice seems to be a bad habit of male athletes, neither spontaneous nor thought out. Yet is there not something natural in the fact that male athletes spit more than women athletes? Men find it easier to fall into this bad habit; hence it is natural in the sense of spontaneous as well as learned. And gratuitous spitting is unnatural in the sense of not befitting the dignity of a perfectly virtuous human being. Virtue attaches to a being, a human being, as to what is best and to what is usual in him. The meaning of virtue is to live according to nature, but it is not very clear what that is. We have to think about how to guide our lives, and most of us make mistakes. We have to accept our necessities but we have a choice as to how. The stereotypes discussed in chapter 2 cannot be clearly divided into what is natural and what is learned. What is natural is partly spontaneous and partly what is best in us, but the spontaneous can be controlled by the best and the best can be diverted by what is spontaneous in us. Both the spontaneous and the best are therefore learned to some extent; nature operates in good part with our cooperation. It is natural for men to spit and not to spit, but not equally natural.

Let us descend from the heights of theory to the naturalness of sexual roles as related to us by Jean-Jacques Rousseau (1712–78). In *Emile* (1762), Rousseau presents himself as tutor to Emile and Sophie, a couple he creates and then advises with almost incredible micromanagement from birth until they meet and marry. His purpose is to present a book "on education" (the subtitle) in the form of the upbringing of a particular model couple. The fundamental social harmony is thus domestic rather than political, and it is achieved by showing that men and women fit together as counterparts rather than through sharing their common humanity. Sexual roles are the basis of society, according to Rousseau, and they are frequently and emphatically said to be formed by or in accord with nature. Rousseau would be dead set against the gender-neutral society, and those today who defend the gender-neutral society are dead set against him.[1] Rousseau argues that the sexes are not just different but strictly complementary, and that treating them so is vital to the harmony and integrity of human life. Rousseau and the feminists do agree on the possibility of sexual harmony, Rousseau by mutual recognition that the sexes are counterparts, and the feminists by recognizing equality and similarity in the other (sex). Rousseau, one could say, invites the feminist critique with his extravagant claim of sexual harmony arising from the very roles that are said now to oppress women.[2] Our task is to see how he uses nature as the guide to manly (and womanly) virtue in order to contrast his way to the way and ways of Plato and Aristotle.

Rousseau also agrees with the feminists on the importance of sex, but for him it is precisely sexual union that originates sexual roles. "In everything not connected with sex, woman is man. . . . In everything connected with sex woman and man are in every respect related and in every respect different."[3] But in *Emile* almost everything is connected to sex. Following immediately from the diversity of the sexual union, then, we are told that the male "ought to be" active and strong, the female passive and weak. The moral difference between the sexes, affecting all their behavior, can be concluded from the bodily difference in sexual union. Women are made by nature to please men, and men to please women? No, women have unlimited desires and men do not; women but not men need and enjoy a natural modesty with which to brake their inclinations. Men need to have their greater strength brought out by the resistance of women, after which women, if they wish, permit themselves to be taken. Rousseau's answer to the feminist question "what don't you understand about the word *no?*" is that it might mean either "get lost" or "try harder." Through the pseudoresistance of modesty, women have "empire" over men, and they have it "not because men wanted it that way but because nature wanted it that way."[4] Men believe they are lording it over women all the while they are actually obeying them. A woman's "docility" is not meekness but actually her means of conquest. It is actually women's weakness that compels them to establish an indirect rule of manipulation over men. When women try to resemble men, they will be mastered by men.[5] Here is a surprise conclusion more irritating to women today than a frank claim of male superiority would be, for women stuck in roles they consider subordinate have no patience for being soothed by assurances that they are really on top.[6]

Further consequences unacceptable to the gender-neutral society are laid down. The double standard in sexual morality, Rousseau says, is natural and necessary. Unfaithful men are bad enough (Rousseau does not excuse them), but unfaithful women dissolve the family and betray both father and children.[7] Women must not only be faithful but also be judged to be so by their husbands and by everyone, so that women live under the dominion of society's opinion in a way that men do not. Yet women are reciprocally judges of men as to their merit (as I argued in chapter 5) even as they seek to please the men they judge.[8] Women require much less education than men, and Rousseau devotes the first four books of *Emile* to Emile and only the last to Sophie and Emile. Emile's education has more to accomplish: it must teach him to handle the male amour-propre that is harder to control than a woman's. A woman's vanity is controlled by her weakness and her subjection to opinion, but a man's must be carefully moderated and given useful or harmless channels of expression. Men need to have wholesome pursuits, such as science and philosophy, to serve as objects for the single-minded passions in which they are superior. "Woman has more wit, man more genius; woman observes and man reasons," claims Rousseau. Whether for good or ill, men are more imaginative, more poetic, more sublime.[9] Our society is now testing his cruel generalizations, and we do not yet have the evidence to prove them wrong.

Rousseau in his *Second Discourse* (1755) provides a history of man through evolutionary stages that seems to remove and replace a fixed definition of human nature. How then can he use the word *natural* with such insistence? Yet the evolutionary biologists of our day do the same, showing that nature evolves all the while using it as a standard to guide behavior as if it were fixed. Rousseau is more aware and more subtle. He was a great thinker and he lived in a time when philosophy, in good part because of him, was more advanced than it is now. He says, "One must not confound what is natural in the savage state with what is natural in the civil state."[10] In the savage state all men and women are naturally fit for each other, but in the civil state they must be matched to each other because they have been formed by education and by nature. Natural differences that were latent in a primitive condition come to the fore in a civil condition in which amour-propre has triumphed over the simple goodness of early man.[11]

Confounding nature in the savage state with nature in the civil state is just what the evolutionary biologists do when they claim that our primitive nature rules our present existence; they pay no attention to the specifically human faculties of reason and amour-propre that, according to Rousseau, cause us to evolve beyond our primitive condition. These scientists are eager to distinguish nature, on one side, and civil or social, on the other side, as if the two were entirely distinct and there were nothing natural in our being civil or social. Rousseau does not agree. He shows that nature indicates things that it does not accomplish by itself without human cooperation. Nature indicates that men and women are naturally matched, but to make the match requires human assistance, in fact, no less assistance than Jean-Jacques himself as an ever-present tutor or even "master" in matchmaking.[12] Matchmaking is neither pure nature nor pure nurture (as if these two elements could be isolated in a laboratory) but nurture of nature, guided by nature. The nature that is nurtured is primitive nature, and it is guided by the nature that makes us free or perfectible only in society, as Rousseau has it.[13]

Still, having made this brief explanation and defense of Rousseau, I have sympathy for the feminist objection that his view of sexual harmony is actually sexual oppression. What Rousseau leaves out is the "battle of the sexes," the characteristically different viewpoints or opinions of the two sexes. Difference in viewpoint appears in different modes of speech, as we saw in Robin Lakoff's and Deborah Tannen's work, but modes of conveying one's opinion do not matter as much as the opinions themselves. In *Emile* for the sake of domestic harmony (just as in *The Social Contract* for the sake of political harmony), Rousseau is anxious to suppress the characteristic opinions of men and women in favor of aggression and peace, respectively. He uses nature as the guide in order to avoid using disputed opinion as the guide, for contradictory opinions would upset the domesticity he wants to build and protect.[14] Actually, women get from him the peaceful household they desire at the cost of the right to dispute — while retaining the right to govern — the aggressive male who apparently dominates the household. So both sexes get what they want, except for the right to express themselves. Women are subjected to the rule of "opinion" in regard to their sexual conduct, that is true, but this is not disputed opinion and it is said to be by nature and thus unequivocal.

It is hard to avoid the conclusion that Rousseau uses "nature" rhetorically as the means to put his matchmaking notion of education beyond dispute, though not for the sake of male domination as his feminist critics would have it.[15] The feminists follow Rousseau in seeking sexual harmony them-

selves. They, too, do not care for the battle of the sexes but for the quite opposite reason that they do not want to be embarrassed by differences between the sexes. They are caught in suspense between their desire not to be
women, a sex they consider subordinate, and their desire to promote the advantage of women so as to stop being subordinate. And although Rousseau
is subtler than Darwin and the Darwinians, he like them puts too much
weight on the division of labor in the sexual union while ignoring or subordinating the difference in outlook between the sexes. We are exploring the
possibility of transcending one's sex, and it is hard to do this if one begins
from the complementary activity of male and female sexual organs. To transcend one's sex one needs to look at the difference of opinion between the
sexes because opinions appeal to reason, which transcends sex.

In appealing to reason, opinions try to picture the whole—a whole in
which aggression or peace, say, is the centerpiece. Opinions confront and
contradict other opinions because each opinion tries—when it is pushed—
to explain everything, whereas sexual organs are stuck with their half of the
bargain. Thus the woman's viewpoint and the man's viewpoint are bound to
come into conflict, and this very fact allows both sexes to transcend their
typical, or natural, viewpoint and to appreciate, if not share, the viewpoint
opposite. Reason, which causes the conflict by pointing it out, also resolves
it by deciding which side is right and in what. Of course, when we speak
of the "battle of the sexes," we mean that it goes on forever and has no resolution, and that is why Rousseau did not want to let it happen. But sometimes the battle—the argument—can be understood, as when a man and a
woman understand something of what moves the other and possibly even
oneself. The result is compromise of a transcendental kind, not so rare in life
as in our somewhat simplistic theories. Happy families enjoy that kind of
compromise.

"Live according to nature" is the byword of Stoicism.[16] But in appealing to
nature as the standard for life, Stoicism seems to confirm rather than transcend manliness. When we hear someone called "stoic," it is another word
for "tough," when being tough is a virtue. To take a step further in company
with Tom Wolfe, let us venture to say that Stoicism is the philosophy of

manliness. Tom Wolfe wrote a novel, *A Man in Full* (1998), with two characters who are candidates for the title, Charlie Croker and Conrad Hensley. Charlie is a wealthy real estate developer who leads the high life in Atlanta and doesn't read books. Conrad is a manual laborer with a family to keep who by a series of unintended injustices gets thrown in prison, where he learns to survive by a chance blessing. By mistake, he is sent a book of Stoic philosophy, and with nothing else to read he begins it. Soon absorbed, he wonders at its truth and its relevance to his situation. Stoicism, he discovers, is the philosophy of inner freedom, of manly confidence learned by living as if you were a prisoner and had to depend for your happiness on nothing external to yourself.

In chapter 17 of Wolfe's novel, Conrad reads passages from Epictetus (c.55–c.135), himself a slave and a prisoner, that we too can follow. Things by nature free, says Epictetus, are in our power, within our will; things not in our power are the body, property, reputation, office — all things we cannot control, that is, *fully* control. The true life according to nature is the life that is your own, and this is guaranteed to you by nature. But to live contentedly and without perturbation, you must avoid any involvement that might bring you into dependence in which you lose your freedom. You must not seek property, reputation or office, and you must not be so attached to your body as to fear death, the cause of the greatest dependence. All your care should be directed to the mind. Epictetus displays Stoicism in its pure form, unadapted to politics (as distinct from Cicero's adaptation),[17] hence completely irresponsible: don't get involved is the lesson. It reminds us of the manly confidence (chapter 1) that remains aloof and does not seek to take charge of risky emergencies.

The Stoic of Epictetus lets disaster occur as it will and remains free by not getting upset. He does not urge others on or upbraid them, let alone boast or draw attention to himself. Silence is his rule. Am I going to say that this is not a philosophy for women? Yes, but because it cares nothing for context; context is external and freedom is internal. Nature makes possible the freedom of human beings so that they can find their guide in nature. Nature is directed toward the human good, and so too is the god, in case humans need more protection than nature provides. For despite their toughness, men may need to know by divination what is going to happen to them. Epictetus distinguishes between the philosopher and the uninstructed, almost as if there were a duty to become instructed in philosophy in order to live according to nature. John Wayne would have a difficult time with this. According to the Stoics, nature is a stage for manliness — but on the condition that manliness be defined as calm responsibility for oneself only and irresponsibility to others. A Stoic would not become a guardian as in Plato's *Republic*.

Epictetus asks too much of Conrad Hensley and leaves nothing for women to do. The manly viewpoint is the only viewpoint, and Stoicism is toughness carried to such an extreme that it is hardly recognizable even to tough guys like Conrad. If we jump to Stephen Crane (1871–1900) and his novella *The Red Badge of Courage* (1895), we get a more balanced picture of manly virtue. For Crane (as for Aristotle) manly virtue is courage in battle, a definition closer to life than Stoic unconcern with externals. Young Henry Fleming, drafted for the Civil War, does not know whether he will run away in battle, his choices being to run or to fight, without the option of unconcern as with Epictetus' Stoic. He does run in his first encounter, but his failure to fight is covered up because he is accidentally wounded (the wound is the red badge) by a soldier on his own side. This leads to his not running the second time when "in a temporary but sublime absence of selfishness" he fights so fiercely that his friends look on him as a war devil, a hero. Before his act of courage the war seemed senseless, having no cause or ideal, an aimless motion of troops and generals not in command. After fighting like an animal, Henry becomes a man, feeling a "quiet manhood": "the world was a world for him." He was now free to stop fighting and love. There the story ends.[18]

Henry was ready to go from one involvement to another, contrary to Stoic advice. At the beginning, when Henry was leaving for war, his mother told him: "Yer jest one little feller amongst a hull lot of others."[19] He had proved her wrong. Or had he? The truth is that he *was* a little feller. Temporarily and luckily, he made himself big. Women with their realism have more truth than men, whose manly virtue is somehow both unselfish and self-important, but the trouble is that women's truth leaves mankind, including women, too insignificant. Of course if we want to know the significance of the American Civil War, we should go first to the speeches of Abraham Lincoln. Despite the absence of those speeches in his book, I do not believe that Stephen Crane disagrees with them. Nor would Lincoln disagree that the unmeaning, bestial courage (or *thumos*) that Crane describes was the condition for the grander meaning Lincoln ascribes to the war. I believe Crane wanted to show how men and women characteristically differ in their viewpoints from too much importance given to human events to too little. Transcending one's sex in this case would mean putting together the two viewpoints presented, a duty for readers of *The Red Badge of Courage*. What is the right amount of human importance?

Now it is time to address the question of nature and nurture in manliness. That question is usually treated as if it were a dispute over fact, though with obvious political overtones. Those who want to reform the status of men and women by creating the gender-neutral society need to believe that manliness is a product of nurture and that it can be removed from the scene by frowning on it or by other methods of de-nurturing and re-nurturing. But there is an issue at stake larger than reform in sex roles. This question has to do with human importance, with how much human beings matter in the grand scheme of things. The manly man thinks and asserts that he matters; for example, it matters whether Henry Fleming runs or fights when faced with battle. It matters to Henry Fleming and his comrades, and it matters to us readers. Manliness, as we have seen, is the assertion of meaning when meaning is at risk. If human events were determined by nature, understood as overpowering accidents, then it would not matter what human beings think or do; the action of one young soldier would not be any more interesting than the daily trail of one ant. If, on the other hand, human events are determined by nurture or human artifice, human events would seem to be all-important: men create their own values and man is the king of the universe.

On second thought, however, we have to reverse that conclusion. When men create their own values, who does the creating? Answer: the strongest. In considering Nietzsche we saw that if will is all, the ruler or superman has the strongest will. Similarly, in Plato's *Republic*, Thrasymachus who says that justice is artificial or conventional soon concludes that justice is the interest of the stronger. But who is stronger, nature or man? Obviously, nature has made us dependent on an environment on earth, which if withdrawn would be fatal to us, and nature gives us inner inclinations that are stronger than our wills. So the strongest will is the will of the strong by nature. A kind of identity emerges between attributing every cause to nature and every cause to nurture, in both cases unfavorable to human importance. Whether Henry Fleming is the victim or the conqueror of his desire to run and save himself, he merely reflects a stronger power than himself.

The two extremes of nature and nurture come to the same conclusion — a denial of human importance. Human importance or dignity cannot be inferred from nature by itself because human importance has to do in every case with individuals like Henry Fleming, and nature does not care for human individuals. Nature cares for the species and for general laws, of which Henry is only an instance. The evolutionary biologists and the social scientists who cannot consider human individuals and care only for generalities do not and cannot understand human dignity. Manliness exists only in its instances; the instances define it better than any definition. Yet on the other side, if we suppose that human importance is humanly made and thus made only in one instance by an act of will, the result is only to repeat the demeaning of humans. The postmodern social constructionists do not discover the human dignity overlooked by the scientists. All the former find is the arbitrary will of the stronger — female or male — that happens to prevail and has no reason for prevailing. What is needed is, as everyone says, a combination of nature and nurture; but more precisely, a nature that leaves humans free to choose and a nurture that can cite a reason for the choice made. Nature must not be simply spontaneous or else it simply determines what we do and even think. Nurture must not be simply arbitrary or else it does not establish itself as a meaningful choice but remains a whim of accident or nature.

Hence nature must be seen as the guide for nurture. If one can cite among the facts presented to us permanent inclinations toward human good, then nurture has a guide and is no longer the arbitrary positing and imposing of one's will. But nature can be a guide only if it is not merely spontaneous in the sense of an invariable law like the law of gravity. Such a law imposes itself and does not permit exceptions. But if nature is to be a guide, it must exist in a sense that permits it to be followed or not, so that one's actions are either natural or unnatural. Nature must then be heterogeneous, consisting of spontaneous inclinations that have to be obeyed—imperious nature—and other inclinations we may call "higher" because one has to reflect about them. In this way nature is hierarchical, consisting of laws we have to obey and inclinations we can judge whether or how to obey. For example, we have to drink to live, but the drink does not have to alcoholic; that's our choice. But you might choose to drink a martini because it tastes good and makes you high. If you had to give a reason for the choice, you might say that the human good is not confined to necessities but by nature includes the care of the soul as well as the appetite. One can neglect these cares but it is unwise to do so; you make yourself a bland, unexpressive creature of no interest or significance. The teetotaler would make a different choice. He would say that water is best because it is pure and does not divert attention from what is by nature the serious business of life, which is self-improvement.

From this example we see that the use of nature as a guide does not supply us with an uncontestable result. Our nature in the sense of our human good is not easy to discern or to convey in a manner that closes off argument. Fine! Then let the human good be arguing about the human good. The extremists on either side of the nature-nurture debate seem to want to put an end to the debate. They think that science or human will can decide what is the human good, and that's it. But in fact, we see that the pursuit of certainty at the expense of accuracy merely produces more uncertainty and pretentious claims of accuracy. It is better to look for the truth of the human good without supposing that one can end debate about it. If you try to look for the human good on which all can agree, you will distort your search by confining it to measurable facts; you will be misled by your insistence that happiness be quantified. Perhaps the truth of the debate between the martini drinker and the teetotaler is to be found in Socrates, who drank a lot without being affected by it.[20] But this is not a universal truth because most of us are affected by alcoholic drink; we have different capacities, and don't forget that men can hold more liquor than women. Don't drink more liquor than you can hold! That is using nature as a guide. It's debatable, since you might have good reason to get drunk, but it's still good sense most of the time. Please don't ask me to quantify "most of the time." I don't mind giving advice, but I don't want to rob you of your duty to think and your freedom to choose.

Let us turn to Aristotle to see what he says — or asserts. For Aristotle makes a distinction between saying something when you could have said something else and asserting something that needs to be urged because it might be contested or disregarded.[21] Asserting, we have learned, is the business of manliness (= courage). Returning to the topic of chapter 3, we now see that manly assertiveness is the crucial factor in the relation between nature and nurture. *Nurture,* in fact, is a misnomer. It is not merely that our natural inclinations must be nurtured but that humans need to make demands on nature, using their inclinations to call attention to themselves in order to receive the justice they deserve. Our nurture (or education) takes place through our politics, which is always in dispute, overt or latent. The feminists are perfectly right to see politics everywhere in our society, reluctant as we are to admit its presence and try as we may to exclude it. How we treat boys and girls in school and out, for example, derives from our notion of democracy, whether restricted to take account of sex differences or expanded so as to ignore them. But manliness is not only one subject among others of the nature-nurture debate; it is also the vehicle by which nature and nurture are combined. Entering that debate, we can go some distance toward resolving it with Aristotle's help and, unfortunately, without Rousseau's. Rousseau is so anxious to dampen our amour-propre that he gives an account of nature and of men and women omitting assertiveness.

Everyone knows that Aristotle defines man as by nature a political animal. "Man" in this definition (near the beginning of Aristotle's *Politics*) is *human being (anthropos)*. But then Aristotle uses the other word for "man," *aner,* meaning a male, when he discusses later topics (in Book 3), such as the difference between the good *man* and the good citizen and whether the best *man* or the best laws should rule.[22] It is as if he had forgotten that human beings, not merely males, are political animals by nature. But Aristotle never nods, so let us look for the reason behind this change of name.

"Man is by nature a political animal." How is it possible to understand that definition today? *Political* to us sounds like something chosen, and *by nature,* we believe, refers to something unchosen or spontaneous. Politics is natural yet it needs something conventional, for Aristotle says that though everyone has an impulse by nature to this sort of community, the one who first made a city was responsible for the greatest of goods.[23] The natural impulse was not enough by itself but needed a founding political act by a god or a human being, this being the convention that gives effect to the impulse. This convention is not spontaneous, for if it were, it would be superfluous — just a bit of talk that accompanies an action. Founding is so far from being spontaneous that it has the character of an assertion, as when the poets (Aristotle says) assert that "it is fitting for Greeks to rule barbarians."[24] It may be that some or many Greeks deserve to rule some or many barbarians, but this is a contestable point — particularly because, as Aristotle hints, the Greeks themselves may have begun as barbarians.[25] That Greeks were superior to barbarians is, as such assertions go, not a bad one, but it belongs to the realm of unscientific propositions that we call stereotypes.

Nature does not divide human beings into Greeks and barbarians; the task of asserting such a division is left to us. Our statement is no doubt unproven, but it is not baseless; it is aided by the desire to believe that our way of life is superior and by the truth that some human beings and their ways of life are by nature superior. The desire and the truth become confused in the assertion, so that the natural superiority (of some humans) is asserted in the conventional superiority of a particular group. Natural superiority does not speak for itself; just as in the example of Antony praising Brutus by arrangement of Shakespeare, natural superiority needs conventional or political representation. It is no surprise that the Greeks assert the claim that they are superior to barbarians, but we should not in our superiority simply dismiss it as self-serving. All such claims are self-serving, including our claim to know better than the Greeks because we are more sophisticated and objective.

Nature supplies the human species with superior individuals who by nature take pride in their superiority. In a wolf pack, one wolf may turn out to be dominant, but with human beings, the difference between best and average is by nature much greater than is the case for other species. But nature by itself is indifferent to the superiority of these few, and it has to be asserted in the face of nature's indifference if human beings are to have any importance. And if human beings are to be important, they must be so as individuals in their own names. In such individuals the rest of us can take pride, so that pride in being superior may be dispersed among humans generally; but pride is always dispersed to some particular part of humanity above the rest, as to Greeks over barbarians. Human assertiveness is always intentionally divisive, our group against yours; hence it is always political. Man the political animal unites himself with other men by dividing himself from other men. Every political association is deliberately partial by excluding the rest of humanity and determinedly partisan by thinking itself to be a superior way of life. Thus the standard of nature is by nature contestable; at least in human affairs, nature does not yield a single, obvious standard for us to see and adopt.[26] Although Aristotle says that man is by nature a political animal, he also says that there are by nature several regimes, not one; bees make one kind of beehive, but humans have a choice of regimes.[27] This does not mean that there is no best regime; there is one, and it is the regime of the wise. But the best regime requires too much virtue and too much philosophy, and it will not be recognized as best by enough people with enough power to bring it into existence and to keep it alive. Those who reject nature as a standard because they believe that a standard, in order to be a standard, has to be unequivocal can be excused, for they share in a widespread error characteristic of modern thinking. But let them investigate the possibility that modern thinking, being too impressed with exactness and too confident of its own superiority, underestimates the need for human assertiveness. The classical thinkers see it better.

Assertiveness has its basis in a brutish quality we have already mentioned, called by Plato *thumos*. In the *Republic* he presents *thumos*, the bristling snappishness of a dog, as the outstanding feature of the guardians or rulers of the just city that he constructs. A dog defends itself, its master, and its turf; and *thumos* is a part of the human soul that performs the similar function of defensiveness. As a dog defends its master, so the doggish part of the human soul defends the human ends higher than itself. In this defense the paradox is that the lower defends the higher and thus asserts the value of the higher. Instead of having reason defend itself in the calm statement of principles and the careful progress of an argument, the reasonable person often gets angry as his *thumos* takes over the defense of its supposed master, reason. In adding up the characteristics of *thumos* detailed by Plato we find ourselves on the rough, not the gentlemanly, side of manliness.

Thumos, Plato says, has no natural end beyond itself; it is blind and wants only independence. It is what gives us personal pride and makes us individuals, as if each of us were self-sufficient. Having no end, it is reactive to outside intrusion and seeks to get even with intruders. Yet *thumos* is also expansive and has sympathy for its own kind. It needs to live with those for whom it has sympathy in order to establish trust, which is *thumos.* It loves to do what it is willing to do; so *thumos* is acting in accordance with one's own will. It is the basis of both friendship and enmity, and Aristotle remarks that one becomes most angry with one's friends. *Thumos* is frustrated when evils are present and at ease when they are absent. Since you cannot question yourself while defending yourself, *thumos* is essentially self-satisfaction. *Thumos* makes the soul insist on itself and, precisely when insisting on itself, offer to sacrifice itself so as to be unbeatable. The ultimate sacrifice is the ultimate defense. When the low in you defends the high in you, it will want to save you by putting all of you, especially the high, at risk. This is the price of using a brutish thing for your self-defense. It would be more rational to restrain your *thumos* from risking your being, but can you successfully defend yourself without risk? *Thumos* is nature's tool for rescuing man from nature's indifference to individuals. Sex allows individuals to reproduce not themselves but other individuals. *Thumos* allows you to insist on yourself, sometimes against the children you have produced when you get angry with them.[28]

Aristotle draws a distinction between *thumos,* which is uncultivated, and the habit of a virtue. For Aristotle, courage (= manliness) is a virtue, the first of the moral virtues that he discusses in his *Ethics.* There he marks off courage from the *thumos* of a wounded beast, with which it is often confused. *Thumos,* Aristotle says, is spurred by pain and blind to danger, and though it cooperates with courage it falls short of it. Courage is distinctively human, as it is a virtue deliberately chosen like the other virtues and for the sake of the noble. Still, Aristotle says that courage, coming from *thumos,* appears "most natural." It appears spontaneously, and the first, most obvious meaning of "natural" is what moves spontaneously by itself. In his *Ethics,* Aristotle is concerned to describe and promote moral virtues that transcend animal spirits and natural temperaments and that require habituation or nurture. In discussing courage, he does not comment on the etymological connection between courage and maleness or on sex differences in courage. He implies that being male is neither sufficient nor necessary for courage. As a virtue, courage transcends maleness as well as brutish *thumos*. In discussing courage as a moral virtue, Aristotle has nurture transcend nature, understood as the brutish, unreflective part of humans, for the sake of the noble, which is only for humans. The noble itself, because it varies, is not said to be natural. Here nature is not the guide, for moral virtue appears to be above nature.[29]

In the part of the *Ethics* on moral virtue (Books 1–6), Aristotle wants to define, preserve, and promote moral virtue as an end in itself and hence noble. He does not want to seem to allow excuses for not exercising a virtue, such as the excuse of being a woman, of having a nature that makes courage difficult. He refers to each virtuous person impersonally, such as "the courageous one," in order not to imply that moral virtue is the possession of the male sex. For the sake of moral virtue Aristotle implies the possibility of a gender-neutral society in which all are required to be virtuous. It is a very different gender neutrality from ours, but it has the similar effect of constraining the pretensions of males. The lesson that not only males are virtuous is less needed today because maleness is no longer in charge of our morality. Yet males, being bumptious and presuming by nature, still need it in some degree. If we convince ourselves that manliness need not be, we will conclude not that males have no nature but that they are by nature sensitive. And so we would blind ourselves to the need to educate them in sensitivity. The practical measures taken in our schools to make boys more like girls are based on the premise that boys by their nature start out unlike girls. Gender-neutral schools have to be schools in gender neutrality.

In Aristotle's *Politics,* however, the picture changes from his *Ethics* and the sex difference becomes relevant. We learn at the very beginning that the city is composed of households and that the household has relationships of male and female and of master and slave. Both these relationships are natural, for Aristotle at this point defines master and slave as equivalent to the mind (ruling) and body (ruled). He adds that although female and slave are "by nature" distinct, the barbarians confuse them, and then, as we have seen, he quotes the poets asserting that it is fitting for Greeks to rule barbarians under the assumption that barbarian and slave are the same. The difference between Greek and barbarian is what might be called an assertive distinction, one in which the first term is asserted as superior and all the rest is herded indiscriminately into the second term.[30] The household, with its two natural relationships that ought to be distinct, suddenly confronts us with a problem, for male and female must be coordinated with master and slave. Male and female as such ought to be equal, both being necessary for reproduction, but the other relationship of master and slave, or mind and body, gets in the way. The barbarians make the mistake of equating female and slave, while the Greeks answer by mistaking barbarian for slave. In coordinating, the barbarians make an error, says Aristotle, and the Greeks make a poetic assertion that is also an error (though not said to be). What is "by nature" is not so clear as we might think.[31]

The situation is clarified later (at the end of Book 1) when Aristotle gets around to discussing the household within the city as opposed to its condition before the establishment of the city. We now see the difference that politics makes for nature and nurture. The government of the household, Aristotle says, is in the hands of males but as ruling over free persons, the husband ruling "politically" over his wife and in "kingly" fashion over the children. The city, the political, compels the males to treat the rest of the household as free, no longer as slaves as in primitive times. Indeed, why should males always rule in the household, Aristotle wonders, since both sexes can share in what he calls "gentlemanliness" (*kalokagathia*)? We might wonder about the same thing and venture to say that husband and wife might rule in different things, but Aristotle says that ruling and ruled differ in kind, not degree. When we look at souls we see that "by nature most things are ruling and ruled," and this applies to the deliberative capacity (which is the capacity for ruling) and the moral virtues. A woman has the deliberative element but it lacks authority (*akuron*).[32] This seems little different from the lack of aggression and assertion in women compared with men that we have studied in the science of our day. As to moral virtues, both men and women have them, as accords with the *Ethics;* yet they have them differently, there being a ruling and a serving courage and similarly with the other virtues. Moral virtue is affected by the fact of ruling — by politics.[33]

To illustrate the point, Aristotle singles out the virtue of moderation and quotes a poet saying (not asserting) that "silence is an ornament to woman," though this is not so for a man (*aner*). Let us rest for a moment on the quotation so as to give an idea of the intricacy and depth of Aristotle's text. The quotation comes from Sophocles' play *Ajax* and from a scene in which Ajax is about to leave his tent to do something extremely foolish that will bring him to ruin. His girlfriend Tecmessa tries to calm him and persuade him to stay, but as Ajax leaves regardless, he calls over his shoulder "silence is an ornament to woman."[34] Here is a woman superior to her man in intellect and in deliberative capacity but in comparison to him *akuron*, lacking in authority, neither for the first nor the last time in the relations between the sexes. The pregnant silence of intelligent women watching men making fools of themselves casts a pall of helpless regret over many manly deeds. One thinks of Raphael's portrait of such a woman, *La Muta* — the Mute who in her eyes understands everything. But the men who rule do not listen.

Wisdom is necessarily impotent, and Aristotle himself is in the same situation as Tecmessa. Unable to rule and lacking authority, the philosopher has to watch manly men be manly and while criticizing their excesses, he tolerates and even endorses their often misguided forwardness. Like a woman, he serves as a measure of manliness, appreciative of its capacities and aware of its limitations. As judge of manliness he transcends it but does not try to replace it. He can offer advice to manly rulers but not with confidence that it will be listened to. As to their title to rule he remains silent, apparently unlike his friend Plato who in the *Republic* proposes replacing them with philosophers. Actually Plato, too, has no reasonable hope that this proposal can ever be effected.

Since for Aristotle moral virtue depends on your station in life, he consents to sexual roles. As women do not have the authority, the political capacity, of men, they are, as it were, elbowed out of politics and ushered into the household. There women find more to do than reproduce, as in the original, primitive household; by rearing children, women now share in the perfection of citizens. Their political nature expands and corrects their primitive nature. Meanwhile the male rules because of his greater authority, even though he may be constituted "contrary to nature" in this regard (for nature does not always achieve its intention). Aristotle notes that the ruler "seeks to establish differences in external appearance, forms of address, and prerogatives"; these are the conventions of male authority known to the Greeks as nobility and to us as "patriarchy" by which, one supposes, male rulers make their authority known or, in some cases, conceal their lack of authority. The conventions of authority give it a certainty that its doubtful natural basis in the greater authority of males does not have. For human purposes nature needs to be supplied with more exactness than it has by itself, yet this addition is made possible by nature, as it accords with the human being's political nature.[35]

Why is male authority so necessary to the city? Male authority supplies the military element in the city, and the military is needed both to maintain the regime and to defend the city against external attack. To maintain the regime, those who want it to continue must be stronger than those who might oppose it; the most stable regime is the one Aristotle calls "polity," the regime dominated by those who bear heavy arms (the hoplites). "For those who have authority over arms also have authority over whether the regime will last or not."[36] These are the ones who also preserve the city against attack, thus preserving the city's freedom and the freedom of all citizens within it.[37]

Which of the several types of regime a city may have is also a matter of assertiveness, and Aristotle examines the claims about justice that are typically present in political debate. Although in every regime those who want the regime must be stronger than those who do not, authority in a regime does not simply come from strength or from the military. Every regime claims to be just as well as having supporters and defenders who are stronger than its enemies. These claims are not merely registered at some office, like a claim of property; they are asserted in a debate or dispute. To all, justice seems to be equality, but it is a *certain* equality, not equality in general. Justice is a certain benefit for certain persons, for example, the well born, the free, or the wealthy, and justice should be equal for persons equal in one or several of these particular qualities. But this certain equality has to be *asserted,* Aristotle specifies, because it will be disputed by another equality opposed to the one asserted, as the claim of the free must be asserted against that of the well born and the wealthy. Aristotle himself in his office of political philosopher enters an assertion on behalf of virtue, usually ignored in political dispute on behalf of the other claims.[38]

Assertiveness in debate does not require the bodily strength of a hoplite or soldier, as an arguing orator may be a scrawny weakling, but it does require a quality of soul, mostly male. In the very justification of power that transcends power by giving a reason for power, the agent of transcendence is a quality mostly male. Men are superior not only in war but also in war-like speech, in what we call "polemics." Every regime is founded on the result of a polemical dispute, featuring rival assertions as to what is meant by justice.[39] We see better now why the women's movement in America, for all the power of its oratory, preferred to make its claims for justice with the much less assertive methods of raising consciousness and changing the language.

In sum, we see how far Aristotle is from Rousseau's blunt differentiation of the natures of women and men that crams the sexes into separable, easily identified "natural" roles. Aristotle does indeed defend sex roles, and he is still further from the gender-neutral society than he is from Rousseau, for, like Rousseau, he deliberately exaggerates their naturalness. But he leaves much more to politics than does Rousseau, and he does not share the aggressive, deterministic naturalism that Rousseau deploys for our ready consent. A quick survey of what Aristotle says of men and women outside the *Politics* and *Ethics* will disclose the complication as well as the upshot of his thought. I do not aim to do more than suggest what a deeper study might discover. To do this much I ask readers to suspend their suspicion of Aristotle on account of his alleged misogyny, his ill repute as the ancient enemy of modern science, and his having lived long ago.[40]

If we begin with psychology, we see that Aristotle, like Darwin, finds similar characters for male and female animals across species. These characteristics are most developed in human beings, but their naturalness is supported by their appearance in other animals too. In content they remind us again of the stereotypes we have discussed, as the central difference seems to be that females are softer and less spirited than males. Being softer, the female is quicker to be tamed, more receptive to handling, and readier to learn; she is naturally a follower in the low sense of being easier to control and in the high sense of being eager to learn. All females are less spirited (have less *thumos*) than the males, except, Aristotle allows, for female bears and leopards, who are "more manly" than the males. Females are also "more vicious, less simple, more impetuous, and more attentive to the feeding of the young," while males, being more spirited, are wilder, simpler, and less cunning. Switching suddenly to wives, Aristotle says that a wife is more compassionate than a man and more given to tears but also more jealous, scolding, and given to fighting. Females love and hate more strongly than males, and they are more shameless and lying, more ready to deceive, more wakeful, more afraid, less active, and eat less than males.[41] Apart from the remark about eating, Aristotle does not refer to the weaker bodies of females. Though they have less spirited souls it does not appear that they have weaker souls. Females have strong desires, but having less spirit, they satisfy their desires indirectly, or as Aristotle says more frankly, with cunning and deceit. Females are more controllable than males, but this means they can control themselves. They must deal with males who have stronger bodies but whose spirit makes them simple and unsuspecting, if more rigid and harder to control. A spirited person, indomitable and therefore full of himself, is more sociable and consequently, perhaps, easier to fool.

All this has the ring of truth. Aristotle reveals what is the natural cause underlying the behavior we see in human beings, and in his sudden insertion of a remark on wives, he also shows how the underlying nature is connected to what we see every day. In maleness and femaleness nature so to speak develops itself, as the male/female characters are most developed in the highest species, where they are mixed with reason — for example, complaints! Of course the complaints of a wife presuppose that she is not a voiceless slave and that her female nature benefits from a degree of freedom. A degree of cultivation must be present. But it also suggests that nature is inescapable and that wives are not going to stop complaining, as indeed they have not. In the gender-neutral society, we have seen, they have all the more reason to complain, given the unequal sharing of household work. More fundamentally, Aristotle suggests to us that the sexes are not autonomous but related, hence that the ideal of autonomy put forth by the women's movement will not work. Women see themselves in relation to men, and men, who are more spirited, have a need for women that they often do not care to admit. The sexes are complementary but men often do not appreciate this and behave as if they were autonomous. Women who would try to imitate men in their supposed autonomy are not well advised, as they trade their womanly sense of reality for a delusion that is not even congenial to them. By referring to wives, Aristotle perhaps indicates his conclusion from male and female characters that women are by nature better suited for the household than for acting in public. But he does not say this. Nature is pliable as well as inescapable.

Aristotle reaches his conclusions about male and female characters without discussing reproduction, as do the sociobiologists, the Darwinians, and Rousseau. Aristotle's survey of the psychology of males and females does not depend on strategies of reproduction, nor does it issue in sexual harmony—quite the reverse, in the mention of complaining wives.[42] Yet male and female do form a unity in generation, discussed in another work of Aristotle's, *Generation of Animals*. Born of male and female, we are, all of us, androgynous as well as male and female: "things are alive in virtue of having in them a share of the male and of the female."[43] Aristotle's account of generation has attracted criticism because he finds the role of the male superior to that of the female. Any male, we believe, who thinks such a thing must be diverted from truth by hatred of women. The form of a human being, he says, gets into the material when the semen of the male implants form in the material of a female, both being necessary but the form more necessary. But Aristotle, as always, has a reason. According to his physics, the form of a thing is in its material, not above it; and the form of a thing, more than the material, is what makes it that thing.

Yet if the form of a thing is in the material, it might seem that females are enough by themselves. Aristotle actually asks the question put by some feminists as to why males are necessary, and to say the truth, his answer is not very powerful.[44] Reason, the specifically human element, is said to come from "outside," not from the male. How can this be if the form is already in the material? Let us leave this puzzle, remarking that Aristotle, like Darwin, has trouble reconciling mind with what is not mind. Does reason come from outside, meaning outside nature, or is it within nature and thus combined with the authority of the male? It's not that men are smarter than women but only that being separate, men are taken to be the source of form though not of reason, which is sexless. Reason needs some way to make itself effective in nature, and perhaps this is done through the authority of the male. Perhaps men, more pushy than women, naturally *think* they are smarter. In the *Metaphysics,* Aristotle says more agreeably to us that men and women are not "other" but in the same species, though different.[45]

From the standpoint of the gender-neutral society, and when Aristotle is not carefully read, he may appear sexist; but in his male-dominated society he does what he can to tame the pretensions of manly males and to let them see the worth and necessity of women. He says in the *Politics* that "moderation and courage differ in a man and a woman," there being a higher standard of moderation for a woman and of courage for a man.[46] We note again that "courage" in Greek is manliness; but moderation is not said to have anything to do with "womanliness." We may guess that Aristotle did not want to spoil moderation for men by using a name that associates it with women, though the same need does not apply to women in regard to courage. Manly men have a prejudice against women that women do not reciprocate with a prejudice against men. Yet despite the sex difference, the result is to hold both sexes to account for moral and citizen virtue. Although yielding something to the natural characters of men and women, Aristotle does not give in to them, and he makes it clear that both sexes are equally human. To do this he uses nature, in a complicated way, as a guide for reforming the male-dominated society he inhabited.

Aristotle says in his *Ethics* that man *by nature makes a pair* more than he is political, and just before this he says that man (*aner*) and wife appear to have friendship *according to nature*. By nature is spontaneous, without reflection, and is evidenced by the fact that the family is more necessary than the city and by the pairing of other animals. According to nature, however, is the use of nature as a guide, with reflection. Nature can be used as a guide by a single individual, but in society it is political; the use of nature is made authoritative for a city by its regime. Democrats will believe that democracy is according to nature and will want a democratic society, including a democratic family; oligarchs, the same with oligarchy. That is why Aristotle in this context speaks of different kinds of family by the names of regimes—monarchical, aristocratic, oligarchic, timocratic, as well as democratic.[47] Thus the family is in a sense more natural than the city, but it is formed politically within a city, hence according to that city's sense of justice. Aristotle says more generally elsewhere, in a dark passage very hard to interpret, that natural justice is part of political justice.[48] He seems to mean that nurture appropriates a view or opinion of nature and makes it authoritative for that city (or, we would say, society). Insofar as nature is merely spontaneous, men transcend nature, making friendship out of pairing, but in doing so they use nature as a guide, not always wittingly but with some degree of reflection, and they impose their interpretation on *nature* as well as on their society.

Nature allows itself to be understood as a whole in partisan interpretations, variously, and by regimes. For Aristotle, human beings transcend nature with the aid of nature and with a view to nature. They do not get altogether above nature nor do they conquer nature.

It is time to return to the definition of manliness now that we have seen it to be both within nature and asserted against nature. It is within nature as spontaneous *thumos,* an animal quality we have not yet finished describing; and it is asserted against nature when human beings, especially males, show their dissatisfaction, above all in politics, with what is given to them and is therefore merely spontaneous. Assertiveness is what makes manliness "transcendent," to use Beauvoir's word in a more adequate way than she, because of her ignorance of Plato and Aristotle or lack of common sense, was capable of. We began provisionally in chapter 1 with a definition of manliness as confidence and competence in the face of risk, expressed sometimes irresponsibly as the disdain of the manly man for the effeminate and incompetent and sometimes responsibly in his willingness to take charge when others hang back. Both disdain and taking charge are assertions of superiority, the one nonpolitical or against politics, the other political. But why do manly men feel so superior? Is the manly assertion of superiority justified?

In the *Ethics* Aristotle declares that courage (= manliness) is a virtue shown in battle. A battle has two sides and courage can be found on either side. Courage does not depend on the justice of the cause in which it is displayed, so that seemingly even a tyranny could have the courage of its soldiers enlisted in its behalf. To go further, even a tyrant could exercise courage in his own behalf. Should we say that courage as such does not care about the use to which it is put? And yet courage is a noble virtue and it is hard to accept that virtue is divided against itself, the virtue of courage being indifferent to that of justice. In *High Noon,* for example, Gary Cooper's courage is distinguished from that of his gunslinger opponents by its union with the justice of defending the town. Although Aristotle wants us to join noble and good in the notion of gentlemanliness (*kalokagathia*) that he often invokes, is it yet possible that what is noble is not necessarily good?

In the *Politics* Aristotle shows that courage is indeed questionable for its character of self-assertion. The "self" being asserted is not only compatible with tyranny but in its desire for superiority has an inherent element of tyranny. To see this let us return to Aristotle's "assertion" that there are several regimes—a point he has to assert because one could easily be tempted to believe that there is only one true regime, the best regime.[49] In these regimes the rulers make claims to rule, for example, in democracies and oligarchies that democrats and oligarchs deserve to rule. These claims are asserted against other regimes and are therefore inherently exclusive, as we now say, of the "other." "For all fasten on a certain justice" but not the whole of it, and so they exaggerate. The democrats claim that all justice is equality, the oligarchs that all justice is inequality. "They judge badly," Aristotle says, because they are judging themselves and most men are bad judges of their own things.[50] Their assertiveness, we see, has become possessiveness. Aristotle does not leave his statement at this, for despite the possessiveness of humans he wants to insist on the distinction between the correct regimes, which aim at the "common benefit," and the deviations that do not. He does not want to let it be concluded that all regimes are bad and that there is no hope for just or decent behavior in politics. Later (in Book 7 of the *Politics*), however, he shows in a discussion of imperialism that the possessiveness of regimes affects the correct ones as well as the deviants. For if some regimes are better than others, and if the political life is the happy life for human beings, why should not the best regime exert itself to rule over its neighbors, or indeed over all inferior regimes anywhere they may be?

Here in Aristotle's imagination would be a world state or empire held by the best regime. And the same applies to an individual: "When another person is superior on the basis of virtue and of the power that acts to achieve the best things, it is noble to follow this person and just to obey him."[51] The latter description applies to the take-charge responsibility of the manly man and the former, to the regime that the logic of his manliness would bring about—a world tyranny. When examined, manly assertiveness reveals an element of tyranny not only in the deviant regimes but especially in the best regime. Politics in its manliness has a problem it cannot resolve: the manly men in taking responsibility for others cannot stop themselves from ruling their inferiors and from treating them as slaves. Their very goodness, when it is responsible, compels them to compel others so as to make them good too. These others may be inferior, but are they not free? And the responsible may be superior, but are they not tyrants? Their assertiveness, it seems, is necessarily self-assertiveness and insofar as it is active involves them in never-ending war to establish and maintain their rule over the irresponsible.

This shocking conclusion (I have made it more explicit) from a supporter of manliness surpasses anything that has been said today by those who want to make manliness obsolete. It might come as a surprise to people who think that supporters of virtue like Aristotle are naïve. But Aristotle does not let it stand. Against this conclusion, he reminds us that war is not for its own sake but for the sake of peace, that the active way of life does not necessarily have to do with relations to others, and thus with responsibility, and that thinking does not have to do necessarily with results but much more with thoughts that are complete in themselves and with study that is complete in itself.[52]

Interesting, is it not, that Aristotle puts the subordination of war to peace in company with the subordination of action to contemplation and of practical thinking to theory? Politics, even or especially the politics of responsible men, cannot keep itself moderate since terrifying imperialism can result not only from the evil schemes of evil men but also from virtuous actions by those superior in responsibility. Politics has to be shown moderation by those who know best how to live in peace, the philosophers. It is not that philosophers are irresponsible, though they do not live as confidently as John Wayne. They show their responsibility as philosophers and also as manly men by setting limits to the responsibility of active men, reminding them as if with the attitude of women that peace is better than war. They make it clear that risks should be taken not endlessly for greater advantage or thrills but for what is less or not at risk, the satisfaction of a good life that is complete in itself by not depending on other men. Their self-sufficiency is the fullest definition of peace available to our reason, for the kind of peace to be found in politics is always compromised by the *deeds* as well as, though not as much as, the *misdeeds* of manly men.

Plato takes a similar view of the perils of courage, and somewhat more openly than Aristotle. Plato has his spokesman in the *Laws* say that respectable regimes like Sparta and Crete go wrong in putting courage first; it is the fourth, the lowest virtue, the smallest part of virtue. In the *Republic,* Socrates adopts courage as the virtue that defends the city by preserving its law and opinion concerning which things are terrible. Courage keeps the people or the guardians of Plato's city believing what they should; it is a kind of color-fast dye that serves as an instrument of the legislator to sustain the laws he makes, an official virtue. But unofficially, without the legal function that provides its cover, courage is far less attractive. When in the *Republic* Glaucon and Adeimantus challenge Socrates to defend justice, they both place courage on the side of injustice: for Glaucon, courage is the character of the perfectly unjust man, and for Adeimantus it is only lack of courage that keeps men from doing injustice. Courage, says Protagoras in the dialogue named for him, is the virtue most isolated from the other virtues because it is often found together with vices. It is the virtue of a man as distinct from a woman, the virtue of being able to carry out the affairs of the city and to have your way by benefiting friends, harming enemies, and not letting others have their way with you, says Meno, another dialogic partner of Socrates. His idea is that pushing other people around, a pleasure not given to women, is what makes manly virtue seem so great. The liberty of doing anything one thinks fit in one's city, for example, killing or expelling those one doesn't like, is just what Polus and Callicles, characters in the *Gorgias,* consider to be tyranny. Plato lets these accusations be made against courage without contradiction from Socrates, who confines himself to praise of official or "political courage." That is Plato's quiet way of confirming the truth that courage is essentially tyrannical. Political courage is a "virtue" made of a vice, a conventional virtue that deserves our quotation marks of doubt. Socrates says that courage will receive a "finer treatment" later.[53]

The finer treatment proves to be the same amazing disclosure we have seen in Aristotle — that there is such a thing as philosophical courage. Socrates says in the *Republic* that courage is the rare faculty of those who are both quick and steady enough "to be able to bear the greatest studies." All others are cowards. In the *Meno* he says that "by supposing one ought to inquire into things he doesn't know, he would be better, more manly, and less lazy" than by supposing that it's impossible or one shouldn't inquire. And in the *Phaedo* he says that "what is called courage" is especially (not only) characteristic of philosophers, as they fear death less than other men.[54] These disparate statements made in different contexts would have to be reconciled, and compared with Aristotle's, in a longer study than I present here. Philosophical courage stands out more starkly in Plato than in Aristotle because Aristotle does not want to call all the nonphilosophers "cowards" as does Socrates; to avoid doing this he has invented "moral virtue" as opposed to "philosophical virtue" in order to shield the virtues of most human beings, because they are necessary though inferior, from direct and constant contrast to the wisdom of philosophers.

Courage (manliness) seems to be the least intellectual of virtues, requiring little reflection and not only available to the stupid but also more congenial to them than to the geeks who spend their days and nights in libraries and laboratories. It has its basis, we have seen, in *thumos,* the quality of bristling that human beings share with other animals. Let us examine *thumos* a little more closely, as it is forgotten or not well understood in modern psychology. As animal bristling, *thumos* defends the body and its environs or territory. To do so, however, it risks the very body it defends. By risking the body it rises above the body, showing willingness to sacrifice the body, to die, for the sake of its defense. In this animal quality we see the transcendence of oneself and one's sex that we have been looking for. *Thumos,* very much embedded in nature, is the means for transcending nature. Beauvoir was wrong to regard transcendence as simply rising above nature, for nature gives us this faculty in common with barking dogs. Of course, human beings develop it further. In us, willingness to sacrifice one's body transforms the body into an ideal, a bodiless cause to which we can be devoted. *Thumos,* with its paradoxical risking of what one wants to defend, is the natural basis of "idealism" in human beings. It is wrong to believe that the desire for self-preservation is more natural than courage because it derives from primitive fear for the body, as in the concept of "self-preservation" that we inherit from the liberalism (the so-called realism) of Hobbes and Locke. Nor is idealism unprompted by nature as in the later liberalism of Kant. The realism to correct and restrain the manly idealism, which is the first, reactive response to a threat to one's body has to be taught, just as much as courage has to be taught to those who would run from danger. Realism has its own ideal in the picture of hard-nosed calculation that does not always come easily to the natural coward in human nature. Realism, too, is in its way a kind of manliness.

Taking the argument a step further, we see that the ideal of manliness established on the basis of *thumos* allows you to think that you are not defined by your body. If you are willing to sacrifice your body, you have a certain abstractedness from it even though you began by defending it. In the act of defending your body you reject it, and your rejection as it becomes an affirmation of your abstract self defines you better than the body you wanted to protect. Following out this thought, one could wonder whether all definitions have to do with bodiless, invisible conceptions resembling Plato's ideas or forms.[55] Is not the *what* of a thing an abstraction from its particular embodiment or name? The *what* of a thing differs from its *who,* as a human being differs from an American. But when an American asserts his or her worthiness to be defended, or his worth, it is as a certain kind of human being. Asserting the who leads to defining the what, and it takes courage or manliness to do either task. Assertiveness in the face of risk is a task of political responsibility requiring that one not be overcome by fear for one's body; defining a universal quality requires finding what is common and necessary while overlooking the accidental and idiosyncratic. There is something aggressive about a manly man, and also something single-minded and abstract. Now we begin to see the connection that social psychology was unable to establish between the two male qualities, low and high, of aggression and single-mindedness.

We have seen that in Aristotle, the philosopher's courage sets limits on the statesman's courage and keeps his sense of responsibility from enveloping everything in his view. In three of Plato's dialogues we have seen it suggested that true courage is being able to bear the greatest studies, that it is inquiring into things one doesn't know, and that the philosopher is the most courageous person because he is the least afraid of death. Having collected these thoughts, we could easily go further, but perhaps it will be enough if we look briefly (as always) at the one dialogue of Plato's, the *Laches,* that is devoted to defining courage. It will show the difference as well as the similarity between philosophical and political courage.

The principal characters in the dialogue are Socrates and two Athenian generals, Laches (for whom the dialogue is named) and Nicias. The two generals are veterans of the battlefield whom one would suppose to be experts in courage, the virtue of the battlefield, but of course they are both easily defeated by Socrates and shown to be completely incapable of defining a thing they ought to know familiarly. The dialogue ends without a definition, leaving readers in the same condition as the generals and, so he says, as Socrates himself. Let us look closely at one example given in a speech by Laches suggesting what courage is. Before speaking of courage Nicias and Laches are asked by Socrates to consider whether learning to fight in armor is worthwhile. Nicias thinks it is, and Laches thinks not. To prove his point Laches tells a story about Stesilaus, a professional in armor-fighting they had just been watching, who had once made himself ridiculous in an incident of war. Stesilaus, holding a spear and fighting from a trireme against another ship, found his spear entangled with the other ship's tackle, and unable to free it, he was dragged along his own ship until he was obliged to let go of the spear and watch it be carried off—to the laughter of the men on both ships.[56]

Here is the case of a weapon that turns against its wielder, so that he does not know whether to hold it or let go. The weapon is a picture of courage, which saves you but also takes hold of you and endangers you unless you drop it, at the cost of ridicule or shame. It is also a picture of philosophical courage in holding on to the logos or logic of a speech even though it endangers your body (your opinions and your self-esteem) and subjects you to ridicule as it carries you away from the deck on which you are standing. Laches and Nicias suffered, like Stesilaus, when Socrates forced them to accept the logic of their remarks and to recognize the contradictions that left them with nothing to stand on. Following the logos as Socrates commands can sweep you away from familiar ground, and to do this while suffering the ridicule of onlookers requires courage. In the *Republic,* Socrates says that urbane folk might ridicule his proposal for having men and women exercise naked together, but the true standard of ridicule should not be convention but what is natural.[57] It takes courage for a philosopher to stand up to the ridicule of those who defend whatever is conventional, to the peer pressure of one's inferiors—a quality Laches lacks and others considered manly often lack. In chapter 4 I said that in following the logos the philosopher abandons the manly desire to win, but it can now be seen that he vindicates it. For to win in manly fashion one must not bluff and avoid argument. The bluffer who merely asserts is actually a kind of sneak who does not truly win.

Yet if it makes sense to speak of philosophical courage, the difference between that and ordinary courage is clear. In the Platonic dialogues Socrates seems always to be in command, yet he frequently reminds his interlocutors that not he but *the logos* is in command. One should always follow the logos, the argument, and not try to bend it to suit one's purposes. Most human beings bend the argument so as to protect their interests, like those who Aristotle says judge badly when speaking of justice. When you try to protect your interests you let go of the argument, as Stesilaus let go of his spear, in favor of your home ground. You drop the what to protect the who. Philosophy being devoted to the what, it abstracts from the who, from the particulars of human life, indeed, from human life itself. Socrates in the *Phaedo* defined philosophy, everyone knows, as learning how to die, that is, learning how to follow the logos or the what, and to abstract from the facts of your particular life. Attention to those facts is what we call realism, especially womanly realism as shown in the following he/she joke. He: "The trouble with women is that they always take things personally." She: "Doesn't apply to me!"

We have likened women to philosophers more than once, but insofar as women take things personally, they are unlike philosophers. Such women are useful for keeping an eye on things philosophers neglect. But those particular allegiances that I collect together and call the who need to be defended as well as watched over, and this is the job of ordinary courage or manliness. Manliness defends and asserts the who, while philosophy criticizes all of one's interests, loyalties, and property from the standpoint of the what that abstracts from them. Ordinary courage abstracts too, but it stops abstracting at a certain point, for example, at Americans, before it reaches the further philosopher's abstraction in human beings or beyond in nature, which contains human beings.[58] Look again at Beauvoir's distinction between transcendent and immanent, which I have criticized: the transcendent being the traditionally male rejection of nature or whatever is given; the immanent being the traditionally female acceptance of it. We see that the philosopher transcends because he rises above the particulars of one's self; but he also criticizes manly transcendence for not getting above those particulars. From the philosopher's standpoint, manliness transcends by the willingness it inspires to risk one's life, yet it is immanent because it remains self-assertive. It refuses to leave the self behind; it insists on the who. Yet the philosopher can see that manly self-assertion is a necessary and on the whole good feature of human life. Why? Because, as we saw, "men need to feel they are important." Someone needs to examine whether this claim is justified, and it is the job of the political philosopher to reconcile the truth of human importance with the assertion of our self-importance — the what with the who. The ultimate is not enough for us human beings; we have our particular identities as well as our human nature. We do not know how to live a universal, abstract life apart from the details, mundane and vivid, that women cling to and men insist on. Women and men are needed together but separately for the appreciation of details in our lives because in clinging one fails to defend and in insisting one fails to cling.

Let us return to the confidence of the manly man who thinks he knows he can handle a risky situation. What kind of knowledge is the basis of his confidence? If the knowledge is an art like other arts consisting of rules that can be taught, then confidence would arise from this art and not from manliness. An example is the movie *Fargo* discussed in chapter 3 in which a woman professional does the work of a policeman without either the erratic boldness or the fuss and display of a manly man. Generalizing to all trades and occupations, we could say that professionalism makes it possible to transcend manliness in the sense of leaving it behind. The possibility was anticipated in Plato's *Republic,* where the rule of the guardians is presented as an art, the art of justice, and the conclusion drawn that the sexes should be treated equally and sex roles abolished.[59] If ruling can be fixed in rules, then all you have to do, to be a policeman or to rule, is to follow them. You need to be prepared, having learned the rules, and you need to keep steady in applying them. But there are rules for learning and for keeping steady in emergencies that women can absorb as easily as men (in *Fargo* it is implied that women are better than men at following rules).

The difference between Plato and *Fargo* is that the former is meant as an impossible utopia and the latter, however far it goes, as contemporary if still imagined fact. The reason for that difference is to be found in the modern notion of rational control discussed in chapter 6, which expands the capacity of rules. No longer does science have to rest content with studying nature and natures like Plato and Aristotle, but it can include within its ambition the application of science in what we call technology. No longer does science have to coexist with chance, and thus tolerate the limited relevance of science to human life, but with technology it can now overcome chance and achieve genuine control and full relevance to human life. Or is this latter condition still an aspiration? It is not a mere aspiration, one can say, because of the successful results produced by modern science. But again, can we replace manliness with a PhD in crowd control? Can manliness be professionalized?

The tests determining a profession or (in Plato's term) an art are that it is teachable and that it produces results.[60] Consider first the teachability of manliness. Among professions we know that an excellent coach in athletics might be a mediocre player, and that a good doctor might be a bad teacher of medicine; in neither case does the discrepancy detract from the profession. Now could a coward teach manliness? That we immediately want to say no shows how much we take manliness for granted. One would have to be manly or courageous oneself, we think, in order to serve as a model to others. Serving as a model is different from teaching because it is prior to teaching, a presupposition that cannot itself be taught. The woman policeman in *Fargo* was a professional who followed the rules and occasionally taught them to her foolish male colleagues, but did she not have a manly spirit in addition? She could easily have served as a role model to some women, at least, who do not believe in sex roles (since you mustn't think of yourself as a woman) but do believe in role models (since you must think of yourself as a woman).

Moreover, manliness, unlike the professions named above, is sometimes good, sometimes bad; this ambivalence seems to be in its character. Machiavelli remarks that "very rarely do men know how to be altogether wicked or altogether good." His example is a certain vicious tyrant of his time guilty of incest and murder — surely a promising beginning — who did not know how to go all the way to killing the pope and attending cardinals on one occasion when he had the chance. He did not know how to be altogether bad, and it is not clear whether the cause was lack of knowledge or lack of the spirit that would prompt him to seek the knowledge.[61] "Virtue" according to Machiavelli seems to be a combination of knowledge and manly spirit, each factor encouraging the other to do its worst, or its best. To be altogether bad you have to be good at being bad, thus good. Manliness is irreducible to knowledge because knowledge does not supply the means to accomplish its end. For that you have to be manly. A more recent writer, Céline, more expert in attaining the altogether bad than Machiavelli's hapless tyrant, published a novel, *Voyage to the End of the Night* (1932), whose hero, Ferdinand, adopted cowardice as his virtue. Ferdinand could find nothing in the world worth defending with courage; so, better to be a coward. But at a certain point his friend Robinson showed him that he lacked the courage to keep his eyes open and "to go truly to the bottom of things."[62] Getting to the end of the night with the most determined cowardice calls for courage.

Manliness, unlike knowledge, is a habit (Aristotle's term) easy for some to acquire and difficult for many others, as it seems to develop a natural predisposition that you either have or lack. The manly or courageous person, we have seen, takes responsibility in a risky situation. In doing so he declares himself indispensable and his manliness impossible to teach to others. If manliness were teachable, one successful pupil would be as good as another, just as one professional can be substituted for another. If manliness is not teachable and yet necessary, a teacher cannot be sure how his teaching will be taken; he cannot be sure whether his pupils will have the gumption to make good use of his lessons. In this way the teacher's responsibility is circumscribed by the pupil's manliness or lack thereof, and you cannot blame the teacher for the pupil's failures.[63] Yet for this very reason the teacher — the political philosopher — must beware of the teaching he puts in the way of manly men. What will manly types do with doctrines that call on their manliness and not their moderation? That is a question philosophers should ponder, especially ones like Machiavelli, Nietzsche, and Céline who set up shop on the road to the altogether bad, or beyond good and evil, or at the end of the night. A word of warning, too, should be delivered to the feminists who are too busy with their own careers to have time to criticize manly men and want to give over that task to psychologists with their "anger management." The many irresponsible thinkers of modern times are divided, roughly, into those who expect too much from reform and those who have given up on reform. In contrast to them and elevated above them stand Plato and Aristotle, from whom one can learn to respect manliness in the measured sense of giving it its due and remaining wary of its dangers.

The other test of an art is producing results. In this, Plato's dialogue offers two possibilities for us to consider, each presented by one of the two generals. Laches says that manly confidence is shown in performance, the speech or reputation of manliness justified by the deeds that follow. Nicias, admirer of Socrates, has a more philosophical view; manly confidence should be judged by its consistency, its speech justified internally by its consistency with other speech. Laches likes it when he finds harmony between someone who is "truly a man [*aner*]" and his speech, as for example Socrates himself, whose worthy speech is validated by his deeds in a battle—a retreat—in which both he and Socrates fought.[64] The harmony Laches speaks of would have to be created by adjusting speeches to manly deeds after they have been done; it would amount to the primacy of deeds and the relegation of speeches to the function of rationalizing deeds. It goes with Laches's view that courage is a quality humans share with wild animals, and it sounds like suspicion, by a John Wayne type, of fine talk as opposed to action. Laches's view makes manliness prior to knowledge and distinct from it—and morally quite dubious. When in our own regard we sink to the level of lions and foxes (two kinds of wild animals, by the way, whose qualities only humans can choose between or combine) we are down there with Machiavelli.

When Socrates asks Laches to define courage, Laches comes up with steadfastness of soul, a virtue that applies not merely to war, he agrees, but to such things as fighting desires and pleasures.[65] Courage in holding fast, it appears, is a virtue to be found in all virtue. Socrates goes after him to show that his definition fails because his speech is inconsistent. Laches wants courage to be steadfastness, but he also wants it to be just and noble, especially noble. Socrates gets him to see that being steadfast in a foolish action is not courageous since folly is not noble and courage is noble. Yet prudent calculation, for example in spending money, is not noble either. Courage seems to require calculation, as to seek the best place to fight, yet utilitarian calculation (as we would say) is the death of courage. Laches cannot find a solution to this difficulty, and Socrates leaves him and us readers at a loss.

Nicias has a solution that says courage is knowledge or science and nothing but knowledge. Courage is wisdom, which is every other virtue as well. For Laches, every virtue is courage because all virtues require steadfastness. For Nicias, courage is wisdom, which is all virtue. Both see courage as universal in human actions, Laches as the prerequisite to all actions and Nicias as part of the end of all actions. When Nicias defines courage as knowledge of terrible things and of things inspiring confidence, Laches intervenes in disgust. Farmers, he asks, know terrible things in regard to farming, but does this make them courageous? Such people, Nicias responds with his mimic of Socrates, would have to know whether it is terrible or not to die. Laches says this is the knowledge of the diviner; the diviner is courageous because he knows whether death is terrible.[66] Thus the knowledge of science needs to be supplemented with divination of things science cannot know; divination has the same function of controlling chance that we see in modern technology. It would destroy courage by transforming it into calculation, in this case utilitarian calculation of the will of the gods. Socrates does not make this point but leaves it to be inferred. He simply shows that Nicias has broadened courage so far that it has lost any definition of its own and become the whole of virtue. Again we are left at a loss.

Plato gives us a choice between animal courage that is too low, unable to state what is human in courage, and scientific courage that is too high, in effect destroying courage by eliminating risk. Unlike Aristotle, who makes courage into a virtue while limiting it to the battlefield, Plato gives it a wide scope but leaves us in a quandary between two wrong definitions. These are two diverse strategies to one end, taming the manliness of the manly males so much admired in ancient times. To us, they may seem too protective of manliness, but our reaction is biased by the fact that we live under modern liberalism with its allegiance to self-preservation, distrust of sacrifice, and calculated campaign against *thumos*.

In this book we have seen three ways of transcending sex differences: repressing the difference between male and female (chapter 5), ignoring that difference (chapter 6), and respecting the difference (chapter 7). Let's drop the first: repressing the difference won't work because manliness is in our nature and cannot be repressed. The very act of repressing it is manly, and in a bad way. Respecting the difference is most in accord with our natures, but then we have seen that nature does not prescribe exactly how she is to be respected. There is room for choice, which means for convention, and the conventions of our day are not those of the Greeks or of the Greek philosophers. We need to respect modern liberalism as well as sex differences; we need to both respect and ignore sex differences. That is a very general statement I shall try to make more specific in my conclusion.

Unemployed Manliness

I am not going to end this book by giving out pointers on how to live, though I suppose I could. I could tell young women not to disparage motherhood in the hearing of a man they want to attract. If you do, you will make a man think his mother is being disparaged and he will compare you to her—just what you want to avoid. I could tell young men that women want to be taken seriously almost as much as they want to be loved. To take women seriously you must first take yourself seriously and after that ask them what they think. And when they tell you, try to *listen*. But this is not a let-me-help-you self-help book. My book is for thinkers, and I say this not so much to flatter ourselves that we can think originally as to get us to address the problem of manliness.

The problem of manliness is not that it does not exist. It does exist, but it is unemployed. It exists in our human nature and in the human nurture that, I have argued, accompanies and cooperates with our human nature. Perhaps you don't agree with what I have told you from Plato and Aristotle, and you would rather have pure, unadulterated nature in the way of modern science. In that case, consider the evidence for manliness in social psychology and evolutionary biology, which show as best they can that the stereotypes of men and women are basically correct. Men and the manliness they exude are still around and are not going away despite our gender-neutral society. There is no need to call for men to be men and demand that manliness be revived as when William James called for a moral equivalent to war. The actions of the Islamic fascists are proof enough that despite our civilization there remain barbaric cutthroats waiting to assault us. To oppose the horrifying excess of manliness we need not just to imagine the moral equivalent of war but to wage a real war. Here is a useful employment for manliness. For this and other uses manliness needs some respect, some wary respect.

Unemployed manliness is nothing new in the world, and in particular it has not been caused by feminism. As we have seen, feminism would rather join in manliness than oppose it. The entire enterprise of modernity, however, could be understood as a project to keep manliness unemployed. The goal of modern liberalism was the rational state (chapter 6), a state that completed the long-standing attempt at the rational control of nature and human life that began with Machiavelli and culminated with Hegel. The rational state does not arise from or depend on manly assertiveness but merely reflects an objective recognition of all the rational advances that in the course of history have become real.

Yet the first modern thinker, Machiavelli, began from the observation that the world in his time suffered from "ambitious idleness."[1] Ambition there was, but it was idle because it had nothing to do. The reason for this was the domination of the world by Christianity, a religion that puts the honor of gaining salvation in the next world above worldly honors that engage the ambition of manly men. The world was effeminate, and Machiavelli set out to revive it. His method was to do his best to exclude or at least minimize the influence of the next world over this one and thus, one might think, restore manliness to its ancient ferocity. He did speak of "virtue" (*virtù*) in a way that would make one think he was taking the lid off moral virtue in Aristotle's sense. But his "altogether bad" (discussed in chapter 7) was not altogether manly. In order to confine human ambition to this world Machiavelli had to strip it of its claim to rise above this world by being good. He saw correctly that anyone who wants to do good will end up yearning for more good than is possible in this world. The yearning for good must be closed off with a new loyalty to this world or to the earth and with a new animus (*animo*) in its defense. Machiavelli's *animo* replaces the classical *thumos* and simplifies it. Whereas *thumos* tends to idealize itself and to offer sacrifice of the body it defends to a higher goal, *animo* has no such paradoxical complication; it is a spirit that keeps its eye solely on the preservation of its own body. Instead of idealizing itself Machiavelli's *animo* reduces itself to a brutish aggression that has no yearning in it. All it wants is more acquisition since however much you have is never surely enough. To acquire more, men must play the fox as well as the lion, and more the fox than the lion. They must resort to fraud as well as to open force, that is, to indirect means of the sort that women use as opposed to manly directness.[2] Men must act "according to the times" or as we would say, according to the situation, with flexibility. Flexible is what a manly man is not, nor does he use fraud. If we compare classical *thumos* and Machiavelli's *animo* (in which fraud is central), we get a better idea of the difference between aggression, a composite, simplifying term that blurs this distinction, and manliness.

With Machiavelli the modern idea of "security" was born, the very antithesis of manliness. Although he began by deploring the fact that manliness sat idle, he ended by keeping it there. Machiavelli tried to simplify manliness so as to make it more effective. Manliness henceforth would be occupied with making humans more powerful rather than making them better. Machiavelli called this "prudence," but I have to say it was not wisdom. Wisdom lies in recognizing our need for perfection as much as for power. Such wisdom can be sought in classical philosophy, but it can be found, too, in the Bible or in the outlook of the ordinary religious person who does not try to simplify human life in order to control it but lives his life more fully and with greater awareness than the Machiavellian.

After Machiavelli the modern notion of rational control took shape. It can be seen developing in the series of philosophers studied in chapter 6, as each of them seeks new and better means toward the same end of "increasing the bounds of human empire without end." That is Francis Bacon's phrase, taken from the motto of his scientific utopia and directed against the church and any other institution or doctrine seeking to limit the bounds of human empire. In the early phase of modernity, rational control meant human as opposed to divine control, and the religious question was foremost. Again it might seem that manliness would be an obvious ally of human government as opposed to divine rule, since we have seen (in chapters 4 and 7) that manliness has among its higher functions the assertion of human importance. But modern thinking does not want to cooperate with manliness and does not care for *thumos*, especially in its ambitious, higher range where it supports a kind of sacrificial idealism. Modern rational control differs from the classical philosophy that we have seen to be rather friendly to manliness and opposed only to its conspicuous vices, not to its essential, paradoxical nature. Our rational control, fearing courage more than fear, will do without manliness and will seek to supplant it and to keep it unemployed by means of measures that encourage or compel behavior intended to be lacking in drama.

Thus we have replaced the manly man with the bourgeois, a character who has several faces, none of them manly. One is the professional already discussed as the model of gender neutrality. A professional is formed by uniform education and judged by objective criteria, not tested by manly deeds. Although one professional may be better than another, all professionals are as such equally professional; one can be substituted for another, and a woman can take the place of a man. "Professional calm," not manly passion, characterizes him or her, and neither he nor she succumbs to anger as do those who might be tempted on occasion to throw a punch at some SOB and thereby behave "unprofessionally." Professionals treat each other with "professional courtesy" but never with chivalry. Another unmanly type we harbor is created by modern technology. We have the same arts as the Greeks, such as carpenters and others, including lifeguards and bodyguards, resembling the fighter in armor of the *Laches,* who turn courage into an art. But with progress in science and technology we have expanded the range of art and added many new arts — the various repairmen, for example, who fix things that break (since rational control needs control over its failures).

People obsessed with their health, divided into devotees of physical or mental health, bring rational control into their own lives. They are unmanly because they want longer or less troubled life rather than a short, eventful life in the noble manner of Achilles. Meritocrats are unmanly to the extent that they think their merit should be recognized and promoted through an educational system that does the manly job of self-assertion for them by giving them honors they do not have to claim or fight for. Rational control is afraid of exposing itself and thereby being compelled to take responsibility for its rule; so it claims only to represent those whom it controls. "Representatives" of all kinds, including lawyers, actors, agents, and various intermediaries, are unmanly because in representing you they discreetly avoid asserting themselves and are content with a mere percentage of the transaction. Politicians who do what they think right are manly; those who do what you think right are unmanly. Commerce is unmanly because it is materialistic, willing to settle for gain rather than victory, for trade-offs rather than justice. The commercial life rejects sacrifice and rests on calculation of advantage. The most famous defense of manly chivalry is an attack on modern calculation. Edmund Burke laments over the imprisonment of Marie Antoinette during the French Revolution, that no one was man enough to avenge her: "But the age of chivalry is gone. That of sophisters, economists and calculators has succeeded; and the glory of Europe is extinguished forever."[3]

Burke's exclamation in praise of chivalry amounts to a defense of aristocracy against the foremost modern revolution on behalf of democracy. It suggests that democracy, too, can be understood as anti-manly. There is manliness in the frank exchange of views characteristic of democracy, where one man meets another, as we say, "on equal terms," if not as a perfect equal. But democracy is anti-manly insofar as it cooperates with modern progress in rational control, for example, the rational control of society so prominent in the French Revolution and its aftermath. When democrats abolish the customs and traditions of the old regime that they believe have kept the people unfree and unequal, they must put a new authority in place, the authority of reason. Reason does away with the anomalies and idiosyncrasies that protected aristocracy so as to treat everyone the same, democratically; hence followed the Napoleonic code, the bureaucracy to enforce it, and the education to form the bureaucrats — all features of rational control.

What in manliness makes it the target of modern progress? We may sum up the characteristics of manliness as they have been developed, for all of them are obstacles to rational control. Manliness must prove itself and do so before an audience. It seeks to be theatrical, welcomes drama, and wants your attention. Rational control prefers routine and doesn't like getting excited. Manliness is often an act of sacrifice against one's interest, hence concerned with honor and shame rather than money and calculation, to which rational control makes its appeal. Whereas rational control wants our lives to be bound by rules, manliness is dissatisfied with whatever is merely legal or conventional. Manliness favors war, likes risk, and admires heroes. Rational control wants peace, discounts risk, and prefers role models to heroes. Manliness is sometimes vulnerable and fragile but doesn't care to admit human weaknesses. Rational control prefers your weakness to your strength, your guilt to your pride. It does not address your reason but looks to your fears and hopes, your passions, to contrive its "incentives" (no one needs or responds to an incentive to be manly). Manliness likes to show off and wants to be appreciated. And it is critical of those who do not measure up to its high standard. It is generous but judgmental. Rational control would rather not be seen in public, and it dislikes high standards because they cannot be stated in rules or made universal. It is more forgiving of avarice than anger, and it saves its praise for the future and its blame for the past.

To be sure, thanks to the failures of rational control, manliness has not disappeared. We have professional sports in which manliness is more apparent than in, say, professional education, but our athletes, so much more concerned for getting money than spilling blood, could never be confused with gladiators or knights. Our meritocracy is qualified by the policy of "affirmative action" on behalf of those who might not make the grade without help. Affirmative action is manly if you do it for yourself, otherwise not. Commerce is unmanly, yet there is manliness in the spirit of commercial enterprise, so that Tocqueville can say that "Americans put a sort of heroism into their manner of doing commerce." The Yankee clipper ships he was speaking of in 1835 went to China and back in order to sell a pound of tea for one penny less than the competition — heroes and mercenaries at the same time.[4] Americans are also salesmen, and salesmanship, one could say, shows the manly side of commerce. When salesmen tout the virtues of the product they represent, they are inclined to exaggerate, and boasting is a good thing from the manly point of view. These facts, especially the popularity of sports, testify to the inevitability of manliness however checked or reduced by rational control.

We see that the disparate features of manliness discussed in this book and just now summarized have in common the fact that they express — better to use my favorite word, *assert* — the importance of the individual.[5] Human importance consists of the importance of human individuals. When human individuals get together, their importance attaches to individual collectivities, a country, for example, or a party, an entity with a proper name. Manliness is responsible for our individuality. And because individuality must be asserted to, and against, other people, its creation is essentially a political act. To make an identity takes effort to impress those who may contest it, sometimes in battle, sometimes through persuasion. Manliness is never selfless; it may be nobly engaged in a cause, but it always has some self in mind.

Rational control tries to free itself from an individual self, which it sees as arbitrary, distracting, entangling, and irrational. So it works to diminish the importance of the individual. Professionalism makes one individual replaceable by another, for example, one doctor by another; technology makes available machines that work for anyone who submits to the requirements of their use; democracy gives authority to the multitude, it used to be said, or to the majority as we say—a certain number of undefined individuals. Individuals such as these are exchangeable for one another as they have no individuality. Lacking individuality is the way rational control likes us to be, so that we can be governed without regard to our foibles and without encountering foolish excuses for resistance. Rational control believes in individualism rather than individuality, an individualism of individuals effectively alike, as in Hobbes's state of nature. Nowadays it often speaks the language of diversity, but it believes in egalitarian justice that leaves manliness, the cause of diversity, unemployed. In speaking of rational control I have personified a concept rather than identify the individual thinkers who in various, often conflicting ways promoted it. I have in mind the modern project that begins with Machiavelli and Bacon, long before feminism got started, we may say, with Mary Wollstonecraft in the late eighteenth century.

The danger in unemployed manliness comes from too little manliness and too much of it. Too little manliness would follow from the success of the modern project of rational control, for the very meaning of rational control is to do away with erratic, obstreperous manliness. The great Tocqueville dwells on this possibility; he sees democracy in a long trend toward similarity in its citizens and conformity in their behavior. He wrote more than a century and a half ago, yet his insight gave his predictions such force that he remains by far the best authority on American or any other democracy. Tocqueville feared the gradual construction of a new democratic despotism, an "immense tutelary power" over the people that "would take away from them entirely the trouble of thinking and the pain of living." To oppose this trend he would rely on every democratic institution of self-government that strengthens individual pride. What we lack most is not humility but pride, and he says he would trade several small virtues for that vice. And although he agreed that democratic equality makes men unwilling to accept anyone's authority, hence intractable, he says he admires "that obscure notion . . . at the bottom of the mind and heart of each man" — can we call it *thumos?* — that serves political independence.[6]

Tocqueville holds on to manliness as the remedy for democratic despotism; it is the spirit behind the democratic institutions and practices he describes. Yet if we turn to Nietzsche, we find the danger of too much manliness. Nietzsche denouncing modern softness sounds much like Tocqueville deploring democratic despotism; in his attack on herd morality he repeats Tocqueville's fear that each nation will be reduced to "a herd of timid and industrious animals of which the government is the shepherd."[7] But in the face of the same threat, Nietzsche turns his back on Tocqueville's moderate politics and calls for a cultural transformation, a transvaluation of values. He remarked, as noted in chapter 3, that men will rather will nothingness than not will, and with his call for will to power, he illustrated the danger he warned of. He would surely not have agreed with the Nazis, but he inspired them. And if he did not inspire the communists, he showed what they were about. The communists spoke of "the struggle for peace," but they were always much more interested in struggle than in peace. They were war lovers as much as the Nazis and with the same ruthlessness. The Islamic radicals of our century overflow with the same spirit; though they say they are pious, they use the name of God to strengthen and serve their own will, not to direct it.

Our judgment on manliness has to take its bearings from the dangers it poses on both extremes, too little and too much. If you keep your eye only on one extreme, you back unawares into the other. The modern philosophers behind the project of rational control were mainly afraid of *thumos* and its incitements to idealism; they laid the ground for a dull, bourgeois society lacking in both love and ambition. Nietzsche, in revulsion against this uninteresting landscape, released manliness from all restraint except the self-restraint needed to strengthen one's self. Of course those who followed him forgot what was noble and embraced what was brutal. Yet our situation is not so different from the one faced by the classical philosophers. True, our extremes are more extreme than in their time. We are, or we claim to be, more rational than they, and at the same time the history of our totalitarian regimes shows us to be more willful as well. The uncompromising reason with which we have destroyed divine authority is accompanied by the untrammeled will that has destroyed self-government and been guilty of genocide. Can it be an accident that the first atheist regimes in human history were the first totalitarian regimes? Still, our experience only confirms the conclusions of Plato and Aristotle on manliness that the true way is in the middle between too much and too little. In this general strategy they can be our guide.

How can we employ manliness usefully in our gender-neutral society? One thing we cannot do is to go back to a society in which women are kept in the home and men are free to leave it. Women restrained, men free; this is how that traditional arrangement looks to us now. One could say, with a nod to Rousseau, that women were more in charge than they appeared to be, and men less. Some conservatives, women and men, may be inclined to go back in this direction, and to see whether this reactionary change might be possible let us look briefly again at Tocqueville. Tocqueville paints a beautiful picture, too beautiful to be true, of how men and women lived separate but equal in America in his day.

Tocqueville congratulates American women for willingly accepting the confines of the household, the "yoke" of marriage, in view of natural differences between the two sexes. American women, he says, tolerate this condition "courageously" because they have chosen it; they often display a "manly reason and a wholly virile energy." So if you were to ask Tocqueville (he imagines) to what he attributes the prosperity and force of the American people, he would answer that "it is to the superiority of its women." Although American women cannot escape the domestic circle, they are never forced to leave it; so they retain "a very delicate appearance and always remain women in their manners."[8] Women with the best of manliness who yet remain women, and democratic too!

Tocqueville's solution to the threat of democratic despotism is to encourage manliness, and part of that is to attribute manliness to American women. American women are manly precisely in bowing to their fate, because in bowing to it they choose it. He insists that their fate is equal to that of American men, though men perhaps are less inclined to look on their public lives as fated. It's a very complimentary statement, a nice try from a gallant and attractive man; but today, in a late stage of the democratic revolution that Tocqueville described so well, our democracy has placed the idea of separate but equal status for women firmly in the past. Praise for their courage in settling for domesticity will not convince them to do it when they are not compelled, and Tocqueville's description of American women — really an indirect argument to them — has been replaced by his friend Mill's statement of the reasonable case for women's equality, which ought now to satisfy reasonable women (see chapter 6). Mill does not explain the character of manliness or allude to the danger of democratic despotism when manly pride is lost; his statement is both radical and shallow but it is at least an argument, shrewd and good enough for us in our situation. For us, perhaps, an argument for women's equality merely adorns and conceals the fact that modern progress has not left much for women to do at home. A determined woman might live wholly absorbed in the tasks set down for her in Cheryl Mendelson's *Home Comforts,* but it would be her own choice, not necessity.[9]

Having firmly set aside the reactionary solution of separate roles, man in public and woman in private, an arrangement "traditional" to be sure — if you mean by that common to all human history — we abandon nostalgia and return to the gender-neutral society. The gender-neutral society was prepared by the series of anti-manly measures I have listed, but it was accomplished by feminism. What, in conclusion, should we think of feminism? Feminism is the culmination of rational control yet at the same time radically opposed to it. It culminates rational control by abolishing the sex differences, facilitating the management of human beings by removing the grand source of irrational insistence, manliness. Women are of course liberated but so are men. Women lose their hindrances, men their inhibitions — the ones that keep them from engaging in some rational activity merely because it's unmanly. This liberation applies not only to the mutual relations of the sexes but to every activity that has hitherto been distorted by manly blindness. Or is this not correct? Most men do not want to be liberated from their rights, now called privileges, though many may not miss their traditional duties. They may let women pick up the check or pay for themselves, but an equal share of the housework is harder to impose on men. To get this, feminists have had to rely on the sensitive male, willing to cooperate in establishing the gender-neutral society, but they have not done much to construct the sensitive male.

Believing in social construction and denying any natural obstacles to it, they think that social construction is necessarily *easy*. They are right to see that a "male" is (in part) a social construction, but they are wrong to suppose that it's easy to transform men against their inclinations. It can be done but it's not easy and will achieve only partial success, as we see in the division of housework. And besides this irritating reluctance in men to do what is clearly their share of a common task, there's the danger of an explosion of extreme manliness such as we see in Islamic radicalism or, less sensationally but more regularly, in instances of male violence.

The danger of extreme manliness is already within feminism itself, which is opposed to rational control as well as a late stage of rational control. If there are no essences, if all nature and human nature have been made amenable to rational control, then there is no reason in the way of the rational controllers to do what they will. The ultimate in rational control destroys the basis for rational control and thus leads to a release of the will from reason. Release of the will is usually dressed up by feminists (and others) in the word "autonomy," a concept from the liberal philosophy of Kant, a highly respectable source. Autonomy as understood by feminists, however, means freedom to make your own law, not considering yourself as a rational being legislating for all other rational beings as Kant supposed, but to suit yourself, or to construct yourself as the not-so-respectable Nietzsche wanted. In practice, autonomy means putting yourself ahead of your husband and your children. If carried to its logical conclusion, autonomy means tyranny, the will altogether unchecked. If carried part of that way, it liberates the manliness in men who after all can believe they are autonomous too and because of their manliness more likely truly and foolishly to believe it.

To be autonomous is the contrary of "contextual," the understanding of women that you get in common sense, social psychology, and Carol Gilligan. Women are contextual because in the context of men and women they are the weaker sex. If you are weaker you have to pay more attention to the context than do those who are stronger. I believe it really matters that women are weaker than men, and that is why I have mentioned the fact more often than a gentleman would have preferred. It matters even today when thanks to democracy women can call the police or get an injunction and thanks to technology they can use a gun. Recall that in the movie *High*

Noon, Grace Kelly was very fortunately able to use a gun in the shootout at the end to save her husband Gary Cooper. But this well-timed deed was exceptional and was meant to be. It shows what women can do, not what they typically do. Since women are weaker and have to look more closely at the context, they are more aware, more realistic than men. So it is not merely a question of power but of outlook. Perhaps—if one thinks in teleological fashion—there is a weaker sex so that one sex would be more realistic and not so self-important as the other, rather than supposing cynically that women have to be realistic because they are weak. Realistic is not inferior; it is a part of strength, especially when joined with manly enterprise.

I have said that the woman's movement was a manly enterprise, an assertive claim to rights long denied. But it was womanly in its choice of means, particularly in the idea of raising consciousness. It was also womanly in the character of the anger that fueled it. In Plato's *Laws,* the Athenian Stranger makes a passing reference to "bitter, women's raging" that invites our consideration.[10] Weaker than men, women have to be indirect in getting what they want; they cannot simply insist. With winning words they have to make others want to accommodate them; hence the different speech patterns of men and women described in chapter 2. When women are frustrated, they sometimes fall into "bitter, women's raging" that differs from men's anger in its implied recognition of vulnerability. They are raging at the necessity to be nice, at the fate they have been dealt. Men, in contrast, lash out, with the desire to punish and overcome the object of their ire as if they were unbeatable and not subject to fate.

Women are misled by feminism into mistaking themselves. They are told they have no weaknesses because they have no essence, no definition; hence they have no limitations. Women can do anything, young women are foolishly assured. They are also told to see their strength as weakness. To be prudent, cautious, modest, persuasive, undemanding, unselfish is unworthy of . . . what? An assertive male? An autonomous entity? Feminism has no understanding of womanhood; it leaves women without a guide and even tries to convince them they need no guide. What womanhood should be in our society I leave to a new feminism less fascinated with manliness than the feminism we have had. The radical feminism I have discussed is not what most women believe or practice, but it is the only feminism there is. Another, better feminism might begin from the idea that women, as many of them say, "want it all." They want a career and they want to be women too. They don't want to be defined, and they do. The challenge to a new feminism is to make sense of those two desires and unite them.

Our gender-neutral society needs to readopt the distinction between public and private that is characteristic of liberalism. In public it should be gender-neutral, in private not. In public it should not permit sex stereotypes to operate; in private it should admit that they are true. True means true as generalities, not in every case. The exceptions are women who want public careers that require and reward manly qualities and men who do not want them. Somehow I think that the female exceptions will be more numerous than the male, because men are by nature more single-minded, hence more public-spirited, than women, but let's not say that in law. The law should offer equal opportunity to men and women, but our expectations should be that men will grasp the opportunity more readily and more wholeheartedly than women. The reason for the difference is manliness, a fact of human nature but not for that reason an unambiguous necessity to which we must submit. We have the choice of how to treat it, and we should exercise that choice reasonably by respecting manliness and giving it employment. Our liberalism is a formal theory, one that offers rights that may or may not be exercised. The rights belong to all citizens, but since one is free to exercise them or not, citizens are defined formally without regard to characteristics that might make it more or less likely for the rights to be exercised. Thus citizens should be defined in gender-neutral terms. But in the private sphere, in society, we should think of men and women really, not formally. The personal, the real individual, should not be the political, the formal individual. Our individuals should not be autonomous choosers free to go either way or in any direction. They should have individuality arising from their many qualities, in particular male and female. Plato provides a model that we can apply to liberalism, so let's look at him one last time.

In one dialogue, the *Republic,* Plato shows a gender-neutral society in which the sexes are held equal because they are judged solely from the standpoint of justice as an art; and from this standpoint, one would choose the best regardless of sex to be educated as rulers. The best of men and the best of women would be chosen. In another dialogue, the *Statesman,* he proceeds quite differently and shows that men and women as counterparts need to be woven together in society.[11] For this purpose the best men and the best women would be chosen. Here Plato's spokesman (the Eleatic Stranger) speaks not directly of men and women but of courage and moderation (their virtues or stereotypes), and he says that the statesman needs to use the art of weaving to put them together. Since the art of weaving is a feminine, domestic art, we have the manly taught by the unmanly to be moderate. And as in weaving the warp and the woof are kept separate while woven together, so in society the two sexes will be mixed while remaining themselves. There is no attempt to make them the same, or androgynous. Each virtue sets limits on the other and in that way defines the other. If there were no moderation, courage would be unrelenting hardness; and if there were no courage, the moderate person would not resist any temptation and moderation would be softness. Each virtue needs the other in order to be itself! Is this not still true of men and women today?

Our liberalism (I mean the society of rights that is precious to us) contains both of these rival solutions in Plato: a neutral equality of sexes in our formal and public laws; an actual weaving together of the sexes in our private lives and in the way we think of the public. No bright line of division is possible in liberal society in regard to manliness, if only because manliness is responsible for bringing private matters to public attention. What is public can change, and the most recent change has been to make the public gender-neutral instead of male-dominated, a change that was the manly work of the women's movement.[12] In the private sphere of society, however, we should not look on people as gender-neutral, autonomous individuals all equally ambitious to become rulers or celebrities. We should consider them as "gendered," having a sex, and not one sex by itself but as the sexes are when they engage each other — as *married.* Of course we have same-sex relationships and even marriages, but the gays and lesbians so united try to compensate for the missing qualities of the other sex and thus show that sex is essentially twofold.

Individuals in our society should live as if, or to some extent as if, they were married, the men protective and authoritative as if they were husbands, the women nurturing and critical as if they were wives. Actually, if you look around, you see that men and women do live in this fashion. Even when not married they live as if they were married, guided by a vague sense of behavior appropriate to one's sex deriving often unconsciously from the behavior expected of one's sex in marriage. To be sure, not every woman is your wife, but she is potentially someone's wife and worthy of respect for that and not just because she is a fellow human being. Marriage is the social construction of the natural inclinations of the two sexes, and it includes, of course, virtues held in common as well as sex differences. Indeed, it is by being married that the partnership of the sexes is revealed, not by a notion of autonomy that finds community only in common, self-centered indifference or exploitation.[13]

Our gender-neutral society is, thankfully, much stronger formally in public law than it is actually in private. But so often in our private lives the two sexes live in embarrassment and confusion. This is the problem of legitimacy in the gender-neutral society that I discussed in chapter 1, with special reference to housework. No doctrine or set of ideas within our liberalism justifies the behavior to which men and women are naturally inclined and in which they need moral education. So both sexes think that they must repress those inclinations rather than develop them, and our public education tries to get boys to play with dolls, and girls to play with . . . no, for some reason not guns. A better education would make children and grown-ups more aware of themselves, and it would be franker and less manipulative than what we attempt now. A better public doctrine would give greater respect to the way we want and ought to live as two sexes in private. It should be expected that men will be manly and sometimes a bit bossy and that women will be impressed with them or skeptical. It should be expected that women will recognize manliness with a smile by checking it while giving it something to do or, on occasion, by urging it on. It should be expected that women, with a woman's art, will weave us together once again.

This is a liberal country, "liberal" in a broad sense that includes the liberals and conservatives of our politics. But in constructing the gender-neutral society it has been following an illiberal impulse by trying to impose the liberal state upon liberal society. The liberal state is based for the sake of impartiality between the sexes on an abstraction; it is neither male nor female. But human beings cannot actually live that way, vigilantly stifling every thought or impulse due to one's sex. To protect women's careers we need a gender-neutral state, but the gender-neutral society gives no respect to the liberal distinction between state and society or between public and private. It assumes that the principle of our public lives must rule our private lives too. It makes women think that they are unfaithful to the cause of women if they do not behave like men. Not so: the point that women are capable in public occupations has been made. Women should be free to enter on careers but not compelled—yet they should also be expected to be women. And men should be expected, not merely free, to be manly. A free society cannot survive if we are so free that nothing is expected of us.

Notes

CHAPTER I. THE GENDER-NEUTRAL SOCIETY

1. Tocqueville, *Democracy in America*, I 2.10, 381. Tocqueville, however, was a critic of both gender neutrality and feminism; *Democracy in America*, I 3.12, 574.
2. Alexander Hamilton, *Report on Manufactures* (1791), in *Papers of Alexander Hamilton*, ed. Syrett and Cooke, 10:255, emphasis added. Cf. Adam Smith, *Wealth of Nations* 1.2, where the difference of talents is said to be the effect, not the cause, of the division of labor—hence not "nature" but social construction.
3. Faludi, *Backlash;* Rothman, "Was There Ever a Backlash against Women?"; Hochschild, *Second Shift*.
4. Williams, *Unbending Gender*, 1–6.
5. Or is that not the case? See Flanagan, "How Serfdom Saved the Women's Movement," 109–28.
6. Burns, Schlozman, and Verba, *Private Roots of Public Action*, 16, 155, 181–87, 375–76. See also Giele, "Gender and Sex Roles," ch. 9 in *Smelser,* ed. *Handbook of Sociology;* Bianchi, Milkie, Sayer, and Robinson, "Is Anyone Doing the Housework?"; Williams, "Family-Hostile Corporation," 41–42; Hochschild, *Second Shift*, 8, 127, 219, 222; Schor, *Overworked American*, 85, 103; Sigel, *Ambition and Accommodation*, 99.
7. Friedan, *Feminine Mystique*, ch. 1; Schaub, "On the Character of Generation X," 15–18.
8. Mansbridge, *Why We Lost the ERA,* 187–99.
9. Okin, *Justice, Gender and the Family,* 171.
10. *Statistical Abstract of the United States*, table 615; the figures are for the year 2000. Query to Ernie Boch, Jr., prominent Boston car dealer: "Why don't more women sell cars?" [Answer:] "They don't apply. They're intimidated by the industry. It's totally male-dominated." Boston *Globe,* July 20, 2003. That is, of course, a totally male interpretation of a kind rarely printed in the newspapers today. See Maccoby, *Two Sexes,* ch. 9.
11. Mendelson, *Home Comforts*. The first chapter of this excellent book begins: "I am a working woman with a secret life," thus gravely compromising her loyalty to the gender-neutral society. For the contrary, official view see Schor, *Overworked Ameri-*

can, ch. 4. According to *this* excellent book, women are unnecessarily devoted to housework because they do not put an economic value on the time they spend doing it. They should look on housework as if they were being paid to do it, as if they were employees and not their own boss.

12. Rhoads, *Taking Sex Differences Seriously,* 9–11, 35, 193–94, 222.
13. Herland began two thousand years ago after a volcano and a slave revolt killed off almost all the men, and the young women then slew the few remaining men, their "brutal conquerors." Gilman, *Herland,* 54. Unlike Plato's *Republic,* which features manliness and accepts war, Gilman's *Herland* is warless as well as manless. It has no *eros,* no *thumos,* and no philosophy.
14. Irving, *Alhambra,* 169. Shakespeare, *Macbeth* 1.5.7; on this, Shakespeare's play most concerned with manliness, see Benardete, "Macbeth's Last Words," 63–75. "Have you no bones?" is what women in New Guinea say to unmanly men; Mead, *Male and Female,* 27.
15. Tocqueville, *Democracy in America,* Intro.
16. Comparing "market work" men do with "family work" women still do, one intelligent observer says, "This is not equality." Williams, *Unbending Gender,* 3.
17. For Garry Wills, John Wayne "became the pattern of manly American virtue." Wills, *John Wayne's America,* 30. In reality as on film the manly villains in Wayne's movies were much more numerous than the heroes. For the unromantic lowdown on the typical American cowboy, see Courtwright, *Violent Land,* ch. 5, "The Cowboy Subculture."
18. Rubin, *Families on the Fault Line,* 74.

CHAPTER 2. MANLINESS AS STEREOTYPE

1. I switch to "sciences" in the plural because they differ in their conclusions. But it is important to remember that science aspires to unity and completeness, to which it will be led, at least in principle, by a single method. That method, requiring the universality and exactness of mathematics, does not respect the difference between "social" and "natural" science—a difference that common sense as distinct from science might want adopt in order to tolerate inexactness in social science.
2. Lippmann, *Public Opinion,* chs. 6, 7.
3. Allport, *Nature of Prejudice.* Allport's social-science view of stereotypes removes the awareness of authority, in this case democratic authority, that is visible in Lippmann's title, *Public Opinion.* All stereotypes collected together would form the beliefs supporting what the Greeks called *nomos,* the ruling law and custom of any society. On the history of the concept "stereotype," see Fiske, "Stereotyping, Prejudice, and Discrimination," in Gilbert, Fiske, and Lindzey, eds., *Handbook of Social Psychology,* 2:357–64; Ashmore and Del Boca, "Conceptual Approaches to Stereotypes and Stereotyping," in Hamilton, ed., *Cognitive Processes in Stereotyping and Intergroup Behavior,* ch. 1; Miller, *In the Eye of the Beholder,* ch. 1.

4. Allport, *Nature of Prejudice,* 33–34, 360–63, 372–77. The anthropologist Margaret Mead had written of sex stereotypes in 1949, in *Male and Female,* 31, 373, before the notion was developed in social psychology.

5. Sigel, *Ambition and Accommodation,* 14.

6. Haig, "Inexorable Rise of Gender and the Decline of Sex," 87–96; this is a survey of the use of sex and gender in more than 30 million titles of academic articles.

7. Maccoby and Jacklin, *Psychology of Sex Differences,* 355.

8. Shields, "Functionalism, Darwinism and the Psychology of Women," 739–54. See the account in Eagly, "Science and Politics of Comparing Women and Men," 145–58.

9. Eagly, "Science and Politics of Comparing Women and Men," 145–58. "Presentations of sex differences are fraught with political danger"; Eagly, "Reflections on the Commenters' Views," 170. See also her earlier book, *Sex Differences in Social Behavior,* 1–6. For similar statements see Williams and Best, *Measuring Sex Stereotypes,* 307; Moir and Moir, *Why Men Don't Iron,* 117, quoting Diane Halpern. And see the account in Rhoads, *Taking Sex Differences Seriously,* 17–22.

10. Eagly, "Science and Politics of Comparing Women and Men," 150; Halpern, *Sex Differences,* 82–9.

11. Tannen, *You Just Don't Understand,* 287. A category that won't go away is an *essence.*

12. Maccoby, *Two Sexes.* She concludes that "gender matters greatly" (287). She favors a "harmonious relationship" between two parents (313) and says that "there is every reason . . . to make each sex's choices as free as possible" (314). But does more choice make for more harmony?

13. Halpern: "It has been estimated that 50% of college women do not know the principle that water level remains horizontal." *Sex Differences,* 72–74.

14. Rhoads, *Taking Sex Differences Seriously,* 27.

15. Hall and Halberstadt, "Smiling and Gazing," in Hyde and Linn, eds., *Psychology of Gender;* and Eagly, "Science and Politics of Comparing Women and Men," 150.

16. Rhoads, *Taking Sex Differences Seriously,* 26–27, 46–54, 96–108; see also the summary in Pool, *Eve's Rib,* ch. 2; Schwartz and Rutter, *Gender of Sexuality,* 46–53; Thompson and Walker, "Gender in Families," 845–71; Geary, *Male, Female,* 146.

17. Rhoads, *Taking Sex Differences Seriously,* 9–11, 18–19, 35–41; Lueptow et al., "Social Change and the Persistence of Sex Typing," 1–36.

18. Rhoads, *Taking Sex Differences Seriously,* 24, 156, 195, 205, 263. Maccoby, *Two Sexes,* chs. 2, 3, p. 120; Williams and Best, *Sex and Psyche,* 36–57; Williams and Best, *Measuring Sex Stereotypes,* 275–87; Harris, *Nurture Assumption,* 218–39; Pool, *Eve's Rib,* 46–50; Tannen, *Argument Culture,* 168, 182.

19. Lakoff, *Language and Women's Place.* See the summary in Crawford, *Talking Difference,* 24–25. Lakoff herself makes a number of jokes in her short book. The Moirs say that women "use jokes as a way of making others feel comfortable," as opposed to men who use "insult, jest and innuendo." Moir and Moir, *Why Men Don't Iron,* 266.

20. Lakoff, *Language and Women's Place,* 7.

21. Tannen, *You Just Don't Understand,* 15.

22. Ibid., 88, 145.

23. Ibid., 225.

24. Ibid., 229

25. Cf. Lakoff: "We could shuck off deferential style just as we did hoop skirts and girdles." Quoted in Crawford, *Talking Difference*, 25.

26. (In a manly way?) I push this point further than Tannen does; see Tannen, *Gender and Discourse*, 7–12.

27. Ibid., 47–48, 85, 228.

28. Ibid., 294–95.

29. Eagly, "Science and Politics of Comparing Women and Men," 147; Halpern, *Sex Differences*, 59–97; Geary, *Male, Female*, 218–21, 289, 312.

30. See Mathell, Vingerhoets and Van Heck, "Personality, Gender, and Crying," 19–28.

31. "Laypeople, once maligned as misguided holders of gender stereotypes, are fairly accurate observers of female and male behavior." Eagly, "Science and Politics of Comparing Women and Men," 152. "This study confirms the folk wisdom concerning how women should act to be attractive to men." Maccoby, *Two Sexes*, 197. "Stereotypes are reasonably accurate assessments of the typical differences between men and women," Campbell, *Mind of Her Own*, 7, 123. See also Swim, "Perceived Versus Meta-Analytic Effect Sizes," 21–36.

32. Maccoby, *Two Sexes*, 40; Rhoads, *Taking Sex Differences Seriously*, 140; Campbell, *Mind of Her Own*, ch. 6. Here we see the intolerance of science for opposites; through misplaced economy it tries to understand insinuation as aggression. Science is also intolerant of exceptions, as when stereotype is defined as applying to "all individuals in the group" instead of most individuals. This is what a stereotype would be if it were a scientific concept; common sense does not try to be so exact. The phrase is quoted in Halpern, *Sex Differences*, 177.

33. Allport, *Nature of Prejudice*, 19, 171, 202.

34. McMillan, Clifton, McGrath, and Gale, "Women's Language," 556.

35. Maccoby, *Two Sexes*, 172–73.

36. Some feminists take a hostile attitude toward objective, modern social science, considering it to be an attempt to impose control and disparaging it as "phallic." I believe, as we shall see, that there is something in what they say, but they should at least in the first instance be grateful to its aid in the construction of the gender-neutral society.

37. Plato, *The Republic* 514a–517c.

38. Fiske, "Stereotyping," in *Handbook of Social Psychology*, ed. Gilbert, Fiske, and Lindzey, 2:357. See also Allport, *Nature of Prejuice*, 31–37, 171–73, who says judgmentally that a stereotype is the work of an in-group wrongly distinguishing itself above others and yet that those (such as he) who do not think in stereotypes use hesitant, "differentiated," categories.

39. Tocqueville, *Democracy in America*, 2 1.3, 3.1–5, 4.2. Manent, *Tocqueville and the Nature of Democracy*, ch. 5.

40. Some studies speak of "clusters" or "patterns" of traits; Ashmore, "Sex Stereotypes

and Implicit Personality Theory," 62; and Pettigrew, "Extending the Stereotype Concept," 313.

41. Mead, *Male and Female,* 34, 45, 47, 134, 143. Mead's book in no way departs from, and frequently reiterates, the general stereotypes we find endorsed by the psychologists' studies that women are nurturing, men are aggressive and achieving.

42. Eagly, "Science and Politics of Comparing Women and Men," 146. Psychology's change to a continuum was not a change on a continuum but a qualitative change.

43. "Men emit more task-oriented behaviors than women," Deaux and LaFrance, "Gender," in *Handbook of Social Psychology,* 1:805. You don't say! But what about Socrates — is he task-oriented?

44. Carol Gilligan remarks, in a "Letter to Readers, 1993" for a reprinting of her *In a Different Voice* (1982), that when asked what "voice" means, she answers: "By voice I mean voice." But in fact she doesn't mean "voice"; she means what people say characteristically when they assert themselves. In her book she says nothing about women's actual, dulcet voices. On Gilligan, see Maccoby, *Two Sexes,* 198–201; Sommers, *War Against Boys,* chs. 4, 5.

45. See Tannen, *Gender and Discourse,* 57, on the misleading character of "operational" definitions.

46. An instance of phenomenology can be seen in the work of Eleanor Maccoby when she distinguishes a clear distinction, male-female, from a "fuzzy set," masculine-feminine. You are either male or not, but you can be more or less masculine. Maccoby infers this distinction among distinctions from the way we commonly speak. But aren't fuzzy sets required for the sake of clarity? See Maccoby, "Gender as a Social Category," 762; also Gottfredson, "Why *g* Matters," 79–132; and Fiske on "moods," *Handbook of Social Psychology,* 2:390–92.

47. See Ashmore, "Sex Stereotypes and Implicit Personality Theory," in Hamilton, ed., *Cognitive Processes,* 40.

48. On occasion, social scientists find that an exception becomes necessary: "Sexual harassment is a pernicious form of gender-related behavior." Deaux and La France, *Handbook of Social Psychology,* 1:815. Steven Pinker insists on the impossibility or impropriety of inferring value from fact when the message of his book is to show the "downsides [value] of denying human nature [fact]." *Blank Slate,* 152, 164, 172, 194, 340.

49. Geary (and others he cites) cannot use unscientific words, such as "beautiful" or "good-looking," and so is obliged to speak of "symmetrical" as if it were the same thing. And why are men and women attracted to symmetry in each other? Because in the evolutionary past if not today, symmetry suggests good health, a useful quality in a mate. This is the imprecision known as reductionism: beauty is reduced to utility. Geary's useful book also contains repulsive nude drawings, resembling composite police photos of wanted criminals, of the ideal of each sex in the eyes of the other. For greater accuracy, why not print the centerfold from a girlie magazine and a photo of Cary Grant? Geary, *Male, Female,* 31, 132, 149, 151.

50. Camille Paglia: "Sexual freedom, sexual liberation. A modern delusion. We are hierarchical animals. Sweep one hierarchy away, and another will take its place, perhaps less palatable than the first." *Sexual Personae*, 3.

51. For example, Geary, *Male, Female;* Buss, *Evolution of Desire;* and Udry, "Nature of Gender," 561–73. Rhoads, a political scientist, speaks more cautiously of what "evolutionary psychologists think"; *Taking Sex Differences Seriously*, 27.

52. Aristotle, *Politics* 1284a15–18. "Where are your claws?" said the lions.

53. Andrew Sullivan, "The He Hormone; Testosterone and Gender Politics," *New York Times Magazine*, April 2, 2000; Rhoads, *Taking Sex Differences Seriously*, 30–34; Udry, "Biological Limits of Gender Construction," 709–22.

54. The very long time during which human nature evolved is known as the "environment of evolutionary adaptation" (EEA), as if in our time evolution had stopped. For practical purposes, it has stopped.

55. Darwin, *Origin of Species*, 16:48–49.

56. "And as Natural Selection works solely by and for the good of each being, all corporeal and mental endowments will tend to progress towards perfection." Ibid., 16:428.

57. Darwin, *Descent of Man* (1870), in *Works*, 21:2, 48–49, 65, 125–26, 128, 147.

58. "Strategies" is a neo-Darwinian term, not Darwin's, that glosses over the difference between an unconscious instinct and a conscious plan. "Genes" were discovered by Gregor Mendel.

59. Whereas human beings are *dominant* over other animals, men are *pre-eminent* over women. Darwin, *Descent of Man*, 21:556, 564, 605, 614.

60. Aristotle, *Nicomachean Ethics* 1162a17–34.

61. Nature's support of the double standard is argued today by neo-Darwinians. Symons, *Evolution of Human Sexuality*, 226–31; Ridley, *Red Queen*, 177–79; Pinker, *Blank Slate*, 251–54; Arnhart, *Darwinian Natural Right*, 136.

62. "The canon in Natural History [is] *Natura non facit saltum.*" *Sed facit species*, one could reply. Darwin also says that the species are "only well-marked and permanent varieties." But varieties are varieties of species. Darwin, *Origin of Species*, 16:233, 416, 425.

63. Darwin, *Origin of Species*, 16:44, 142; *Descent of Man*, 22:25, 61.

64. "The great break in the organic chain between man and his nearest allies, which cannot be bridged over by an extinct or living species, has often been advanced as a grave objection to the belief that man is descended from some lower form; but this objection will not appear of much weight to those who, from general reasons, believe in the general principle of evolution." Darwin, *Descent of Man*, 21:156.

65. Gould attempts to address the difficulty in gradualism with his theory of "punctuated equilibrium" in which evolution proceeds by stages instead of gradations. This is a step back toward Aristotle. Gould, *Structure of Evolutionary Theory*.

66. Note the greater precision of Thomas Aquinas over Darwin's "survival": "every substance seeks the preservation of its own being according to its nature," *Summa Theologica*, I–II, 94.2.

67. See the last pages of *The Origin of Species*.

68. *The Origin of Species* ends: "From so simple a beginning endless forms most beautiful and most wonderful have been, and are being, evolved." Matt Ridley, a neo-Darwinian, has written a book titled *The Red Queen* after the character in Lewis Carroll's *Through the Looking Glass* who runs very hard without getting anywhere because the surroundings move with her. The postmodern point is that when one species adapts, the others return the favor and the advantage originally gained is lost; progress, being relative, is not really progress. Progress requires a fixed standard of perfection. Ridley, *Red Queen.*

69. Darwin, *Origin of Species,* 16:145.

70. "The Female of the Species" has thirteen stanzas of which the seventh supplies this explanation for the phenomenon.

71. "Man is a social being," to be sure; but this is a species-characteristic of "inherited tendencies" acquired through evolution. Yet Darwin admits, without referring to politics, that animal (including human) sociability extends "only to those of the same association." *Descent of Man* 21:97, 108–9, 115.

72. Wilson, *Sociobiology;* Gilder, *Men and Marriage* (a popular treatment).

CHAPTER 3. MANLY ASSERTION

1. "The very essence of the male animal, from the bantam rooster to the four-star general, is to strut." Daniel Patrick Moynihan, *The Negro Family* (U.S. Department of Labor, March 1965), ch. 3.

2. Hemingway, *Old Man and the Sea,* 26, 66, 84, 103.

3. "Ernest Hemingway can *just* do it!"

4. *Death in the Afternoon* (1932) shows too that manliness is about knowledge and courage together, but the knowledge mixes the ways of bulls with the conventions of bullfighting.

5. See Bickford Sylvester's ingenious observations on Cuba and baseball in the book, "The Cuban Context of *The Old Man and the Sea,*" 165–84.

6. Hemingway, *Old Man and the Sea,* 65, 105, 107, 121. On the Christian symbols, see the essays by critics published in Bloom, ed., *Hemingway's The Old Man and the Sea,* some of whom are too quick to assume that referring to the Bible means agreeing with it.

7. Sylvester remarks on the "human community's discomfort with those rare individuals upon whom the survival of the many depends"; "Cuban Context," 183.

8. The judgment of William Faulkner: "His best. Time may show it to be the best single piece of any of us, I mean his and my contemporaries. This time, he discovered God, a Creator." Bloom, ed., *Hemingway's The Old Man and the Sea,* 5.

9. In *Death in the Afternoon,* Hemingway argues with an uncomprehending old lady about bullfighting.

10. For what follows on Achilles, I rely on the work of the late Seth Benardete, *Argument of the Action,* ch.2; *Bow and the Lyre,* 2, 4, 44; "Achilles and Hector," 31–58, 85–114.

11. *Iliad* 7:96.

12. Ibid., 12:23.

13. Ibid., 1:7, cf. 1:24.

14. Ibid., 1:134–39, 243–44, 303; 2:100–108.

15. See the seven claims to rule given in Plato, *Laws* 690a–c.

16. *Iliad* 1:416, 18:95.

17. Ibid., 9:10–16. Did Achilles have a choice or was it fated that he would die young? See Brann, *Past-Present,* 317–22.

18. See Stove, "Intellectual Capacity of Women," 113–36. No experiments on this matter, he says, would weigh with him "if their results were inconsistent with the verdict of ordinary experience" (132). But Stove does not make a point of our lack of experience with women philosophers. (In speaking of philosophers, here and elsewhere, I am not referring to philosophy professors but rather to thinkers of the highest rank.)

19. *Iliad* 1:240, 412. Whether a ruler can always honor the best is a question, as Achilles comes to see.

20. It is not, however, as different as Margaret Mead said; see Caton, ed. *Samoan Reader.*

21. In 1878 the Supreme Court ruled that polygamy is not protected by the Constitution in part because it "leads to the patriarchal principle"—obviously not thought to be in force at that time; *Reynolds v. U.S.* 98 U.S. 145 (1878).

22. Aristotle, *Politics* 1253a1–18.

23. See the discussion of Aristotle's *Politics* in ch. 7, below.

24. See Courtwright, *Violent Land,* 9–11: "I begin with . . . a statistical syllogism. Young men are prone to violence and disorder; America attracted unusually large numbers of young men; therefore America . . . was a more violent and disorderly place." Wilson and Herrnstein show the combination of youthful adventurousness with male aggression in the highest crime rates; Wilson and Herrnstein, *Crime and Human Nature,* 104–25, 141–44, 178–79. Campbell maintains that robbery is a distinctively male crime and that the thrill of a stickup is to prove your superiority; Campbell, *Mind of Her Own,* 212, 220.

25. The scientific term is *territory;* see Wilson, *Sociobiology,* 256–78. Lorenz, *On Aggression,* 34–39.

26. Machiavelli calls a person in this situation a "hereditary prince" and warns him to watch out for rising new princes. He puts no stock in manly protectiveness. *The Prince,* chs. 2, 6, 8.

27. See Krause, *Liberalism with Honor,* 21.

28. Kant, *On the Proverb,* 294n.

29. Oh social scientist! You long for a study that will say how many Grace Kellys and how many Gary Coopers will rise to the occasion, how many will cringe in helpless fright. If only there were a study, we wouldn't have to go to the movies.

30. What is it about the word *no* that you don't understand? goes the feminist query. Answer: whether no is final or refers only to the first date, or to the first request. A woman's modesty enables both sexes to live their lives with nuance in which a woman's grace and intelligence have scope to operate. If she is too blunt, she will

accept or reject too quickly. But we seem to be living under the principle, not favorable to women, that honesty comes before good sense. The sort of honesty I refer to was introduced by Nietzsche (see chapter 4).

31. See Crawford, *Talking Difference*, ch. 3.

32. Crawford notes that although women need to be more assertive, men need to be less so: "However, the male half of the model received little attention." Training men to be less assertive is the traditional "assertiveness training" done by women. In the words of the song from *Guys and Dolls*, "marry the man today and change his ways tomorrow." But if women are in training to become more assertive, they don't have time or inclination for this. Crawford, *Talking Difference*, 51. Tannen approves of assertiveness training for women as part of her campaign for greater flexibility through understanding the other sex. But learning to be assertive would seem to make you less flexible. Tannen, *You Just Don't Understand*, 120–21.

33. What makes this reversion to the past a "New Age" is the suppression of cherubs, demons, and gods—male counterparts to female spirits.

34. James Boswell, *Life of Samuel Johnson*, July 31, 1763; Aristotle, *Nicomachean Ethics* 1125a13–16.

35. Crawford, *Talking Difference*, 45.

36. See the long list of films in the last decade featuring women killers in DeMott, *Killer Woman Blues*, 68–69.

37. On Aristophanes' *The Assembly of Women* (*Ecclesiazousai*), see Leo Strauss, *Socrates and Aristophanes*, ch. 9; Saxonhouse, *Fear of Diversity*, ch. 1.

38. Aristotle, *Nichomachean Ethics* 1115a25–35.

39. On the conservative side: Browne, "Women at War," 51–247; Gutmann, *Kinder, Gentler Military*; Yarbrough, "Feminist Mistake," 48–52. On the liberal side: Abrams, "Gender in the Military," 217–41; Morris, "By Force of Arms," 651–781; Stiehm, ed., *It's Our Military Too!*

40. One of many studies: Cornelius and Averill, "Sex Differences in Fear of Spiders," 377–83.

41. Browne, "Women at War," 205.

42. Morris, "By Force of Arms," 751.

43. *United States v. Virginia* 518 U.S. 515, 533 (1996).

44. Burns, Schlozman, and Verba, *Private Roots of Public Action*, 111; Kaufmann and Petrocik, "Changing Politics of American Men," 864–87.

45. Edlund and Pande, "Why Have Women Become Left-Wing?" 917–61; Greenberg, "Race, Religiosity, and the Women's Vote," 59–82.

46. Graglia, *Domestic Tranquility*, ch. 2; Rhoads, *Taking Sex Differences Seriously*, 38; Burns, Schlozman, and Verba, *Private Roots of Public Action*, 157–60.

47. "Big Government" is nonpolitical in the sense of providing entitlements that are intended to remove security issues from partisan dispute. As a result women, who are less political and less partisan than men, paradoxically favor Big Government. Another reason why women may like Big Government is that it likes them: more women than men have jobs in or close to government, 26.6 percent of women vs.

7.8 percent of men; and 49.1 percent of women receive payments from government, vs. 32.8 percent of men. (Andersen, "Gender Gap," 19) Yet Big Government has to be established and maintained by political action, requiring partisan dispute and thus providing employment for manly types.

48. Men have more political information generally, but women know better the name of the head of the local school system. Burns, Schlozman, and Verba, *Private Roots of Public Action,* 101–5. On women as organizers, see also Welch, "Women as Political Animals?" 721.

49. If the participatory factors were equalized, "it would follow as the day the night" that sex differences in political participation would disappear. Burns, Schlozman, and Verba, *Private Roots of Public Action,* 385. Ignorance, or as the Marxists used to say, "false consciousness," might seem to stand in the way, but instructed by this book, women could recognize that nothing inherent to them prevents them from participating in politics equally with men. Once this happens, they could then leap ahead of the participatory factors, seize control of their fate, and not wait to be declared equal before behaving as equals.

50. Is education a "private root" of public action? It seems rather that the American democracy educates its citizens to democracy in democratic fashion (partly indirectly), so that the public is more cause of the private than effect.

51. For women holding office, the gender gap in political opinion is much wider than in the electorate. Successful ambition in women makes them more womanish in the sense of representing women's views. Burns, Schlozman, and Verba, *Private Roots of Public Action,* 112. Ambition, which might seem to be the perfection of political participation, is not treated by Burns et al., who speak slightingly of "some unmeasured taste for various kinds of activity that explains political participation." (256, 273) To be is to be measurable by social science, they say.

CHAPTER 4. MANLY NIHILISM

1. In the movie *Patton* (1970) the American general in an early scene discloses that he is the author of the poetry celebrating himself.

2. See Bloom, ed. and trans., *Republic of Plato,* Interpretive Essay, 351–60; Benardete, *Socrates' Second Sailing,* 66–68; Strauss, *City and Man,* 90, 97–99.

3. Plato appears to be the inventor of the word *theology,* which he puts in the mouth of Adeimantus questioning Socrates; *Republic* 379a5. See Benardete, *Argument of the Action,* 1–2.

4. *Republic* 386c.

5. Or is there a place for manliness in the natural right Achilles implies in his challenge to Agamemnon? Perhaps the nihilism of poets (and the corresponding promotion of cosmos by philosophers) is exaggerated, for the sake of explaining justice, in Socrates' discussion here.

6. Plato, *Republic* 379a–383c.

7. James, *Writings,* 1281, 1289–90.

8. Ibid., 1293.

9. Ibid., 481, 506–7.

10. Ibid., 491, 533, 535. Nietzsche, *Beyond Good and Evil,* 1:6, 19, 23.

11. James, *Writings,* 509.

12. Ibid., 579.

13. Ibid., 613.

14. Ibid., 617.

15. Townsend, *Manhood at Harvard,* 243–45.

16. Roosevelt, *American Ideals and Other Essays,* 51.

17. Roosevelt, *Strenuous Life,* 1.

18. Edmund Morris, *Rise of Theodore Roosevelt,* 40, 60.

19. Roosevelt, *Autobiography,* ch. 4. A New Yorker by birth, TR made himself into a Westerner by deliberate intent or, should I say, sheer willpower. In 1889, at the age of thirty-two, he published a two-volume work, *The Winning of the West,* celebrating the manly spirit of democratic heroes who extended civilization by leaving it behind. See Burton, *Theodore Roosevelt,* 15–27.

20. Maccoby, *Two Sexes,* 51–53.

21. See Susan Faludi's bluff-book *Backlash.*

22. Roosevelt, *Autobiography,* 314.

23. Ibid., 313.

24. Ibid., 120.

25. Ibid., 347. See also "The Great Adventure," in *Works of Theodore Roosevelt,* 19:243. What TR means by "fear of living" corresponds to what Socrates meant by fear of death, but TR's "living" consists of facing risk rather than seeking awareness. See *Apology* 29a; *Republic* 387d, 486b, 540b.

26. Roosevelt, Speech at Yellowstone National Park, 1903.

27. Ibid., 318.

28. Roosevelt, *American Ideals,* ch. 3, "The Manly Virtues and Practical Politics," 34–41.

29. Roosevelt, *Autobiography,* 161–63; and his speech "On American Motherhood," 1905.

30. Silverman, *Theodore Roosevelt and Women,* ch. 4.

31. Roosevelt, "The New Nationalism," Speech at Osawatomie, Kansas, August 31, 1910: "But when I say I am for the square deal, I mean not merely that I stand for fair play under the present rules of the game, but that I stand for having those rules changed so as to work for a more substantial equality of opportunity and reward for equally good service." A year earlier Croly contrasted the "conservative" notion of equal rights under the law with the "radical" notion (of which he partly approved) of "equal opportunities" for exercising such rights, establishing "equality of opportunity" for the "virile democrat"; Croly, *Promise of American Life,* 180–83. See Stettner, *Shaping Modern Liberalism,* 42–43.

32. See Mansfield, "Liberty and Virtue in the American Founding," 9–15.

33. Thomas Jefferson, Letter to John Adams, October 28, 1813.

34. Roosevelt, *Autobiography,* 389.

35. Luke 19:20; see Mansfield, *Taming the Prince,* 15, 302n38; Yarbrough, "Theodore Roosevelt and the Stewardship of the American Presidency," 536–48.

36. Machiavelli, *Discourses on Livy,* 3:13.3.

37. *The Letters of Theodore Roosevelt,* ed. Elting E. Morison, 2:853, 892, 894–95, 901–2, 907, 909, 919.

38. Haggard, *King Solomon's Mines,* 49; see 28, 62, 65, 135, 215, 306. Says the narrator at the beginning: "I'll scratch that word 'niggers' out, for I don't like it" (9).

39. Ibid., 56.

40. Ibid., 237.

41. Ibid., 135.

42. Ibid., 54.

43. Ibid., 292; see also 155, 279, 287. "I myself am not a gentleman. If I were, I would almost certainly not be writing this book, for one of the marks of a gentleman is that he seldom mentions the question of gentility." Raven, *English Gentleman,* 7.

44. Ibid., 7, 23, 223, 233. Yet Quatermain killed sixty-five lions until the sixty-sixth wounded him; 8, 240.

45. Ibid., 68.

46. Ibid., ch. 17, "Solomon's Treasure Chamber," contains nature's most valuable gems which only men know how to treasure. Nature does not care about them, nor do the blacks.

47. Ibid., 246.

48. Contrary to Wendy Katz, Haggard's fatalism is favorable to human action because as far as humans can know, what is fated comes as chance. See Katz, *Rider Haggard and the Fiction of Empire,* ch. 4.

49. Burroughs, *Tarzan of the Apes,* 41. Thanks to Hugh Liebert for his insights throughout this section on Tarzan. On the difference between the movie and the book, see Kirkham and Thumim, *You Tarzan,* 107.

50. Burroughs, *Tarzan of the Apes,* 56.

51. Ibid., 48–49, 52, 101.

52. Ibid., 206.

53. Ibid., 95, 98.

54. Ibid., 163. Presence of mind is lacking in women and in the "insane rage" of male animals (57).

55. Ibid., 100.

56. Ibid., 143.

57. Ibid., 166, 179. Burroughs accords the status of natural to polished gentlemanliness, for in Darwin's theory "civilized," being an evolution, is just as natural as the "savage" from which it is evolved.

58. Ibid., 250, 259–60. Bederman misses this point in her perceptive discussion of Tarzan, which is less friendly than mine. She wants to understand Tarzan's revenge as lynching and his civilization as racism. For her, manliness is on the one hand an ideological construction, hence nothing essential, but on the other hand it is vio-

lence and rape, hence essentially objectionable. Bederman, *Manliness and Civilization*, 218–32.

59. *The Second Jungle Book* (1895), with its poem, makes a theme of the law of the jungle. Kipling's *Just So Stories for Little Children* (1902) are about animals in Ethiopia.

60. This is the last word of Kipling's poem, "The Law of the Jungle."

61. "The Ballad of East and West" in *Barrack Room Ballads* (1892).

62. "Gunga Din," in *Barrack Room Ballads* (1892).

63. See Cantor, *Creature and Creator*, 111.

64. Stevenson, *Strange Case of Dr. Jekyll and Mr. Hyde*, 5.

65. Ibid., 7.

66. Ibid., 5, 8, 10, 30. Dr. Lanyon, Dr. Jekyll's friend, gets a good look at Mr. Hyde and notes its effect on himself with cool self-awareness (38–39).

67. Ibid., 50.

68. Ibid., 23.

69. Whatever insight may be found in this section comes from the late W. Carey McWilliams, the manly professor at Rutgers University. See also Zuckert and Zuckert, "'And in Its Wake We Followed,'" 59–93.

70. Twain, *Connecticut Yankee*, 65. It does not appear that Franklin Roosevelt borrowed this phrase in 1932.

71. Ibid., 43, 48–49, 77, 101, 244.

72. Manliness, manhood, being a man are referred to frequently; ibid., 14, 39, 64, 89, 181–82, 190, 195, 212, 215.

73. Ibid., 5.

74. Ibid., 11.

75. Ibid., 190.

76. Ibid., 91.

77. Ibid., 236–37, 245–46.

78. For a contrary view, see H. L. Mencken, "Roosevelt I." In 1920 Mencken dared to say that Roosevelt "owed a lot to Nietzsche," that "Theodore . . . swallowed Friedrich as a farmwife swallows Peruna [a patent medicine] — bottle, cork, label and testimonials" (42).

79. Nietzsche, *On the Genealogy of Morals*, 3:24; *Thus Spoke Zarathustra*, 4, "The Shadow." Nietzsche does not *say* it is his definition, but in his spirit of interpretation I put it in his mouth.

80. Plato, *Crito* 46b; *Gorgias* 457e–458a.

81. Marx, *Theses on Feuerbach*.

82. Plato, *Republic* 380a; Homer, *Iliad* 20:1–74. The reference to warring gods alludes to the question, "Which of the warring gods should we serve?" by Max Weber, "Science as a Vocation," 153. Weber was in many ways a follower of Nietzsche, not least in the concept of charisma that does some of the work of manliness for him.

83. See the section "War and Warriors" in *Zarathustra*, 1:10; *Human All Too Human*, 1:77; "I greet all the signs that a more manly and warlike age is commencing," *Gay Science*, 283, see also 362; *Will to Power*, 125; *Beyond Good and Evil*, 293; *Twilight of*

the Idols, 38. Nietzsche scholars have not paid much attention to the manliness in the thought of their hero, so impressed are they with its sublimation into philosophy. But the appeal of Nietzsche comes in great part from his blatant, if not quite genuine, manliness. See, however, Pangle, "Warrior Spirit," 140–79; Bentley, *Century of Hero-Worship.*

84. *Zarathustra,* 1:10. See Goyard-Fabre, *Nietzsche et la question politique,* 15–29.

85. Nietzsche, *Beyond Good and Evil,* 209.

86. *Beyond Good and Evil,* 227; *Zarathustra,* 1, "Of the Afterworldsmen"; 4, "The Leech"; 4, "The Sorcerer"; 4, "Of the Higher Man"; *The Dawn of Day,* 536; *Nachlass,* 1:65, 1056; 2:554, 605, 1077.

87. Aristotle, *Nicomachean Ethics* 1127a33–1127b34.

88. Nietzsche, *Twilight of the Idols,* 1:8.

89. Nietzsche, *Zarathustra,* 2, "Of Self-Overcoming."

90. Nietzsche, *Nachlass,* 2:1077. "Each of [the Greek philosophers] was a warlike, brutal tyrant," *Human, All Too Human,* 1:261.

91. Nietzsche, *Beyond Good and Evil,* preface.

92. Nietzsche, *Beyond Good and Evil,* 263; *Human, All Too Human,* 1:224, 235, 240, 251.

93. Nietzsche, *Human, All Too Human,* 1:3. This book is in Nietzsche's pro-scientific phase but it fits with the whole of his thought.

94. Nietzsche, *Gay Science,* 293. Today "no one lives philosophically, with that simple manly constancy." Nietzsche, *Advantage and Disadvantage of History for Life,* 5.

95. Nietzsche, *Zarathustra,* 1, "Of Old and Young Women."

96. Nietzsche, *Zarathustra,* 2, "Of Redemption."

97. Nietzsche, *Beyond Good and Evil,* 236.

98. Appel, "Ubermensch's Consort," 512–30. Nietzsche, *Human, All Too Human,* 1:259, 377, 411; 2:272, 274.

99. Nietzsche, *Human, All Too Human,* 1:411; *Gay Science,* 68.

100. Nietzsche, Zarathustra, 1, "Of Old and Young Women."

101. Nietzsche, *Beyond Good and Evil,* 144, 238–39. How long must we wait for social science to test that one?

102. Nietzsche, *Human, All Too Human,* 1:169, 213.

103. Nietzsche, *Beyond Good and Evil,* 145.

104. Nietzsche, *Human All Too Human,* 1:425; *Gay Science,* 363.

105. Plato, *Republic* 387e. In the *Birth of Tragedy,* Nietzsche wished to find Greek manliness and instead, we learn from Plato, came upon self-pity, which he confused with manliness.

106. See the lecture by Leo Strauss, delivered in 1941 and printed only recently; "German Nihilism," 353–78. Aschheim, *Nietzsche Legacy in Germany,* ch. 8; Manent, *Cours Familier,* 269–80.

107. Hitler, *Mein Kampf,* 56, 174–75, 214, 237, 342, 392–93, 750.

108. Ibid., 175.

109. *Lieber will noch der Mensch das Nichts wollen als nicht wollen; On the Genealogy of Morals* 3:28.

CHAPTER 5. WOMANLY NIHILISM

1. We must first concede, as is obvious, that the ideas of feminism are not the sole cause of the gender-neutral society. Many things, including the technology of birth control and advances in public health, have reduced the special demands of morality and reproduction on women and thus brought the sexes closer to one another.

2. Note the value derived from a fact.

3. Cott, *Grounding of Modern Feminism,* 13.

4. Wollstonecraft, *Vindication,* 30, 44, 219.

5. Ibid., 13, 205–23.

6. Ibid., 4.

7. Tocqueville's American woman is both knowing and modest, however; "she has pure morals rather than a chaste mind." *Democracy in America,* 2 3.9.

8. Wollstonecraft, *Vindication,* 219.

9. Ibid., 6.

10. *Stanton-Anthony Reader,* 49. Stanton assumes that woman has a "deeper interest" than man in the home; see also a speech by Susan B. Anthony on the single woman's capacity for homemaking, praising her "pure love of home"; *Stanton-Anthony Reader,* 146–51, 225.

11. Ibid., 212.

12. Ibid., 30, 136.

13. Ibid., 121. See Banner, *Elizabeth Cady Stanton,* 71, 83. The same is true of the feminism in Charlotte Gilman's Herland, which is a community held together by a religion of motherhood. To a male visitor, a woman of Herland asks with horror: "'Destroy the unborn — !' she said in a hard whisper. 'Do men do that in your country?'" Gilman, *Herland,* 66, 69–70.

14. See also Anthony's "constitutional argument"; *Stanton-Anthony Reader,* 152–65.

15. Being alone is good because it obliges the individual woman to develop herself in all regards, however, not in order to make her own choices. "Life must ever be a march and a battle." But if so, why is Stanton so opposed to war? And soldiers do not fight alone. *Stanton-Anthony Reader,* 247–49.

16. Sir Robert made his money in the building of the Suez Canal, and the villainess Mrs. Cheveley tries to blackmail him into supporting an Argentine Canal in which she has a corrupt interest. The key to the play is to note that the Suez Canal was for the common good and the Argentine Canal was not (see act 1).

17. Henry James, *Bostonians,* in *Novels, 1881–1886,* 1154.

18. Ibid., 1115.

19. Ibid., 1210.

20. Ibid., 819.

21. Verena, it turns out, too easily discovers "almost unsuspected truths" on Basil's side. Ibid., 1162.

22. Ibid., 913, 958, 1048.

23. Ibid., 1015.

24. Ibid., 856.

25. Ibid., 1047.

26. Ibid., 1010; see Wardley, "Woman's Voice," 639–55; and Catherine H. Zuckert, "American Women and Democratic Morals:, 148–72. Let it be noted for elaboration in ch. 7 that James's women in this novel and others are *American,* which to him means *democratic.* "Social construction" for him is political. See James's essays, "The Speech of American Women" and "The Manners of American Women," published in Henry James, *French Writers and American Women*; and *The American Scene,* 638–43.

27. Henry James, *Bostonians,* 978, 1111.

28. Ibid., 978, 1212.

29. Ibid., 927–28.

30. Ibid., 944.

31. Among features of our contemporary landscape that can be found in *The Bostonians* are: women's rejection of men's courtesies; the professional woman; new truths vs. old (stereotypes); the equality vs. the superiority of women; elite women vs. the working girl; radical vs. moderate feminists; the unerotic character of feminism; the coarseness of manners.

32. Beauvoir, *Second Sex.* "Of all feminist theorists de Beauvoir is the most comprehensive and far-reaching." Firestone, *Dialectic of Sex,* 16. For the American reception see Bair, *Simone de Beauvoir,* 432–39.

33. Beauvoir's chapter "The Mother" begins with nine pages on abortion (*Second Sex,* 484–93); later she says provocatively, "When woman suffocates in a dull gynaeceum — brothel or middle-class home" (603); and the reader comes upon nothing about women's responsibility for morality but rather finds remarks like this: "marriage is directly correlated with prostitution" (555).

34. Beauvoir, *Second Sex,* 118–21.

35. See, e.g., Deckard, *Women's Movement;* Mitchell and Oakley, *What Is Feminism?;* Cott, *Grounding of Modern Feminism* (but see 45, 151); Fraisse and Perrot, eds., *History of Women in the West.*

36. Beauvoir, *Second Sex,* 61.

37. To acquiesce in immanence is "false consciousness" (a neo-Marxian term) or "bad faith" (a usage of Jean-Paul Sartre); Krause, "Lady Liberty's Allure," 5.

38. For Aristotle, male is that which generates in another; female, that which generates in itself. *Generation of Animals* 716a.

39. Beauvoir, *Second Sex,* 267. The statement begins a chapter on childhood, which is followed by a chapter on the young girl. Every woman, it seems, is first a child, then a young girl; she can't go in reverse. Is this not a natural becoming that Beauvoir takes for granted, quite distinct from the historical becoming on which she dwells? But historical becoming also presupposes natural becoming, and in this is not distinct from it. A woman *is* born a woman so that she can become a woman.

40. Beauvoir, *Second Sex,* 714.

41. Tocqueville, *Democracy in America*, 2 3.10.
42. Beauvoir, *Second Sex*, 627.
43. In Donald Symons's words: "Among all peoples, copulation is considered to be essentially a service or favor that women render to men, and not vice versa." This is the last of the seven sex differences that he finds in all societies. *Evolution of Human Sexuality*, 27–28.
44. Beauvoir, *Second Sex*, 529.
45. "The woman who achieves virile independence has the great privilege of carrying on her sexual life with individuals who are themselves autonomous and effective in action, who — as a rule — will not play a parasitic role in her life, who will not enchain her through their weakness and the exigency of their needs." *Quelle illusion!* Beauvoir, *Second Sex*, 695.
46. Ibid., 682.
47. See Bertholet, *Sartre*, passim.
48. See J. Michael Bailey's excellent book, *The Man Who Would Be Queen*.
49. Karl Marx and Friedrich Engels, *The Communist Manifesto*, 2 (end).
50. On Beauvoir's "need for a male figure," see Evans, *Simone de Beauvoir*, 76, 79, 94.
51. *L'Arc* 61 (1975): 3–12. Said Beauvoir of this exchange, "I questioned him [Sartre] on his relations with feminism. He answered with the greatest good will but rather superficially." Beauvoir, *Adieux*, 82.
52. Beauvoir, *Second Sex*, ch. 11.
53. These were the sexist questions Fidel Castro put in a speech to the Cuban women who had fought in the revolution that installed him in power and are deplored by Germaine Greer, *Female Eunuch*, 319–20.
54. Ibid., 1, 51, 56, 61, 68, 77, 196, 259, 349.
55. Millett, *Sexual Politics*, 62–63; the index of the book has an entry for "double standard" but not for "morality."
56. Firestone, *Dialectic of Sex*, 135–38, 223. See also Betty Friedan's praise of Freud within a criticism of his traditional outlook on women; *Feminine Mystique*, 104–5.
57. Cf. Ingrid Bengis, who hates men because she cannot through sex get them to stay with her: she wants transcendence, they want nature. What she calls transcendence (more than an orgasm) Beauvoir calls immanence, and what she calls nature (orgasm alone) Beauvoir calls transcendence. Which one is right? *Combat in the Erogenous Zone*, 95.
58. Millett, *Sexual Politics*, 161–68; Greer, *Female Eunuch*, 156–57; Firestone, *Dialectic of Sex*, 74. Greer in her saucy way hopes that in the future "children might grow up without the burden of gratitude for the gift of life which they never asked for." In her own case, she says that as children, "we could see that our mothers blackmailed us with self-sacrifice" (249, 157). But don't we owe gratitude for gifts we don't ask for? For the gift of life that makes it possible to ask for things?
59. Firestone, *Dialectic of Sex*, 218.
60. Greer, *Female Eunuch*, 181.

61. The assumption is contrary to fact because in cases of sexual encounter women are liable (1) to become pregnant, (2) to suffer more from sexually transmitted disease, and (3) to feel more emotional hurt afterwards.

62. Firestone, *Dialectic of Sex*, 126.

63. Ibid., 141.

64. Ibid., 215–16.

65. Ibid., 172.

66. Millett, *Sexual Politics*, 94. Greer appears to agree; *Sexual Eunuch*, 21.

67. Greer, *Female Eunuch*, 32–40, 92; the title of her book refers to Freud's view that a woman is a castrated man. The intelligent Ms. Firestone, who called Freudianism "the misguided feminism," also said: "*Freud grasped the crucial problem of modern life: sexuality*" (emphasis in original); *Dialectic of Sex*, 46, 48, 46–72. Millett, *Sexual Politics*, 176–203.

68. Freud, *Three Essays*, 87; *General Introduction*, 185–86. Marcuse, *Eros and Civilization*, 49–50.

69. Greer, *Sexual Eunuch*, 347, 351. Note the contradiction between "spontaneity" (347) and "the purposive employment of energy in a self-chosen enterprise" (351).

70. Millett, *Sexual Politics*, 25, 27.

71. Firestone, *Dialectic of Sex*, 139.

72. Aristotle, *Politics* 1252b5.

73. Greer, *Female Eunuch*, 7, 349.

74. Sarachild, "Consciousness Raising," 145. See also MacKinnon, "Feminism, Marxism, Method and the State," 519–20 for a discussion of the difference between feminist consciousness-raising and Marxism.

75. A fact Friedan later tried to conceal, according to a recent biographer; Horowitz, *Betty Friedan and the Making of the Feminine Mystique*, 10–12, 92–94, 217.

76. Friedan, *Feminine Mystique*, ix.

77. Ibid., 32, 258.

78. Ibid., 329.

79. Making others conform to oneself is the factual truth of Kant's categorical imperative, which was then turned into a principle by Nietzsche. For Kant, the categorical imperative was meant to have a moderating influence on one's will by subordinating it to the will of a rational being, but in effect, and with Nietzsche's interpretation, the categorical imperative identified one's own will with that of a rational being and abandoned the moderation of self-discipline.

80. See Friedan's criticism of Adlai Stevenson, who in an address at Smith College in 1955 actually addressed "the problem that has no name" but in doing so betrayed his belief that woman's true role is as wife and mother; *Feminine Mystique*, 60.

81. Ibid., 61.

82. I am encouraged by Bailey's *The Man Who Would Be Queen*, 180, in the belief that "better looking" can be a term of social science.

83. Think of the difference between a man's man, such as Clint Eastwood, and a ladies' man like Warren Beatty.

84. Naomi Wolf, *Promiscuities*, xxii. In her book *Misconceptions*, Ms. Wolf relates her discovery that motherhood is hard work requiring creativity and calls for a new "motherhood feminism" that would seek better appreciation and more government programs for mothers.

85. Shalit, *Return to Modesty;* Gurstein, *Repeal of Reticence.*

86. Aristotle, *Politics* 1259a39.

87. Nietzsche, *Beyond Good and Evil*, 23.

88. Gilligan, *In a Different Voice*, 18.

89. Ibid., 157–63.

90. Ibid., 23.

91. "For [the phallus] is a signifier intended to designate as a whole the effects of the signified, in that the signifier conditions them by its presence as a signifier." "The Signification of the Phallus" (1958), in Lacan, *Ecrits*, 285. Lacan has inspired a considerable literature on "masculinity" that sees the male organ as signifying power while ignoring its two more obvious natural functions; see, e.g., Hooper, *Manly States*, 60.

92. See Diamond and Quinby, eds., *Feminism and Foucault*, xi–xix; Fraser, *Unruly Practices*, 17–34.

93. "All men by nature desire to know" is the opening sentence of Aristotle's *Metaphysics*.

94. For an introduction to Foucault, see Foucault, *Power/Knowledge.*

95. Benhabib, "Feminism and Postmodernism," 17–34, and Butler, "Contingent Foundations," 35–37.

96. As Butler says: "subjects who institute actions are themselves instituted effects of prior actions." "Contingent Foundations," 43.

CHAPTER 6. THE MANLY LIBERAL

1. Goldwin, *Why Blacks, Women and Jews Are Not Mentioned in the Constitution.*

2. *Liberalism* is a nineteenth-century term, but I use it anachronistically to designate seventeenth-century philosophers, above all John Locke, who laid down the principles and practices that later came to be called liberal.

3. Hobbes, *Leviathan,* ch. 15, where the laws of nature are said to be moral virtues; see also *Elements of Law,* 1.17.15; *De Cive,* 3.32. At one point in *Leviathan,* ch. 15, courage is put under justice: "That which gives to humane actions the relish of Justice, is a certain Noblenesse or Gallantnesse of courage (rarely found), by which a man scorns to be beholding for the contentment of his life, to fraud, or breach of promise." Hobbes's political philosophy is complicated by the fact that he stated it as a whole three times and in regard to manliness or courage struggled throughout either to deny or to reformulate it as it had been previously conceived in the tradition of philosophy. In an earlier formulation Hobbes is closer to courage, while still omitting it as a virtue: "The sum of virtue is to be sociable with them that will be sociable, and formidable to them that will not. And the same is the sum of the law

of nature; for in being sociable, the law of nature taketh place by the way of peace and society; and to be formidable, is the law of nature in war." *Elements of Law,* 1.17.15.

4. Hobbes, *Leviathan,* chs. 6, 10. See Strauss, *Political Philosophy of Hobbes,* 13, for discussion of why Hobbes did not unequivocally lay down vanity as the basis of his political science.

5. Hobbes, *Elements of Law,* 1.9.21.

6. Hobbes, *De Cive,* 1.5. The vanity Hobbes is most concerned with is "a vain conceipt of ones owne wisdome, which almost all men think they have in a greater degree, than the Vulgar; that is, in all men but themselves, and a few others, whom by Fame, or for concurring with themselves, they approve." *Leviathan,* ch. 13.

7. The term *dominators* is from Kavka, *Hobbesian Moral and Political Theory,* 97–107. Kavka shows that the existence of a minority of dominators is necessary to Hobbes's reasoning that the state of nature is a state of war. See Hobbes, *Elements of Law,* 1.15.10; and Sullivan, *Machiavelli, Hobbes and the Formation of a Liberal Republicanism in England,* 95.

8. Strauss, *Political Philosophy of Hobbes,* 133.

9. Hobbes, *Leviathan,* chs. 4, 11, Review and Conclusion; *De Cive,* Epistle Dedicatory and Preface; *Elements of Law,* Epistle Dedicatory, 1.13.3; Strauss, *Political Philosophy of Hobbes,* 138.

10. Hobbes, *Leviathan,* chs. 17, 28.

11. Ibid., chs. 13–15.

12. Ibid., chs. 16, 21.

13. "Eloquence, whose end . . . is not truth (except by chance) but victory." *De Cive,* X.11; see *Elements of Law,* 2.8.14. The rhetoric Hobbes opposes in passionate orators is to be distinguished from the "powerful eloquence, which procureth attention and consent" that he practices himself; *Leviathan,* Review and Conclusion; see *De Cive,* 12.12. The former is a hindrance to sovereignty because it supposes that justice is arguable; the latter spreads the truth of Hobbes's civil science, which gives the decision of disputable questions to the sovereign. See Skinner, *Reason and Rhetoric,* 297–300, 435; Herzog, *Happy Slaves,* 75; Polin, *Politique et Philosophie,* 207–9.

14. Hobbes, *Leviathan,* ch. 21.

15. Ibid., chs. 14, 21, for the exception to perfect nonresistance when you are about to be taken by the executioner. At this point justice permits manly (or desperate) resistance.

16. Ibid., chs. 10, 15; see the extensive discussion in Tuck, *Natural Rights Theories,* ch.6.

17. It was Hobbes, not Kant, who invented the priority of right to good.

18. Hobbes, *Leviathan,* ch. 15, Review and Conclusion. See Strauss, *Natural Right and History,* 188; and Strauss, *Political Philosophy of Hobbes,* 18, 49–50, 114–15, 120; Herzog, *Happy Slaves,* 87. See also *Leviathan,* ch. 30, discussed by Dietz, "Hobbes's Subject as Citizen," 108–11.

19. Hobbes, *Leviathan,* ch. 14. See Tarcov, *Locke's Education for Liberty,* 38.

20. See Okin, *Women in Western Political Thought,* 197–99; Pateman, *Sexual Contract,* 44, 222. Pateman recognizes Hobbes's attack on "masculine right," but both writers are so indignant at his sexism that they fail to appreciate his repression of manliness.

21. Hobbes, *Leviathan,* ch. 19; see also chs. 20, 22, 25, 26, 30; see also *Elements of Law,* 2.4.2, 14; *De Cive,* 9.3; and a statement in the Latin version of *Leviathan:* "authority does not take account of masculine and feminine." *Leviathan,* ch. 42.

22. Descartes, *Passions of the Soul,* 153–56; Hobbes, *Leviathan,* ch. 14; Spinoza, *Ethics* IIIP6–9, P17, P59, IVP67; Spinoza, *Political Treatise,* 10.8; see Smith, *Spinoza's Book of Life,* 112–22.

23. Spinoza, *Short Treatise,* I/71.

24. Spinoza, *Political Treatise,* 11.4. Did Spinoza overlook Aristotle's criticism of the women of Sparta: "What is the difference between women ruling and rulers who are ruled by women?" *Politics* 1269b33.

25. Spinoza, *Political Treatise,* 2.4–5, 3.9, 4.6, 5.4, 5.6, 6.10, 7.6, 25, 10.8; *Theological-Political Treatise,* 5.22–25, 16.2–7, 24, 18.16.

26. Machiavelli, *The Prince,* ch. 9; *Discourses on Livy,* 1.4–6.

27. Locke, *Two Treatises of Government,* 1 1.

28. Ibid., 2 235.

29. Hobbes says: "For the actions of men proceed from their opinions, and in the well-governing of opinions consisteth the well-governing of men's actions, in order to their peace and concord"; *Leviathan,* ch. 18. See Tarcov, *Locke's Education for Liberty,* 47–48.

30. Locke, *Some Thoughts Concerning Education,* 114; see also 35, 104, 109. Tarcov, *Locke's Education,* 132–33, 152–53.

31. Locke, *Some Thoughts Concerning Education,* 115; *Essay Concerning Human Understanding,* 2 21.30–31, 71.

32. Locke, *Some Thoughts Concerning Education,* 70; cf. 115.

33. Locke, *Two Treatises,* 1 62; 2 80–82.

34. Ibid., 2 34, 37.

35. Edmund Burke, *Reflections on the Revolution in France,* in *Works,* 8 vols., 2:282–83, 331, 352.

36. Ibid., 2:348–49.

37. Burke, *A Letter to a Noble Lord,* in *Works,* 5:125. See Mansfield, *Statesmanship and Party Government,* ch. 7.

38. See the formulation of the categorical imperative as the law of nature: "Act as if the maxim of your action were to become through your will a universal law of nature." Kant, *Groundwork of the Metaphysics of Morals,* 4:421.

39. Kant, *Anthropology from a Pragmatic Point of View,* 7:303–11. See Shell, *Embodiment of Reason,* 88, 157, 220, 225, 254, 310.

40. See esp. Kant, *Conjectural Beginning of Human History,* 8:114–15; Shell, *Embodiment of Reason,* 285, 307, 310.

41. Hegel, *Philosophy of History,* 4 3.3; *Philosophy of Right,* 342–48.

42. "Certain passages in the argument employed by Hegel in defining the relation of master to slave apply much better to the relation of man to woman." Beauvoir, *Second Sex*, 64. That possibility is raised but not elaborated in Alexandre Kojève's interpretation; *Introduction à la lecture de Hegel*, 13.

43. Susan Okin introducing John Stuart Mill, *The Subjection of Women*, v.

44. Mill, *On Liberty*, 86–97. In *Considerations on Representative Government*, ch. 3, Mill disparages "mere unmanliness and want of spirit" in those without the ambition to improve.

45. Mill, *On Liberty*, 48.

46. Note Mill's dismissal of the "cowardice" of not acting on one's opinions; ibid., 55.

47. Yet Mill admits that mankind's truths are for the most part but "half-truths." Ibid., 84.

48. Ibid., 54.

49. Mill, *Subjection of Women*, 61.

50. Ibid., 54, 74, 81, 64, 63, 106.

CHAPTER 7. MANLY VIRTUE

1. Okin, *Women in Western Political Thought*, chs. 5–8; Pateman, *Sexual Contract*, 9, 96–102. Postmodern feminists have been more friendly to Rousseau because of his recognition of women's subtle powers. See Zerilli, *Signifying Woman*, ch. 2; Wingrove, *Rousseau's Republican Romance*, 6–8. See Wollstonecraft's early criticism (1792) of Rousseau, *Vindication of the Rights of Women*, 28–29, 45–49, 84, 88–105: "I have, probably, had an opportunity of observing more girls in their infancy than J. J. Rousseau" (49).

2. Jean-Jacques Rousseau, *Emile*, 377.

3. Ibid., 357.

4. Ibid., 360.

5. Ibid., 370, 408. For the "indirect rule" of women, see Schwartz, *Sexual Politics*, 84–89; and Melzer, *Natural Goodness of Man*, 245–48.

6. "Woman's empire is an empire of gentleness, skill, and obligingness; her orders are caresses, her threats are tears." Rousseau, *Emile*, 408. How satisfying an empire is that? But then the male empire of vaunting and strutting is a delusion; why should women want that?

7. Ibid., 361, 364, 398. See also Rousseau, *Letter to D'Alembert*, 8:82–90.

8. Ibid., 398.

9. Ibid., 387; see Shell, "Emile," 291–94.

10. Ibid., 406.

11. See Bloom, *Love and Friendship*, 103, 121, 138.

12. At the end of *Emile* (480), Emile addresses Rousseau as "my master."

13. Thus Rousseau's use of nature does not introduce a "perpetual circularity," as Wingrove claims (*Rousseau's Republican Romance*, 27). To say this one must believe that there is no nature to be seen or studied but only chaos that can be willfully or politically ordered by tyrannical human beings. Yet for some reason the chaos of

human nature is divided into female and male chaos; i.e., human nature is perceived and isn't chaos.

14. The "quarrels" and "spats" of Emile and Sophie are quickly resolved and shown to be due to the illusions of pride; Rousseau, *Emile,* 426, 447.

15. Rousseau's notion of "nature," by putting the relations of the sexes beyond dispute, actually facilitates the indirect rule of women over men. It satisfies complacent males with an assurance that they dominate while excusing women from having openly to assert their claim to rule.

16. Nietzsche: "'According to nature' you want to *live?* O you noble Stoics, what deceptive words are these!" *Beyond Good and Evil,* 9.

17. Cicero's adaptation of Stoicism is in his *Republic, Laws* and *Offices;* his thoroughgoing criticism is in *De Finibus* 4.

18. Crane, *Red Badge of Courage,* in *Stephen Crane: Prose and Poetry,* ed. Levenson, 175, 183, 212. See also Crane's story "A Grey Sleeve," 632–46.

19. Ibid., 85.

20. Plato, *Symposium* 176c, 23c–d.

21. Winthrop, "Aristotle," 18.

22. Aristotle, *Politics* 1253a2; 1276b13, 1286a9, 1287b13, 1334a11–13.

23. Ibid., 1253a29–31.

24. Ibid., 1252b8. The quotation is from one poet, Euripides, who in *Iphigenia in Aulis* puts it in the mouth of Iphigenia, a woman. The poets broadcast the assertions of human beings, and Aristotle, a philosopher, repeats and endorses this assertion.

25. Ibid., 1252b10–12, 21–23. Aristotle quotes and names both Hesiod and Homer (*Works and Days* 405; *Odyssey* IX 114ff.) to suggest that besides asserting, poets disclose hidden truths. See also Thucydides I 3.3, 6.

26. By contrast, Rousseau insists that natural law "must speak immediately with the voice of Nature" so that it can gain agreement. *Discourse on Inequality,* preface.

27. Aristotle, *Politics* 1253a8, 1278a17.

28. Plato, *Republic* 373e–376d; and Benardete, *Socrates' Second Sailing,* 54–58. Ludwig, *Eros and Polis,* 192–212. See also Aristotle, *Politics* 1327b40–1328a1.

29. Aristotle, *Nicomachean Ethics* 1094b14–19, 1117a6, 1144b4–18.

30. Plato, *Statesman* 262d. Aristotle even asserts the meaning of nature, that the complete thing is the nature of the thing; *Politics* 1252b34.

31. Aristotle, *Politics* 1252a25–b9.

32. Ibid., 1260a13. Does this mean that women lack authority in their own souls or among men or both? See Saxonhouse, *Women in the History of Western Political Thought,* 74; and Salkever, "Women, Soldiers, Citizens," 177.

33. Aristotle, *Politics* 1259b34, 1260a13.

34. Ibid., 1260a31. On Tecmessa, see Nichols, "Women in Western Political Thought," 252–53; and Davis, *Politics of Philosophy,* 25–26.

35. Aristotle, *Politics* 1259b7–8. Aristotle compares the advantages males seek to establish over females to the "story" told by Amasis, a man of low origin who became king of Egypt and sought to confirm his authority by having his subjects worship

the image of a god made from a golden footpan. See Herodotus 2:172; Nichols, *Citizens and Statesmen*, 31–32.

36. Aristotle, *Politics* 1329a13, 1265b29, 1279b2, 1297b2.

37. Ibid., 1329a13, 1265b29, 1279b2, 1297b2. See Salkever, *Finding the Mean*, 197–98; and Salkever, "Women, Soldiers, Citizens," 187.

38. Aristotle, *Politics* 1283a36–9.

39. Ibid., 1282b14–24, 1283a25–30, 36–39.

40. In what follows I am indebted to Swanson, "Aristotle on Nature, Human Nature, and Justice," 225–48; *Public and the Private*, 44–68. See also Freeland, *Feminist Interpretations*.

41. Aristotle, *History of Animals* 608a33–b19.

42. After the passage on male and female characters Aristotle goes on to discuss conflict between and within the species. Ibid., 608b20ff.

43. Aristotle, *Generation of Animals* 732a11–12.

44. Ibid., 741a7–9.

45. Aristotle, *Metaphysics* 1058a29–b26.

46. Aristotle, *Politics* 1277b20–23.

47. Aristotle, *Nichomachean Ethics* 1162a16–17; 1160b25–1161a25.

48. Ibid., 1134b18–1135a6.

49. Aristotle, *Politics* 1278b14, 1288a33.

50. Ibid., 1280a7–15.

51. Ibid., 1325a34–41, 1325b10–11.

52. Ibid., 1325b16–23.

53. Plato, *Laws* 630c–631d, 963e; *Republic* 361b, 366d, 429c–430c, 549d; *Meno* 71e; *Protagoras* 349d–e; *Gorgias* 469c, 483a–b, 491b, 512c. On "manliness" in Plato, see Strauss, *Political Philosophy of Hobbes*, 147.

54. Plato, *Republic* 503c–504a; *Meno* 86b; *Phaedo* 68c.

55. See Benardete, *Socrates' Second Sailing*, 100, on "the spirit of eideticization."

56. Plato, *Laches* 183c–184a. On the *Laches*, see Blitz, "Introduction to the Reading of Plato's *Laches*," 185–225; Rabieh, *Best Part of Valor*; Tessitore, "Courage and Comedy," 115–33.

57. Plato, *Republic* 452a–e.

58. There are humanitarians who assert the rights of humanity, but they do so against the opponents of those rights and do not speak for all humanity.

59. Plato, *Republic* 454c–e.

60. Plato, *Laches* 185a–b, 185e–186a.

61. Machiavelli, *Discourses on Livy*, 1:27.

62. Céline, *Voyage*, 314.

63. Plato, *Laches* 179d, 180c, 200e–201a.

64. Ibid., 181b, 188c–189b. In another dialogue we learn from Alcibiades that Laches himself cut a poor figure in this battle; *Symposium* 221a.

65. Plato, *Laches* 192b–d.

66. Ibid., 195b–196a.

CONCLUSION

1. *Ozio ambizioso;* Machiavelli, *Discourses on Livy,* 1:pr.
2. For Machiavelli's appreciation of women, see his song of praise to Madonna Caterina Sforza in *Discourses on Livy,* 3:6.
3. Edmund Burke, *Reflections on the Revolution in France,* 2:348.
4. Tocqueville, *Democracy in America,* 1 2.10, 387.
5. As noted in chapter 7, I learned about the notion of assertion from my wife, Delba Winthrop, but I have *asserted* (stolen) it.
6. Tocqueville, *Democracy in America,* 2 4.6, 663; 2 3.19, 604; 2 4.1, 640.
7. Ibid., 2 4.6, 663.
8. Ibid., 2 3.10, 566; 2 3.12, 574, 576.
9. That much-to-be recommended book is for the professional housewife and applies rational control to every aspect of her life, but it deliberately presupposes a woman's outlook.
10. Plato, *Laws* 731d; see also 781a, 802e, 814a–d.
11. Besides Plato's *Statesman,* one finds weaving to describe social mixing in the *Phaedo,* in Aristophanes's *Lysistrata,* and in Homer's *Odyssey.*
12. In the *Laws* Plato presents a third possibility of a regime that is somewhat reluctantly but still officially male dominated. See Kochin, *Gender and Rhetoric.*
13. Aristotle, *Nicomachean Ethics* 1162a16–34.

Bibliography

Abrams, Kathryn. "Gender in the Military: Androcentrism and Institutional Reform." *Law and Contemporary Problems* 56 (1993): 217–41.

Allport, Gordon W. *The Nature of Prejudice.* Cambridge: Addison-Wesley, 1954.

Andersen, Kristi. "The Gender Gap and Experiences with the Welfare State." *PS: Political Science and Politics* 32 (1999): 17–19.

Appel, Fredrick. "The Ubermensch's Consort: Nietzsche and the 'Eternal Feminine.'" *History of Political Thought* 18 (1997): 512–30.

Arnhart, Larry. *Darwinian Natural Right.* Albany: State University of New York Press, 1998.

Aschheim, Stephen. *The Nietzsche Legacy in Germany, 1890–1990.* Berkeley: University of California Press, 1992.

Ashmore, Richard. "Sex Stereotypes and Implicit Personality Theory." In *Cognitive Processes in Stereotyping and Intergroup Behavior,* ed. David L. Hamilton. Hillsdale, N.J.: Erlbaum, 1981.

Ashmore, Richard, and Frances Del Boca. "Conceptual Approaches to Stereotypes and Stereotyping." In *Cognitive Processes in Stereotyping and Intergroup Behavior,* ed. David Hamilton. Hillsdale, N.J.: Erlbaum, 1981.

Bailey, J. Michael. *The Man Who Would Be Queen.* Washington, D.C.: Joseph Henry, 2003.

Bair, Deirdre. *Simone de Beauvoir: A Biography.* New York: Summit Books, 1990.

Banner, Lois W. *Elizabeth Cady Stanton, A Radical for Woman's Rights.* New York: HarperCollins, 1970.

Beauvoir, Simone de. *The Second Sex,* trans. H. M. Parshley. New York: Random House Vintage Books, 1989.

——. *Adieux: A Farewell to Sartre,* trans. P. O'Brian. London: Deutsch, 1984.

Bederman, Gail. *Manliness and Civilization: A Cultural History of Gender and Race in the United States, 1880–1917.* Chicago: University of Chicago Press, 1995.

Benardete, Jose A. "Macbeth's Last Words." *Interpretation* 1 (1963): 63–76.

Benardete, Seth. "Achilles and Hector: The Homeric Hero." *St. John's Review* 36 (1985): 31–58, 85–114.

——. *The Argument of the Action*. Chicago: University of Chicago Press, 2000.

——. *The Bow and the Lyre: A Platonic Reading of the Odyssey*. Lanham, Md.: Rowman and Littlefield, 1997.

——. *Socrates' Second Sailing: On Plato's Republic*. Chicago: University of Chicago Press, 1989.

Bengis, Ingrid. *Combat in the Erogenous Zone*. New York: Knopf, 1972.

Benhabib, Seyla. "Feminism and Postmodernism: An Uneasy Alliance." In *Feminist Contentions: A Philosophical Exchange*, ed. Seyla Benhabib et al. New York: Routledge, 1995.

Bentley, Eric. *A Century of Hero-Worship*, 2nd ed. Boston: Beacon Press, 1957.

Bertholet, Denis. *Sartre*. Paris: Plon, 2000.

Bianchi, Suzanne M., Melissa A. Milkie, Liana C. Sayer, and John P. Robinson. "Is Anyone Doing the Housework? Trends in the Gender Division of Household Labor." *Social Forces* 79 (2000): 191–228.

Blitz, Mark. "An Introduction to the Reading of Plato's *Laches*." *Interpretation* 5 (1975): 185–226.

Bloom, Allan. *Love and Friendship*. New York: Simon and Schuster, 1993.

Bloom, Allan, ed. and trans. *Politics and the Arts*. New York: Free Press, 1960.

——. *The Republic of Plato*, 2d ed. New York: Basic Books, 1991.

Bloom, Harold, ed. *Ernest Hemingway's The Old Man and the Sea*. Philadelphia: Chelsea House, 1999.

Brann, Eva. *The Past-Present*. Annapolis: St. John's College, 1997.

Browne, Kingsley R. "Women at War: An Evolutionary Perspective." *Buffalo Law Review* 49 (2001): 51–247.

Burns, Nancy, Kay Lehman Schlozman, and Sidney Verba. *The Private Roots of Public Action: Gender, Equality, and Political Participation*. Cambridge: Harvard University Press, 2001.

Burroughs, Edgar Rice. *Tarzan of the Apes*. New York: Modern Library, 2003.

Burton, David H. *Theodore Roosevelt: Confident Imperialist*. Philadelphia: University of Pennsylvania Press, 1968.

Buss, David M. *The Evolution of Desire: Strategies of Human Mating*. New York: Basic Books, 1994.

Butler, Judith. "Contingent Foundations: Feminism and the Question of 'Postmodernism.'" In *Feminist Contentions: A Philosophical Exchange*, ed. Seyla Benhabib et al. New York: Routledge, 1995.

Campbell, Anne. *A Mind of Her Own*. Oxford: Oxford University Press, 2002.

Cantor, Paul A. *Creature and Creator: Myth-Making in English Romanticism*. Cambridge: Cambridge University Press, 1984.

Caton, Hiram, ed. *The Samoan Reader: Anthropologists Take Stock*. Cambridge: Harvard University Press, 1990.

Céline, Louis-Ferdinand. *Voyage au bout de la nuit*. Paris: Gallimard, 1981.

Cornelius, Randolph R., and James R. Averill. "Sex Differences in Fear of Spiders." *Journal of Personal and Social Psychology* 45 (1983): 377–84.

Cott, Nancy F. *The Grounding of Modern Feminism*. New Haven: Yale University Press, 1987.

Courtwright, David T. *Violent Land: Single Men and Social Disorder from the Frontier to the Inner City*. Cambridge: Harvard University Press, 1996.

Crane, Stephen. *The Red Badge of Courage*. In *Stephen Crane: Prose and Poetry*, ed. J. C. Levenson. New York: W. W. Norton, 1984.

Crawford, Mary. *Talking Difference: On Gender and Language*. London: Sage, 1995.

Croly, Herbert. *The Promise of American Life*. Cambridge: Harvard University Press, 1965.

Darwin, Charles. *The Origin of Species* and *The Descent of Man*. In *The Works of Charles Darwin*, ed. Paul H. Barrett and R. B. Freeman. London: Pickering, 1986.

Davis, Michael. *The Politics of Philosophy: A Commentary on Aristotle's Politics*. Lanham. Md.: Rowman and Littlefield, 1996.

Deaux, Kay, and Marianne LaFrance. "Gender." In *The Handbook of Social Psychology*, 4th ed., 2 vols., ed. Daniel T. Gilbert, Susan T. Fiske, and Gardner Lindzey. New York: McGraw-Hill, 1998.

Deckard, Barbara Sinclair. *The Women's Movement*, 2nd ed. New York: Harper and Row, 1979.

DeMott, Benjamin. *Killer Woman Blues*. Boston: Houghton Mifflin, 2000.

Diamond, Irene, and Lee Quinby, eds. *Feminism and Foucault: Reflections on Resistance*. Boston: Northeastern University Press, 1988.

Dietz, Mary G. "Hobbes's Subject as Citizen." In *Thomas Hobbes and Political Theory*, ed. Mary G. Dietz. Lawrence: University Press of Kansas, 1990.

DuBois, Ellen Carol, ed. *The Elizabeth Cady Stanton–Susan B. Anthony Reader*. Boston: Northeastern University Press, 1992.

Eagly, Alice H. "Reflections on the Commenters' Views." *American Psychologist* 50 (1995): 169–71.

———. "The Science and Politics of Comparing Women and Men." *American Psychologist* 50 (1995): 145–59.

———. *Sex Differences in Social Behavior: A Social-Role Interpretation*. Hillsdale, N.J.: Erlbaum, 1987.

Edlund, Lena, and Rohini Pande. "Why Have Women Become Left-Wing? The Political Gender Gap and the Decline in Marriage." *Quarterly Journal of Economics* 117 (2002): 917–61.

Evans, Mary. *Simone de Beauvoir*. London: Sage, 1996.

Faludi, Susan. *Backlash: The Undeclared War against American Women*. New York: Crown, 1991.

Firestone, Shulamith. *The Dialectic of Sex: The Case for Feminist Revolution*. New York: William Morrow, 1970.

Fiske, Susan T. "Stereotyping, Prejudice, and Discrimination." In *The Handbook of Social Psychology*, ed. Daniel T. Gilbert, Susan T. Fiske, and Gardner Lindzey. 4th ed. New York: McGraw-Hill, 1998.

Flanagan, Caitlin. "How Serfdom Saved the Women's Movement." *Atlantic Monthly* (March 2004): 109–28.

Foucault, Michel. *Power/Knowledge,* ed. Colin Gordon. New York: Pantheon Books, 1980.

Fraisse, Geneviève and Michelle Perrot, eds. *A History of Women in the West.* vol. 4. Cambridge: Harvard University Press, 1993.

Fraser, Nancy. *Unruly Practices: Power, Discourse and Gender in Contemporary Social Theory.* Minneapolis: University of Minnesota Press, 1989.

Freeland, Cynthia, ed. *Feminist Interpretations of Aristotle.* University Park: Penn State University Press, 1998.

Freud, Sigmund. *Three Essays on the Theory of Sexuality,* ed. and trans. James Strachey. New York: Avon Books, 1965.

———. *A General Introduction to Psychoanalysis.* New York: Liveright, 1935.

Friedan, Betty. The Feminine Mystique. New York: W. W. Norton, 1963.

Geary, David L. *Male, Female: The Evolution of Human Sex Differences.* Washington, D.C.: American Psychological Association, 1998.

Giele, Janet Z. "Gender and Sex Roles." In *Handbook of Sociology,* ed. Neil J. Smelser. Newbury Park: Sage, 1989.

Gilder, George. *Men and Marriage.* Gretna: Pelican, 1986.

Gilligan, Carol. *In a Different Voice.* Cambridge: Harvard University Press, 1982.

Gilman, Charlotte. *Herland.* New York: Pantheon, 1979.

Goldwin, Robert A. *Why Blacks, Women and Jews are not Mentioned in the Constitution.* Washington, D.C.: American Enterprise Institute, 1990.

Gottfredson, Linda. "Why *g* Matters: The Complexity of Everyday Life." *Intelligence* 24 (1997): 79–132.

Goyard-Fabre, Simone. *Nietzsche et la question politique.* Paris: Sirey, 1977.

Gould, Stephen Jay. *The Structure of Evolutionary Theory.* Cambridge: Harvard University Press, 2002.

Graglia, F. Carolyn. *Domestic Tranquility.* Dallas: Spence, 1998.

Greenberg, Anna. "Race, Religiosity, and the Women's Vote." *Women and Politics* 22 (2001): 59–82.

Greer, Germaine. *The Female Eunuch.* New York: Bantam Books, 1972.

Gurstein, Rochelle. *The Repeal of Reticence.* New York: Hill and Wang, 1996.

Gutmann, Stephanie. *The Kinder, Gentler Military: Can America's Gender-Neutral Fighting Force Still Win Wars?* New York: Scribner, 2000.

Haggard, H. Rider. *King Solomon's Mines.* Oxford: Oxford University Press, 1989.

Haig, David. "The Inexorable Rise of Gender and the Decline of Sex: Social Change in Academic Titles, 1945–2001." *Archives of Sexual Behavior* 33 (2004): 87–96.

Hall, Judith A., and Amy G. Halberstadt. "Smiling and Gazing." In *The Psychology of Gender: Advances through Meta-Analysis,* ed. J. S. Hyde and M. C. Linn. Baltimore: Johns Hopkins University Press, 1986.

Halpern, Diane. *Sex Differences in Cognitive Abilities,* 3rd ed. Mahwah, N.J.: L. Erlbaum Associates, 2000.

Hamilton, Alexander. *The Papers of Alexander Hamilton,* 27 vols., ed. Harold C. Syrett and Jacob E. Cooke. New York: Columbia University Press, 1961–87.

Harris, Judith Rich. *The Nurture Assumption.* New York: Free Press, 1998.

Hemingway, Ernest. *The Old Man and the Sea.* New York: Scribner, 1995.

Herzog, Don. *Happy Slaves.* Chicago: University of Chicago Press, 1989.

Hitler, Adolf. *Mein Kampf,* trans. not given. New York: Houghton Mifflin, 1939.

Hooper, Charlotte. *Manly States.* New York: Columbia University Press, 2001.

Hochschild, Arlie Russell. *The Second Shift.* New York: Avon, 1997.

Horowitz, Daniel. *Betty Friedan and the Making of the Feminine Mystique.* Amherst: University of Massachusetts Press, 1998.

Irving, Washington. *The Alhambra.* London: Darf, 1986.

James, Henry. *Novels, 1881–1886,* ed. William T. Stafford. New York: W, W, Norton, 1985.

———. *French Writers and American Women,* ed. P. Buitenhuis. Branford, Conn.: Compass Publishing, 1960.

———. *The American Scene.* In *Collected Travel Writings: Great Britain and America,* ed. Richard Howard. New York: W. W. Norton, 1993.

James, William. *Writings, 1902–1910,* ed. Bruce Kuklick. New York: W. W. Norton, 1987.

Kant, Immanuel. *Anthropology from a Pragmatic Point of View.* See *Kants Werke,* Akademie Textausgabe. Berlin: Walter de Gruyter, 1902. 7:117–334.

———. *Conjectural Beginning of Human History,* Akademie Textausgabe, 8:107–24.

———. *Groundwork of the Metaphysics of Morals,* Akademie Textausgabe, 4:385–464.

———. *On the Proverb: That May Be True in Theory but Is of No Practical Use.* Akademie Textausgabe, 8:273–314.

Katz, Wendy. *Rider Haggard and the Fiction of Empire.* Cambridge: Cambridge University Press, 1987.

Kaufmann, Karen, and John Petrocik, "The Changing Politics of American Men: Understanding the Sources of the Gender Gap." *American Journal of Political Science* 43 (1999): 864–87.

Kavka, Gregory S. *Hobbesian Moral and Political Theory.* Princeton: Princeton University Press, 1986.

Kipling, Rudyard. *The Second Jungle Book* (1895).

———. *Just So Stories for Little Children* (1902).

Kirkham, Pat, and Janet Thumim, eds. *You Tarzan: Masculinity, Movies, and Men.* London: Lawrence and Wishart, 1993.

Kochin, Michael. *Gender and Rhetoric in Plato's Political Thought.* Cambridge: Cambridge University Press, 2002.

Kojève, Alexandre. *Introduction à la lecture de Hegel.* Paris: Gallimard, 1947.

Krause, Sharon R. "Lady Liberty's Allure: Political Agency, Citizenship and *The Second Sex.*" *Philosophy and Social Criticism* 26 (2000): 1–24.

———. *Liberalism with Honor.* Cambridge: Harvard University Press, 2002.

Lacan, Jacques. *Ecrits: A Selection,* trans. Alan Sheridan. New York: W. W. Norton, 1966.

Lakoff, Robin. *Language and Women's Place.* New York: Harper and Row, 1975.

Lueptow, Lloyd B., Lore Garovich-Sabo, and Margaret B. Lueptow, "Social Change and the Persistence of Sex Typing: 1974–1997." *Social Forces* 80 (2001): 1–36.

Lippmann, Walter. *Public Opinion.* New York: Macmillan, 1922.

Lorenz, Konrad. *On Aggression*. New York: Harcourt, Brace, 1963.

Ludwig, Paul W. *Eros and Polis*. Cambridge: Cambridge University Press, 2002.

Maccoby, Eleanor E. *The Two Sexes: Growing Up Apart, Coming Together.* Cambridge: Harvard University Press, 1998.

Maccoby, Eleanor E., and Carol N. Jacklin. *The Psychology of Sex Differences*. Stanford: Stanford University Press, 1974.

MacKinnon, Catharine. "Feminism, Marxism, Method and the State: Toward a Feminist Jurisprudence." *Signs* 8 (1982): 635–59.

Manent, Pierre. *Cours familier de philosophie politique*. Paris: Fayard, 2001.

———. *Tocqueville and the Nature of Democracy*, trans. J. Waggoner. Lanham, Md.: Rowman and Littlefield, 1996.

Mansbridge, Jane. *Why We Lost the ERA*. Chicago: University of Chicago Press, 1986.

Mansfield, Harvey C. "Liberty and Virtue in the American Founding." In *Never a Matter of Indifference: Sustaining Virtue in a Free Republic*, ed. Peter Berkowitz. Stanford: Hoover Institution, 2003.

———. *Statesmanship and Party Government: A Study of Burke and Bolingbroke*. Chicago: University of Chicago Press, 1965.

———. *Taming the Prince: The Ambivalence of Modern Executive Power*. New York: Free Press, 1989.

Marcuse, Herbert. *Eros and Civilization: A Philosophical Inquiry into Freud*. Boston: Beacon Press, 1955.

Mathell, Peter, Ad Vingerhoets, and Guus L. Van Heck. "Personality, Gender, and Crying." *European Journal of Personality* 15 (2001): 19–28.

McMillan, Julie R., A. Kay Clifton, Diane McGrath, and Wanda S. Gale. "Women's Language: Uncertainty or Interpersonal Sensitivity and Emotionality?" *Sex Roles* 3 (1977): 545–61.

Mead, Margaret. *Male and Female*. Westport, Conn.: Greenwood, 1949.

Melzer, Arthur M. *The Natural Goodness of Man: On the System of Rousseau's Thought*. Chicago: University of Chicago Press, 1990.

Mencken, H. L. "Roosevelt I." In *Theodore Roosevelt: A Profile*, ed. Morton Keller. New York: Hill and Wang, 1967.

Mill, John Stuart. *On Liberty*, ed. Alan Ryan. New York: W. W. Norton, 1997.

———. *The Subjection of Women*, ed. Susan Okin. Indianapolis: Hackett, 1988.

Miller, Arthur G. *In the Eye of the Beholder: Contemporary Issues in Stereotyping*. New York: Praeger, 1982.

Millett, Kate. *Sexual Politics*. Urbana: Illinois University Press, 2000.

Mitchell, Juliet, and Ann Oakley, eds. *What Is Feminism?* New York: Pantheon, 1986.

Moir, Anne, and Bill Moir. *Why Men Don't Iron*. New York: Citadel, 1999.

Morris, Madeline. "By Force of Arms: Rape, War and Military Culture." *Duke Law Journal* 45 (1996): 651–781.

Morris, Edmund. *The Rise of Theodore Roosevelt*. New York: Ballantine, 1979.

Newell, Waller R. *The Code of Man: Love, Courage, Pride, Family, Country*. New York: ReganBooks, 2003.

Nichols, Mary P. *Citizens and Statesmen: A Study of Aristotle's Politics.* Savage, Md.: Rowman and Littlefield, 1992.

——. "Women in Western Political Thought." *Political Science Reviewer* 13 (1983): 241–61.

Okin, Susan M. *Justice, Gender and the Family.* New York: Basic Books, 1989.

——. *Women in Western Political Thought.* Princeton: Princeton University Press, 1979.

Paglia, Camille. *Sexual Personae.* New York: Vintage Books, 1991.

Pangle, Thomas L. "The Warrior Spirit as an Inlet to the Political Philosophy of Nietzsche's Zarathustra." *Nietzsche-Studien* 15 (1986): 140–79.

Pateman, Carole. *The Sexual Contract.* Stanford: Stanford University Press, 1988.

Pettigrew, Thomas F. "Extending the Stereotype Concept." In *Cognitive Processes in Stereotyping and Intergroup Behavior,* ed. David L. Hamilton. Hillsdale, N.J.: Erlbaum, 1981.

Pinker, Stephen. *The Blank Slate; the Modern Denial of Human Nature.* New York: Viking, 2002.

Polin, Raymond. *Politique et philosophie chez Thomas Hobbes.* Paris: Presses Universitaires de France, 1953.

Pool, Robert. *Eve's Rib.* New York: Crown, 1994.

Rabieh, Linda. "The Best Part of Valor: A Study of Plato's Treatment of Courage in the *Laches* and the *Republic.*" PhD diss., University of Toronto, 2001.

Raven, Simon. *The English Gentleman.* London: Panther Books,1966.

Rhoads, Steven E. *Taking Sex Differences Seriously.* San Francisco: Encounter Books, 2004.

Ridley, Matt. *Red Queen.* New York: Penguin, 1993.

Roosevelt, Theodore. *American Ideals and other Essays, Social and Political.* New York: Putnam, 1997.

——. *An Autobiography.* New York: Scribner's, 1913.

——. "The Great Adventure." In *Works of Theodore Roosevelt,* 20 vols. New York: Scribner's, 1926.

——. *The Letters of Theodore Roosevelt,* ed. Elting E. Morison. Cambridge: Harvard University Press, 1951.

——. *The Strenuous Life.* New York: Century, 1905.

Rothman, Stanley. "Was There Ever a Backlash against Women?" In *The Presentation of Gender in the Mass Media: Neither Victim nor Enemy, Women's Freedom Network Looks at Freedom in America,* ed. Rita J. Simon. Lanham, Md.: University Press of America, 1991.

Rousseau, Jean-Jacques. *Emile, or: On Education,* ed. and trans. Allan Bloom. New York: Basic Books, 1979.

——. *Letter to D'Alembert.* In *Politics and the Arts,* ed. and trans. Allan Bloom. New York: Free Press, 1960.

Rubin, Lillian B. *Families on the Fault Line: America's Working Class Speaks about the Family, the Economy, Race and Ethnicity.* New York: HarperCollins, 1994.

Salkever, Stephen G. *Finding the Mean: Theory and Practice in Aristotelian Political Philosophy.* Princeton: Princeton University Press, 1990.

——. "Women, Soldiers, Citizens: Plato and Aristotle on the Politics of Virility." In *Essays on the Foundations of Aristotelian Political Science,* ed. Carnes Lord and David K. O'Connor. Berkeley: University of California Press, 1991.

Sarachild, Kathie. "Consciousness Raising: A Radical Weapon." In *Feminist Revolution,* ed. Kathie Sarachild. New York: Random House, 1978.

Saxonhouse, Arlene W. *Fear of Diversity.* Chicago: University of Chicago Press, 1992.

——. *Women in the History of Western Political Thought.* New York: Praeger, 1985.

Schaub, Diana. "On the Character of Generation X." *Public Interest* (fall 1999): 3–25.

Schor, Juliet B. *The Overworked American: The Unexpected Decline of Leisure.* New York: Basic Books, 1991.

Schwartz, Joel. *The Sexual Politics of Jean-Jacques Rousseau.* Chicago: University of Chicago Press, 1984.

Schwartz, Pepper, and Virginia Rutter. *The Gender of Sexuality.* Thousand Oaks, Calif.: Pine Forges, 1998.

Shalit, Wendy. *A Return to Modesty.* New York: Free Press, 1999.

Shell, Susan Meld. *The Embodiment of Reason: Kant on Spirit, Generation and Community.* Chicago: University of Chicago Press, 1996.

——. "Emile: Nature and the Education of Sophie." In *The Cambridge Companion to Rousseau,* ed. Patrick Riley. Cambridge: Cambridge University Press, 2001.

Shields, Stephanie A. "Functionalism, Darwinism and the Psychology of Women." *American Psychologist* 30 (1975): 739–54.

Sigel, Roberta A. *Ambition and Accommodation: How Women View Gender Relations.* Chicago: University of Chicago Press, 1996.

Silverman, Eliane L. "Theodore Roosevelt and Women." PhD diss., University of California at Los Angeles, 1973.

Skinner, Quentin. *Reason and Rhetoric in the Philosophy of Hobbes.* Cambridge: Cambridge University Press, 1996.

Smith, Steven B. *Spinoza's Book of Life: Freedom and Redemption in the Ethics.* New Haven: Yale University Press, 2003.

Sommers, Christina Hoff. *The War against Boys.* New York: Simon and Schuster, 2000.

Stettner, Edward A. *Shaping Modern Liberalism: Herbert Croly and Progressive Thought.* Lawrence: University Press of Kansas, 1993.

Stevenson, Robert Louis. *The Strange Case of Dr. Jekyll and Mr. Hyde.* New York: Dover Editions, 1991.

Stiehm, Judith Hicks, ed. *It's Our Military Too! Women and the U.S. Military.* Philadelphia: Temple University Press, 1996.

Stove, David. "The Intellectual Capacity of Women." In *Against the Idols of the Age,* ed. Roger Kimball. New Brunswick, N.J.: Transaction, 1999.

Strauss, Leo. *The City and Man.* Chicago: University of Chicago Press, 1964.

——. "German Nihilism." *Interpretation* 26 (1999): 353–79.

——. *Natural Right and History.* Chicago: University of Chicago Press, 1953.

——. *The Political Philosophy of Hobbes.* 2nd ed. Chicago: University of Chicago Press, 1984.

——. *Socrates and Aristophanes.* New York: Basic Books, 1966.

Sullivan, Vickie B. *Machiavelli, Hobbes and the Formation of a Liberal Republicanism in England.* Cambridge: Cambridge University Press, 2004.

Swanson, Judith A. "Aristotle on Nature, Human Nature, and Justice." In *Action and Contemplation,* ed. Robert C. Bartlett and Susan D. Collins. Albany: State University of New York Press, 1999.

——. *The Public and the Private in Aristotle's Political Philosophy.* Ithaca: Cornell University Press, 1992.

Swim, Janet K. "Perceived Versus Meta-Analytic Effect Sizes: An Assessment of the Accuracy of Gender Stereotypes." *Journal of Personality and Social Psychology* 66 (1994): 21–36.

Sylvester, Bickford. "The Cuban Context of *The Old Man and the Sea.*" In *Ernest Hemingway's The Old Man and the Sea,* ed. Harold Bloom. Philadelphia: Chelsea House, 1999.

Symons, Donald. *The Evolution of Human Sexuality.* New York: Oxford University Press, 1979.

Tannen, Deborah. *The Argument Culture.* New York: Random House, 1998.

——. *Gender and Discourse.* New York: Oxford University Press, 1994.

——. *You Just Don't Understand.* New York: Ballantine Books, 1990.

Tarcov, Nathan. *Locke's Education for Liberty.* Chicago: University of Chicago Press, 1984.

Tessitore, Aristide. "Courage and Comedy in Plato's *Laches.*" *Journal of Politics* 56 (1994): 115–34.

Thompson, Linda, and Alexis J. Walker. "Gender in Families: Women and Men in Marriage, Work and Parenthood." *Journal of Marriage and the Family* 51 (1989): 845–71.

Tocqueville, Alexis de. *Democracy in America,* trans. Harvey C. Mansfield and Delba Winthrop. Chicago: University of Chicago Press, 2001.

Townsend, Kim. *Manhood at Harvard.* New York: W. W. Norton, 1996.

Tuck, Richard. *Natural Rights Theories.* Cambridge: Cambridge University Press, 1979.

Twain, Mark. *A Connecticut Yankee in King Arthur's Court.* New York: Bantam, 1981.

Udry, J. Richard. "Biological Limits of Gender Construction." *American Sociological Review* 53 (2000): 709–22.

——. "The Nature of Gender." *Demography* 31 (1994): 561–73.

Wardley, Lynn. "Woman's Voice, Democracy's Body, and *The Bostonians.*" *English Literary History* 56 (1989): 639–55.

Weber, Max. "Science as a Vocation." In *From Max Weber,* ed. H. H. Gerth and C. Wright Mills. New York: Oxford University Press, 1946.

Welch, Susan. "Women as Political Animals? A Test of Some Explanations for Male Female Political Participation Differences." *American Journal of Political Science* 21 (1977): 711–31.

Williams, Joan. "The Family-Hostile Corporation." *The Responsive Community* 13 (2003): 40–48.

——. *Unbending Gender: Why Family and Work Conflict and What to Do about It.* New York: Oxford University Press, 1999.

Williams, John, and Deborah L. Best. *Measuring Sex Stereotypes*. Newbury Park, Calif.: Sage, 1990.

——. *Sex and Psyche*. Newbury Park, Calif.: Sage, 1990.

Wills, Garry. *John Wayne's America: The Politics of Celebrity*. New York: Simon and Schuster, 1997.

Wilson, Edward O. *Sociobiology*. Cambridge: Harvard University Press, 1975.

Wilson, James Q., and Richard J. Herrnstein. *Crime and Human Nature*. New York: Simon and Schuster, 1985.

Wingrove, Elizabeth R. *Rousseau's Republican Romance*. Princeton: Princeton University Press, 2000.

Winthrop, Delba. "Aristotle: Democracy and Political Science." PhD diss., Harvard University, 1974.

Wolf, Naomi. *The Beauty Myth; How Images of Beauty Are Used against Women*. New York: William Morrow, 1991.

——. *Misconceptions: Truth, Lies, and the Unexpected on the Journey to Motherhood*. New York: Doubleday, 2001.

——. *Promiscuities*. New York: Random House, 1997.

Wollstonecraft, Mary. *A Vindication of the Rights of Woman*. London: J. M. Dent, 1995.

Yarbrough, Jean M. "The Feminist Mistake: Sexual Equality and the Decline of the American Military." *Political Review* 48 (1985).

——. "Theodore Roosevelt and the Stewardship of the American Presidency." In *History of American Political Thought*, ed. Bryan-Paul Frost and Jeffrey Sikkenga. Lanham, Md.: Rowman and Littlefield, 2003.

Zerilli, Linda M. G. *Signifying Woman: Culture and Chaos in Rousseau, Burke and Mill*. Ithaca: Cornell University Press, 1994.

Zuckert, Catherine H. "American Women and Democratic Morals: *The Bostonians*." In *The New Egalitarianism*. Port Washington, N.Y.: Kennikat, 1979.

Zuckert, Catherine H., and Michael Zuckert, "'And in Its Wake We Followed': The Political Wisdom of Mark Twain." *Interpretation* 3 (1972): 59–93.

Index

abortion, 132, 156, 260n33

Achilles, 55–58; complaint against Agamemnon, 60–61, 69, 254n5; and Socrates, 39, 85–86

adultery, 135, 142, 195

aggression, 42, 50, 84, 142; and assertiveness, 62, 77–78; and Darwinism 86–88; Hobbes on, 166–68, 170; in women and men, 64, 135, 151, 155

Alda, Alan, 13

Alport, Gordon, 33, 35; *Nature of Prejudice*, 26

ambition, 80, 121, 126–27, 152, 161, 182, 254n49

America, 88–89, 94, 163–65, 260n26; founding fathers of, 96, 163–64

amour-propre, 196, 204. *See also* vanity

andreia, 18, 75, 204. *See also* courage

anger, 175, 226

anthropology, 139

anthropos: and *aner*, 55, 63, 204

Antoinette, Marie, 181, 233

Antony, Mark 19–20, 38, 205

anxiety, 18, 92–93, 167. *See also* fear

Aristophanes: *Assembly of Women*, 73–74, 187

Aristotle, 204–18; and Darwin, 43, 45, 47; *Ethics*, 207–9, 212, 215–16; *Generation of Animals*, 214; *History of Animals* 212–13; on men and women, 133, 149, 191–92, 265n24; *Metaphysics*, 214; on

moral virtue, 69, 75, 114, 120, 173, 207–10, 226; on nature, 75; on philosophy, 127, 210, 221, 223, 263n93; *Politics*, 204, 208–9, 212, 215; on politics, 62–63, 71, 77, 177, 186, 204; on psychology, 212–13; on war, 88

assertiveness, 50–51, 57, 204; and aggression, 62–63, 77–78, 87; and the human individual, 99, 104, 112, 134, 145–46, 171, 234; in men and women, 64, 67–69, 71, 157; in politics, 79, 205–6, 211, 216–18, 221; training, 50, 67, 71, 253n32

Astor, Lord, 70

athletes, male and female, 193–94

Austen, Jane, 70, 152; *Pride and Prejudice*, 4

authority, 17, 56, 172, 177, 209–11

autonomy, 136, 153–55, 164, 169, 213, 239. *See also* freedom: moral

Bacon, Francis, 112, 231

battle of the sexes, 197–98

Beatty, Warren, 13, 262n83

beauty, 74, 116, 154, 158–59, 249n49

Beauvoir, Simone de: on Hegel, 266n42; influence, 15, 148, 152, 260n32; and Nietzsche, 122, 163, 188; and Sartre, 138, 150–51, 261n51; *Second Sex*, 24, 131–38; on transcendence, 142, 158, 161, 190, 216, 220, 223